Perspectives of British colonial rule in the Fiji Islands

The biography of Ram Charitra, a local civil servant

Binod Charitra

Copyright © 2025 Binod Charitra

ISBN: 978-1-917778-71-8

All rights reserved. Except for brief quotations, you may not copy, store, distribute, reproduce or otherwise make available this publication (or any part of it) in any form, or by any means (electronic, digital, photocopying or otherwise) without the prior permission of the publisher.

Dedication

To our granddaughter

Maria Rukmini

and

in memory of Maria's great-grandfather, whose principles and dedication to work and family laid the foundations for the family's secure future.

"Memories are created by what we do, not by what we think."
Byron Pulsifer

Ram and Tapeshwari Charitra
At 73 Knollys Street (formerly 11 Herbert Street),
Suva, Fiji, 1957
[photo: Prasad's Studios]

If you want to understand today, you have to search yesterday.
Pearl S. Buck

WHITE MAN'S BURDEN

> Take up the White Man's burden –
> Send forth the best ye breed –
> Go, bind your sons to exile
> To serve your captives' needs.
> On fluttered folk and wild –
> Your new-caught sullen people,
> Half devil and half child.
> *Rudyard Kipling*

How your different impulses are orientated, how your whole nature is adjusted, how you are able to attain tranquillity of being, how you are able to penetrate behind all the layers and understand the purpose for which this universe is created and to co-operate with that purpose; to understand the mind of events; to understand the will of the age; to understand contemporary trends; to understand that we are born here to work together, not to hate one another; to understand that we are all co-partners in one task and not rivals, for that something deeper is necessary. You must develop that tranquillity of being, that composure of spirit, that calmness which comes to you by deep reflection on the implications of your sciences, of your feelings and of your actions. It is only then that it will be possible for you to direct the energies of that feeling and will to a common purpose.
Dr S. Radhakrishnan, True Knowledge
(Orient Paperbacks, 1994), p. 21

TABLE OF CONTENTS

Glossary of Fijian words	xi
Preface	xii
Introduction	xiv

Chapter — *Page*

1. The First Fijians. — **1**
The approach to annexation. The Chiefs of Fiji. Ratu Sukuna. Education for Fijians.

2. Events leading to Colonisation. — **20**
European Settlers. Settlers seek settlement with Britain.

3. Americans and Fiji's Future. — **24**
Commercialisation & Expansion. Fiji's Future: Sugar?

4. Europeans Create New World Order. — **30**
Transmutation of Slavery to Indenture System. The Indenture System

5. A New Colony is Shaped. — **36**
Fijian Land Ownership

6. Rebellion Crushed. — **40**
Coaching Fijians

7. Origins of Sugar Industry. Indentured Labourers — **46**
The Final Decision. The First Shipload leaves India. The "Agreement" & the Work. Women & Mortality Rates.

8. Social Workers from India: Self-Emancipation. — **58**
Time to Act. Labourers Indomitable Spirit

9. First Sugar Mill Established. — **67**

10. Political Security. — **69**
Democracy. Demands for Change.

11. Impact of 2nd World War on Fiji's economy. — **77**
What Next?

12. Fiji's New Era & New Problems. — **85**
Managing Education. Essentials of Political Process Denied to Fijians. Impact of Immigration.

13. The Future is Here. — **95**
Testing Times ahead.

14. 1963: A Watershed Year. — **98**
Societal Changes.

15. Political Developments & Role of Education. — **104**

16. Fijians & the Future. — **108**

17. Early Years. 113
Education & Challenges. Impact of Vashist Muni on Education. Change of Direction. The Next Move.

18. Home Life. 125
Toorak, Suva. Grandfather's influence

19. Vuci. 129
The New Era of Post-Indenture Fiji. Property Developer.

20. Colonial Civil Service. 136

21. 1947: Invited to Join Civil Service. 140
Questions for Mr Watson.

22. Ram Sets his Terms. 146
Civil Services Application. The Outcome. Post of Income Tax Inspector.

23. First Day at the Office. 155
Indications of tensions head.

24. Terms of Employment Changed without Notice. 158
The Significance of the changes.

25. Recommended for Professional Status. 164
Recommended for post of Assessor. Revised Terms exploited. Senior Positions out of Reach. 1951: Appointed Acting Senior Assessor. Appointment not published. Corruption in the Colony. Appointment ignored. Change at the top: a series of irregularities. Mr Drysdale's unpredictable actions. The Secretariat declines Mr Drysdale's nominees

26. Further attempts to Expel 179
Exam anomalies. Efficiently discharged his duties. Unwarranted removal of designatory letters. Probationary period extended. Courtesy title removed. Income tax incorrectly assessed. The Appeal.

27. Disciplinary Action and Commission of Inquiry. 195
Mr Philbrick's Final Mission. Causes of Threats. Insubordination.

28. The Accountant-General's Department. 204
Accused of substandard work. Attack as a mode of defence. Causes of discord.

29. Return to Inland Revenue Department. 227

30. Final Thoughts 236

About the Author

Binod Charitra is the eldest son of the late Ram Charitra. He worked for seven years in Ram's accounting firm before leaving to study at the University of London. He established Bramin Financial Services, a firm of Independent Financial Advisors, IFAs, in Mill Hill, London, which specialised in pensions and investments and finance. He retired in 2009 at the age of 70.

For thirty-two years, Binod served as the Hon. Secretary of the Fiji Cultural & Social Club, London. In addition to his social and cultural interests, a hobby that consumes most of his spare time is Indian history, with an emphasis on the ancient learning institutions of Taxila, now in Pakistan, and Nalanda, as well as Udantpuri and others in India and Bangladesh. Nalanda, the world's first residential college, is considered to be the likely origin of the concept of the decimal system and other mathematical innovations under the aegis of Aryabhata and others.

Binod lives in London with his wife Rukmini. He enjoys the company of his family: Bareen, Rohan, his daughter-in-law Ana, and his very special granddaughter Maria.

Acknowledgements

Consultations with friends, relatives and the expertise of specialists form an essential part of composing a biography. I am grateful for the ready help that was available to me at an early stage, especially -

To Dr Dominik Schieder for the initial suggestions and encouragement that I had a story to tell, and guidance about what was important and relevant.

To Dr Amelia Bonea for her interest in the subject matter; her discovery of Ram's documents in the British National Archives at Kew provided the impetus that only a surprise discovery can bring.

To Clare Cottingham and Robert Cottingham of Mill Hill for their interest, for reading the early drafts, and for their many helpful suggestions.

To my relatives Aneel Kumar and Gayatri Kumar of Sydney, Australia, for their suggestions and corrections, as I inched forward with this project over the years.

To Dr Parshu Ram of Melbourne for his encouragement throughout to keep to the storyline and to record faithfully the outstanding abilities of his father-in-law, Ram, including his perseverance and tolerance of his colleagues during his thirteen years in the Fijian civil service.

To my brothers, Peter and Dr Roy Charitra of Melbourne, for our many discussions, and to Roy for suggesting, in the first place, that the travails and achievements of our and other families' early years should be recorded. Both our grandmothers had played pivotal roles with meagre resources but abundant courage and resolution to clear hurdles. With Peter's discovery of the old files, the project took on a new meaning and direction.

Finally, I'd like to thank David Morrison and everyone at *PublishNation* for their expertise in the preparation and publication of this book.

Glossary of Fijian words, *Pronunciation* & **Terminology**

Bavadra *(Bavan-dra)*
Buli - a mid-ranking chief, who could be the head of a district.
Burebasaga *(Buray-basanga)* - a confederacy comprising the provinces of Rewa, Nadroga *(Nan-dronga)*, Serua, parts of Ba, and Namosi.
Cakobau *(Thako-mbau)*
i'Taukei *(ee-Taukei or just Taukei)* - an indigenous Fijian
Kabuna - a confederacy comprising the provinces of Tailevu, Naitasiri, Lomaiviti, Ra, Rotuma, and parts of the western province of Ba.
Koro a Fijian village.
Labasa *Lam-basa*
Matanitu a confederacy.
Mataqali *(Matang-gali)* - a clan or landowning unit of people.
Nadi *(Nandi)* – as in Nadi International Airport.
Rabuka *(Ram-buka)*
Ratu title for a hereditary chief.
Talanoa conversation
Tauvanua ordinary people; commoners.
Tovata a confederacy comprising provinces in the northeast of Fiji, covering Bua, Macuata *(Madu-wata)*, and Cakaudrove *(Tha-kon-drovay)* on Vanua Levu, and the Lau Islands.
Tui title for a high chief or king as in Tui Viti: "King of Fiji".
Turaga *(tu-ranga)* **Bose** *(bo-say)* **Levu** - Great Council Chiefs.
Vuci *(Vu-thee)*
Viti Fiji.
Vunivalu Fijian nobility title.

Terminology

The terminology used here to describe the races in Fiji is based on terms used during the colonial era for clarity and relevance. The indigenous peoples are called "Fijians".

The other communities are referred to by their orientation: Rotuman, Chinese, Indian, or European.

On 30 June 2010, the cabinet approved the *Fijian Affairs [Amendment] by Decree*, to describe **all** people born in Fiji as "Fijians".

The indigenous Fijians would revert to their cultural and traditional descriptions and be referred to as *iTaukei*, meaning "indigenous Fijian" or "owner of the land".

Preface

"Thank you for sharing your manuscript with us. I have certainly become better informed about the social, political and cultural evolution of the various races of people that lived in Fiji during this period. Some of the insights you provide, particularly on the subservience of the Chiefs, are quite revealing. Anecdotes on other important personalities and pioneering developers and entrepreneurs is quite informative...Hats off for the brave and stoically principled character of your Dad – a person that your family should hold in great esteem. It is inconceivable how he was able to last 13 years in such toxic work environment; knowing full well that his incompetent superiors were hell-bent on destroying him. The family, and all those who would have known him, consider themselves fortunate to have had such an upright and far-sighted elder; now that you have thoroughly compiled the highlights of his illustrious career..." Aneel and Gayatri Kumar on reviewing the manuscript.

The origins of this book began during a telephone conversation with my younger brother Roy in Melbourne. His response to some family history we had been discussing was "Oh, that is interesting . . . I did not know that." Well, Roy is nine years younger than I am. I thought that he had much catching-up to do and that the best course of action to deal with this gap was to recount the family's background in the context of Fiji's tortured history; and, in doing so, to reflect on the country, its people, and the impact the British colonial administration's policies had on our father, the late Ram Charitra.

The causes of Fiji's unhappiness in recent times were laid at the inception of the British colony and later policies that created artificial barriers through imagined fears of one race for another.

To appreciate the conduct, performance, and mindset of expatriate civil servants during the post-war colonial era, Chapters 1 to 16 examine aspects of Fiji's history that shaped the administration's policies and plans for the colony's future, set against the backdrop of its ethnically diverse population.

These chapters also expose the demeanour and attitude of the expatriate officers and others who were able to perform only according to their preconceptions and prejudices of the period: for them, the lives of other people, their aspirations, and happiness were less important than the well-being and welfare of the Europeans of the day.

The documents discovered after Ram's passing surprised us, but they also inspired us. He had maintained his daily routine of family life and never brought home his concerns to infect us with hatred or dislike of others.

The documents also motivated me to share his story, ensuring that his struggles would not be forgotten and that they might inspire others to emulate his integrity and patience.

Apart from using those yellowing documents, I have also drawn upon my conversations with Ram over many years, especially during the period when I worked with him as his assistant at his firm, Charitra Accounting and Taxation Service, till I left for London seven years later. He had founded the business after his retirement from the civil service.

He never criticised anyone based on their race or the colour of their skin. He supported the empire; his experiences as a senior law clerk had taught him a healthy respect for the British legal system, and he never equivocated despite the unhappy period in the departments of the Inland Revenue and the Treasury.

To not describe the unsavoury aspects of the administration's doings would have been a dereliction of my responsibilities. However, no slur or offence is intended or implied on the surviving relatives of the expatriate officers of the day. Whatever the motives for their actions, they were, after all, executives of the Empire that conducted the affairs in a manner that suited the period and the stage in the development of colonialism and people's attitudes.

The subsequent generations of the Charitra family, especially those of our granddaughter Maria Rukmini and her cousins, may wish to pause for a moment or two on these pages, deriving inspiration from them and learning to emulate the courage of their forebears. My hope is that they will persevere, prosper, and contribute to the welfare and prosperity of the nations in which they live.

Binod Charitra
London

May 2025

Introduction

Winston Churchill, my first Prime Minister, said that the further backwards you look, the farther forward you can see.[1]

The British Empire conducted its affairs in questionable ways, notably in the Departments of Inland Revenue and the Treasury in the Colony of Fiji. British fair play was partial. The Governor's role as the font of justice and the chief administrator lacked commitment to good governance.

This is a biography of the late Mr Ram Charitra, an accountant and tax consultant, the son of an indentured labourer, who joined the colony's civil service at the government's request as an Inspector of Taxes.

He rose to the post of an assessor and acted on several occasions as a senior assessor. He won legal arguments on interpretations of income tax ordinances. His progress belied his tribulations: the undercurrent of ambushes from his colleagues, including disciplinary action, which the investigating committee dismissed; and the manipulation of his personal tax returns by the Commissioner because he could "afford it". Existential racial intolerance marred his otherwise steady advance as a civil servant.

He was seconded to the Accountant-General's department, the Treasury, as an assistant accountant and returned to the Inland Revenue, where he continued with his principled stance against his detractors, until he retired on government pension in 1961.

The documents he left chronicled a level of desperation and frustration. The offending officers flouted General Orders, Colonial Regulations, and rules of common decency, such as when, in frustration at not being able to dismiss him on trumped-up charges, the Commissioner and the Deputy Commissioner of Inland Revenue decided to remove Ram's courtesy title of "Mr"

---

[1] Elizabeth II, BBC broadcast, Christmas Day, 1999.

from official communications! They operated at this level with impunity and ease.

Peaceful Transfer of Power

Fijian chiefs unconditionally and peacefully transferred sovereignty to Britain in 1874. No other state vied for the attractions of the lush, idyllic South Pacific islands. British interest lay in the islands' location as a staging post to serve its dominions nearby. Instead of lucrative resources to exploit, there were liabilities galore to consider that kept most other Europeans away. Britain accepted responsibility for the islands and set out to reorganise and modernise the social and political structures devised by the warlords, hitherto recognised as cannibals [2].

Under the new regime, the Fijians were segregated and confined to communal arrangements overseen by chiefs or *bulis*. The villagers who lived in these controlled areas undertook and performed repetitive tasks. Effectively isolated from other communities during most of colonial rule, commerce, professions, finance, and other modern concepts remained out of reach for most of them.

The results of this decision took a heavy toll on the indigenous Fijians' prospects and their understanding of modern concepts of commerce, which totally eluded them during the colonial period. The consequences of their segregation led to divisions within the colony's multi-ethnic society.

The Chiefs

It is essential to note that the chiefs of Fiji hold a special place in the hearts and minds of ordinary Fijians, known as the *tauvanua*. The chiefs are revered, and no one may cross their paths, interfere with or contradict them. This belief in their god-like status demands that others stoop and bow their heads in a chief's presence.

The colonial administration was quick to recognise this; it implemented its administrative policies to rule through the

---

[2] Rev. Joseph Waterhouse. The King and People of Fiji – Containing a Life of Thakombau. Wesleyan Conference, London. 1866. p. 311.

agency of the chiefs. The unquestioning support and loyalty were admirable, but it achieved little in material progress for the commoners. Their chiefs, however, received particular attention in various forms - from a high-level education to nominal responsibilities and accolades. The chiefs repaid this special treatment with everlasting devotion and gratitude – even at the expense of their own people.

The ideologically driven, archaic colonial political system and the unjustified rhetoric bound the chiefs to the settlers' apron strings. This situation damaged the faith and the trust between the two major ethnic groups of the islands: the Fijians and the Indians.

It would not be possible to comprehensively understand Fiji's problems without understanding the colony's ethnic make-up and the disparities that were engendered and exploited, which ensured the administration never faced a united front among the peoples.

The First Settlers and the New Administration

During the twilight period when the British, French, and Germans were loitering in the Pacific, settlers from Australia had established plantations on land acquired through dubious transactions. Their muskets had captured the attention of the warring chiefs, who crushed opponents with ease using these modern weapons. The new arrivals had thus gained a toehold in the land, with political advantages to come.

The British had their work cut out for them nonetheless; during the early 1870s, they established a presence under the leadership of Mr J. B. Thurston, who guided the settlers and the inhabitants in their future arrangements with Britain.

The new administration undertook to guarantee the rights and customs of the Fijian peoples, the paramountcy of the chiefs, and to some extent, the protection of land from unscrupulous European settlers.

Before 1874, the country was a collection of belligerent factions defined by regional confederacies (*matanitus*). These political entities were formed by the most powerful chiefs to unify and protect their clans. The most successful of these were the confederacies of Kabuna, Burebasaga, and Tovata.

The Kabuna Confederacy comprised the Kingdom of Bau, and its chief, Cakobau, was seen as the most powerful warlord of Fiji; the Burebasaga Confederacy covered the Rewa region; and the Tovata Confederacy was formed by two smaller alliances. Chief Ma'afu, an influential warlord and prince of Tonga, was sent by the King of Tonga to oversee the Tongan residents in the Lau group of Fiji in 1867. He had larger ambitions of his own. He attempted to destabilise Cakobau's General Assembly and persuade the Chiefs of Lau, Cakaudrove and Bua to unite as a Confederation of North and East Fiji as a bulwark to control Cakobau's expansion. Ma'afu and his ad hoc collection of supporters were no match for Cakobau's organisation under Thurston.

The time had come for Thurston to act. He stepped up to the plate and formed a government with European settlers, Cakobau now confirmed by his cabinet as the King of Fiji, and some minor chiefs, in an attempt to stabilise the chaotic situation and present an organised front (a government) to negotiate with the British. Other influential warlords distanced themselves from the new regal personage. In protest, some individuals chose not to participate in the treaty ceremonies.

However, the British presence and semblance of a duly constituted state prevailed. Eventually, a treaty without conditions that satisfied London, King Cakobau, and the other remaining chiefs was signed, and the Deed of Cession transferred the islands to Britain.

The new administration's priority was to organise Fijian society into a settled and peaceful state, under the secure, albeit nominal, leadership of Fijian chiefs and under the watchful eyes of the district commissioners and district officers. The system worked, but it locked the fate of the Fijian people. In the seamless transition, people believed that nothing had changed: their chiefs appeared to be back in charge; occasionally, they would see a white man in a suit accompanying their leader, which seemed comforting as traditional ceremonials of welcome and other traditional rituals continued.

Lord Lugard, High Commissioner in Nigeria, 1900 – 1906 and Governor General from 1912 to 1919, is credited with the concept of "dual mandate" – a system of central control of indigenous affairs through the Chiefs [3] and their local infrastructure and traditions – a system which Sir Arthur Hamilton-Gordon, the new Governor and John Bates Thurston, effectively his assistant set in place, and secured the services of the now redundant traditional chiefs, was occasioned by a shortage of trained colonial officers; this move proved to be pragmatic and useful and indeed, momentous.

Education and Missionaries

In Britain by 1880, education was made compulsory for every child between the ages of five and ten; they were all required to attend school. The British government had a duty of care to its citizens to provide education. The colonial government of Fiji had a duty of care only to European children.

It was exceptional, in the circumstances, to find a chief speak of the importance of schooling. Timothy Macnaught quotes a Fijian commoner, Ro Tuisawau: *"Education is the most useful thing of all for the present age and the future."*[4] This view of a thoughtful and responsible person was very much his wishful thinking. He was a commoner, and this thinking didn't count. He exemplified the values he had absorbed through education and pointed to a solution to Fiji's problems. He got to the kernel of the matter and crystallised the cause of Fiji's difficulties. Tuisawau deserves a statue.

The unconstrained, detached, and well-resourced European settlers demanded more and more resources for

---

[3] For fuller explanation of Lugard's "The Dual Mandate" concept, see Margery Perham's *Lugard* by Margery Perham, two volumes (London, Collins, 1956-1960) and *the diaries of Lord Lugard* edited by Margery Perham and Mary Bull, four volumes (London, Faber and Faber, c.1959).

[4] Timothy J. Macnaught, *The Fijian Colonial Experience: A Study of the Neotraditional Order under British Colonial Rule Prior to World War II* Australian National University. Chapter 9, http://doi.org/10.22459/FCE.06. 2016. First published 1982. This edition: 2016. p.147. https:// Academia.edu 40632455

schools, public baths and clubs. Schooling and sources of social enlightenment were derived through the gifts of the missionaries, who, with meagre resources, managed to instil basic concepts of a foreign culture, ethics, and beliefs – their introduction to the twentieth century.

Many became literate, but, unfortunately, no further advances in educational facilities deprived the more promising students of an introduction to a more promising and profitable new world. But at least the people were now literate, if not numerate.

The missionaries had been present in the islands for about forty years already; their work (mainly conducting Bible studies) continued with the blessings of the government.

The curriculum of the Methodist Wesleyan missionaries was parochial and unimaginative. The vernacular was the medium of "education", which primarily conveyed the Bible's message and completed the missionaries' brief and responsibility. Education with a broader curriculum to broaden the scope and potential of young Fijians was never considered necessary by the Wesleyan missionaries, the administration, or the chiefs, until that is, the advent of the Roman Catholic missionaries, who were almost immediately at odds with Protestants on this issue. Their curriculum differed significantly as the Catholics taught English, which opened the door to other topics and subjects. The apparent benefits would boost self-assurance and broaden the scope of work, and open doors to other opportunities.

The Catholics appeared dedicated to providing the people with a more comprehensive education, beyond the primary mandate of converting them from ancient faiths and rituals to Christianity. They laid the foundations for future vocational or professional achievement. This course of action proved more practical and realistic, with its broader application in teaching, learning trades, and improving the general ability to communicate with others.

The government favoured the Catholics' broader programme and communicated this view to the Methodists, who were reluctant to follow the "perverts of Rome". Eventually, under pressure, they were obliged to introduce the English language.[5]

Economic Woes. Arrival of Indentured Labourers

The colony's economy was almost non-existent. Cotton was grown, but the inexperienced growers soon chose the wrong variety, leaving the investors out of pocket and the islands without a credible source of income.

For the new government under Governor Gordon, growing bananas and coconuts (for the dried coconut meat – copra – to make oil) was not a sustainable programme to raise Fiji's financial and economic profile. Development and laying the groundwork for Fiji's modernisation programmes began in earnest with the Governor Gordon in 1875. He would call on his experiences he gained from his other assignments in British territories to benefit the economy and the social structure of the Fijian community, especially.

A delicate issue for the Governor was a comprehensive review of the possibilities for an agricultural industrial setup. Labourers imported from the Solomon Islands and the New Hebrides held much promise but led to disappointments during the trials of the 1860s. Cotton in Fiji had been growing since the 1830s, but in the latter half of the century, it had acquired a bitter notoriety as an industry that many loved to hate. Although growing wild, the Fijians had little use for it.

The once-promising cotton industry was plagued by multiple fundamental issues, including a lack of knowledge of tropical agriculture and inadequate capital, though most of the intrepid planters were confident enough in the outcome to risk everything as they

> "were compelled to mortgage their crops and their plantations to the storekeepers in Levuka who lent money at a ruinous rate of interest…"[6]

---

[5] Macnaught, *The Fijian Colonial Experience*, p. 130.
[6] Evelyn Stokes. The Fiji Cotton Boom in the 1860s. University of Waikato. p. 175.

The industry was further disadvantaged by the outbreak of the Franco-Prussian War in 1870 and the return of American cotton to European markets, which led to lower prices in London and had serious consequences for the local industry.

The colony looked at other sources. Sugar, which was grown by some settlers on a smaller scale, was found to be less susceptible to the vagaries of the weather locally. However, economies of scale demanded larger-scale production, which would require a greater certainty of labour supply of a higher quality. Based on his experiences in other territories, Governor Gordon got together investors and growers and recruited labourers from India.

They landed on Fiji's shores under the indenture system. After ten years, they would be free to return home, with paid fares. The government and the plantations encouraged them to remain in the colony and become independent farmers, leasing land in the short term.

The Governor's decision to bring in the labourers was justified, judging by the success of the enterprise and the reluctance of the government and the plantations to return the "freed" labourers to India. The colony's economy was now established, as sugar became the primary industry within a couple of decades of the new contingent's arrival. The stability and consistency sought by the managers and the government were now a reality, and Fiji's finances would never look back.

The exertions of the work took their toll on the labourers' lives. Health and welfare were serious issues. Neither did they have political rights, nor did they have formal recognition as entities with legal entitlements to any social assistance. They had choices: work, starve, or get beaten up. Many chose suicide.

The next generation dispersed and sought clerical posts in firms, opened businesses, and became producers of goods and services for the new generation of Fiji's farming fraternity.

Their demands for education for their children fell on deaf ears. Their solution to a better life was through education, and they were determined to get their way, even if it meant taking the initiative themselves.

Before decolonisation, London reassured the Indians that they were secure as citizens of Fiji, but their persistent demands for the introduction of universal suffrage in the colony were never realised during British rule. With political parity, all races would have an equal say in substantive matters, ensuring that no particular race would be at a disadvantage solely because of its racial identity or socioeconomic status.

These fundamental political issues, the bedrock of society's stability and freedom from exploitation, were mainly projected by Indian leaders. The untimely passing of A. D. Patel[7] put paid to those fundamental and unshakeable beliefs that nothing short of a universal franchise in Fiji would bring the communities together economically, socially, and politically. In the twenty-first century, it seems odd that such a simple and fundamental political prerequisite was withheld in the colony, despite fervent calls for its introduction.

The indigenous people, on the other hand, continued their peaceful occupations in the villages, happily oblivious to their potential in the rapidly moving post-war world.

Multiracial Nation

When we consider the origins of the races in Fiji, we begin to understand the complexities and the disparate personalities of the human races that came together to unite and create a new society with its unique "culture". We are all a little bit less Indian, a little bit less European or Chinese or iTaukei. The sum total of our differences has contributed to producing the best in human spirit.

We explore the journey the indigenous Fijians undertook more than three thousand years ago from Africa; then to the Europeans who landed on Fiji's shores through a variety of reasons: those who were shipwrecked or escaping incarceration

---

[7] The colonial administration and the chiefs had a myopic, regressive view of A. D. Patel's political aspirations. His lifelong struggle for non-racial politics in Fiji lay in ruins at his demise, on the eve of Fiji's freedom. His stubborn political stance for most of a half century was only vindicated after numerous coups and the racial trauma in 2014, when the government adopted his sentiments and political philosophy for a united nation.

and those who left New Zealand following the Anglo-Maori wars and the second-generation Australians looking for new pastures and adventure and last of all the *"blackbirders"* - the perpetrators of kidnapping or deceiving people into working as slaves. They were usually owners of ships based in Australia and other parts of the Pacific, or opportunistic captains seeking a quick and assured return. Followed later by the Chinese and Indians, who arrived at the invitation of the colonial administration. The Chinese were initially assigned to sugar cane farms. Although hard-working and dedicated, they were deemed unsuitable for longer-term employment in the cane fields. They reverted to market gardening and other undertakings and set up successful ventures in retail and wholesale.

With only fifty per cent of the labour required potentially available in the colony, the plantations continued to rely on imported labour. The Fijians found no attractions in the cane fields, and cash was tosh. They moved tribally and communally and had security in food, and lived a happy life with little responsibility or expectations for material progress. As former specialists in warfare, they were now deprived of the only pursuit they had ever indulged in; apart from tilling and sowing, that was their calling during the peaceful interludes when demanded by their respective village chiefs and warlords. They saw no benefit in being farmers or labourers, planting foreign vegetation not for their consumption. Issues of discipline notwithstanding, they had no need for cash as that concept did not exist. Trials using Fijians in commercial farming methods failed despite the sustained efforts of dedicated, well-meaning settler entrepreneurs.

The importation of labour set the economy on course for sustained growth. However, the manner in which the indentured labourers were recruited and hired could have been more humane and objective. Many were misled into signing their contracts with false information about their journey, the type of work involved, and the site's topography. They discovered agony and torment, which led many to end their lives soon after arrival. The government and the plantation owners took no interest in the complaints, and so the labourers' final act was defiance and a strike, which took place in 1920.

They had no support, neither financial nor moral. Fijians of the day were generally sympathetic and understood the causes of the dispute. Their chiefs, influenced by government propaganda, however, advised them not to fraternise with the strikers or support any Indian group because they – the Indians - were planning *to seize* the islands and to subjugate and enslave Fijians!

Many immigrants were desperate to return to India, where their hardships were more tolerable than the hell–*narak* they suffered in Fiji. However, the sugar industry could not hire Fijian labour as they were now well protected from any enforced labour attempts from outside; nor could it give in to the strikers' demands.

The deadlock was resolved through force. At the request of the Governor, the New Zealand Prime Minister, Mr Massey, sent a gunboat to Fiji to deter the strikers. The newspaper reported that

> "The man in the street would call this intimidation to force the Indians to come to the White man's terms so that the exploitation of the past may comfortably continue..."

The farmers at best had picks and shovels. The strong-arm tactics and threats eventually yielded to submission.

To ensure justice, a fair deal for the workers and security, political concerns were becoming an issue for the Indians; they wished to have a permanent resolution to their problems, to strengthen their rights as citizens, and to ensure the government paid attention to their needs.

Emerging leaders – the descendants of indentured labourers - firmly believed that the existing racially based electoral system was damaging to the colony's long-term prospects as a stable and peaceful nation.

However, uniting the various peoples was never a realistic proposition. Indeed, it was the antithesis of the empire's fundamental administrative prerequisite to maintain segregation to facilitate control and domination. Demands for social or political changes were dismissed or ignored and not discussed in an open and transparent manner.

Fiji's social and recreational clubs were organised along racial lines: the Defence Club in Suva was the pre-eminent European-only club; the Indians formed the Union Club and the Merchant's Club, but welcomed *all* races. At the *Regal Theatre* in Suva, the management divided the seating arrangements during the children's matinee showing of films. One section was set aside for European children; the remaining patrons occupied the seats lower down. Mr Crawford – a charming entrepreneur who ran the outfit at the time, before he opened *The Phoenix* cinema in Walu Bay - made sure that children did not mix. He inspected the seating around the white children and sent packing any black or brown child – the author included – who was sitting with European children. All this despite the colony's public perception that there was no racial discrimination anywhere that kept races separate and apart on account of the colour of their skin, in public or in private.

The Suva Sea Baths presented a more challenging scenario. Although the elite European settlers enjoyed a higher standard of living and could afford a private swimming pool for their community, they assumed almost total usage of a publicly funded pool in Suva, next to the old Town Hall. Eventually, the joint efforts of Indian members of the Suva City Council forced desegregation.

In 1956, the baths opened to other races at specific times. During those times, the European community stayed away from the pool. Ms Liebling Marlow recounts an instance when two siblings came to use the baths: the brother appeared to be white, but his sister "looked a bit Indo-Fijian". The girl was not permitted to enter the pool. A kindly white lady approached the official in charge and protested, and she successfully got the girl admitted.[8]

Administrative Service and Localisation

---

[8] https://fijitimes.com.fj/suva-sea-bath-the-go-to-place/ accessed 20 September 2023.

The British civil service laid the foundations of government in the territories it controlled in the image of the Westminster parliamentary model. Justice was based on the British legal system and the rule of law, and "fair play" was generally accepted as a principle across the communities. However, many contradictions in the system were also accepted as the norm; for instance, no one questioned the instances of discrimination mentioned above.

The Governor administered the colonies, representing the monarch, as the sole arbiter and lawgiver. He embodied the interests of the elite settlers of the day, as well as the corporations and chiefs, whose attachment to the establishment provided them with the protection and status they craved.

Since Fiji's inception as a British Crown Colony, civil servants on the islands were recruited from abroad. Local officers had minor roles, and none had achieved a high-level posting in the Inland Revenue until 1948, when a brown man, Ram Charitra, was recruited into this white-ruled world of corruption, inequality, and injustice as an Inspector of Taxes.

Ram Charitra's Inland Revenue colleagues' reactions to his admission to a relatively high-level posting surprised him. He had *not* sought this position; rather, his expertise in tax matters had attracted the department's attention. Mr Watson, the Assistant Commissioner, approached Ram and recruited him into what was, until then, the preserve of the settler and expatriate communities.

As will be seen later, Mr Watson and Mr Ackland, the Commissioner, had observed Ram's presentations of his employers' and his clients' tax returns, and his dealings with their department for nine years, before they were convinced, they had found a suitable local person.

The perception of "justice" that pervaded the colony as fair to all was a hollow notion in official circles. During his tenure at the Accountant-General's and Inland Revenue Departments, he discovered that the values and ideals behind colonial policies were worthless: they had no impact on the senior officers, who ran their departments as fiefdoms. It sounds dramatic, but that is how they seemed to get away with so much.

However, Ram was not deterred and pursued his detractors. As required by General Orders, he turned to the governor [9] presiding during the period, as the holder of the scales, a person of colour had little, if any, demand on the time of the Chief Executive. The hours spent drafting and writing petitions, along with all the necessary evidence, were to no avail. They were ineffective. His complaints were ignored. The governors were unable to take a stand against the expatriate white officers on behalf of a brown officer, who was, after all, one of "Your new-caught sullen peoples, half devil and half child." [10]

Recruitment into higher administrative appointments was confined to European settlers and those imported from Britain or, more typically, from Australia or New Zealand. The absence of a pool of trained indigenous civil servants to assume responsible posts only entrenched the white immigrant community's position in the colony. Their reasons for appointing Europeans were that no locals were qualified to fill the positions.

For thirteen years, he tolerated continual, unproductive confrontations resulting from the department's ethnically driven racist agenda. He decided to take early retirement in 1961.

Ram's detractors never succeeded in their numerous attempts to remove him, although they did successfully interrupt and prevent his rise to a higher position. As a taxation expert, he excelled, and no one could find fault with his assigned work and responsibilities, and no one could remove him solely based on the standard of his work.

The Secretariat (a department of the colonial administration's Executive Council), headed by the Colonial Secretary, continually accepted insubstantial and implausible reasons from departmental heads to pursue their aims to oust Ram. At no time did the Colonial Secretary seek evidence of

---

[9] 1947 - 1952 Sir Brian Freeston
1952 - 1958 Sir Ronald Garvey
1958 - 1964 Sir Kenneth Maddocks

[10] Rudyard Kipling. "White Men's Burden".

negligence or question their motives before instituting proceedings against Ram.

The National Archives at Kew in London hold his records from 1952 to 1961 (FCO 141/4784, FCO 141/4783, FCO 141/4782, and FCO 141/4781). Documents from 1947 to 1951 relating to his pre-application negotiations with Fiji's Commissioner of Inland Revenue are missing.

These included letters from Ram about the terms on which he would accept the offer of work in the civil service and the Secretariat's first letter of offer of employment to Ram.

About five weeks after he entered the department, the Secretariat changed the terms without informing, discussing or agreeing to the new terms now being thrust upon him without his consent. It subsequently denied all knowledge of the existence of the first letter of appointment. It was therefore my first act to find out from the Archives if there were other files dating from 1947 to 1951. The answer was negative. However, if these documents are ever discovered, they would incriminate the Colonial Secretary in an illegal act.

The colonial administration presumably destroyed these sensitive documents prior to Fiji's independence in 1970.

Responsible governments operate under the rule of law and do not engage in, connive with, or foster infringements of the law. The colonial government did just that.

He was subsequently seconded to the Accountant-General's office - the Treasury Department, and soon chanced upon some files. He went through them and found errors that he considered serious enough to bring to his superior's notice. These had potential consequences for the department and the taxpayers, who, in effect, funded the government pension scheme, as well as the officers whose pensions would be financially affected one way or the other.

The Accountant-General, however, dismissed the findings as of no concern to Ram, who was not proved to be wrong in his assessments. At Ram's request, the matter was put to the Attorney-General, who concurred with Ram's interpretations of the ordinance concerned, but it cut no ice with the Accountant-General.

Ram Charitra was born to immigrant parents in Navua, a small sugar-cane-growing township at the southern tip of Viti Levu, the largest island in the Fijian archipelago. He was raised and educated to be a loyal, law-abiding British-born subject. The colonial environment in which he grew up had its own shortcomings. Schools, an important factor for any parent with concerns for their child's wellbeing and welfare were almost non-existent. And the government showed no concerns about these things. Education was a costly affair, and after all, labourers did not need education. Fiji was short of labourers, and they would better serve the colony by working on plantations.

The Europeans' proclivities and the cultural differences that suggested the superiority of one race over another contributed to an improper functioning of the government institutions. No one who understood, experienced, or even suffered the effects of colonial policies ran the risk of upsetting the apple cart.

The benign perspectives fostered and encouraged by the deep and happy relationship of the Fijian chiefs with the colonial administration perpetuated the hype.

The London Conference

During the Independence Conference in London, Ratu Sir Kamisese Mara, the head of the Fijian [11] delegation, challenged the Indians' claim to political rights in Fiji. The responsibility to grant or not grant any rights, political or otherwise, remained with the British. Indians had been in Fiji since 1879, and they started to pursue their demands for political rights within decades of their arrival.

With the world's eyes on Britain during the 1960s, its policies and timetables for freedom were scrutinised in depth; the schedule gathered pace, with the United Nations calling for the release of Britain's overseas "possessions". The Fijians, however, were adamant that British rule in Fiji would never end and that, if independence did rear its ugly head, Fiji should revert to

---

[11] July 1965.

indigenous Fijian control. Indians would be surplus to requirements and deported to India.

Britain firmly reminded Ratu Sir Kamisese Mara (who was to become independent Fiji's first prime minister) and the chiefs that the Indians were full citizens of Fiji.[12] They would not consider their request to return Fiji only to the indigenous Fijians: Fiji was acknowledged as a multicultural colony, and nothing could change that.

"Full citizens" seemed a hollow term. The reticence of the chiefs and the colonial government's rejection of universal suffrage as the basis for political reforms for a post-independence nation meant the future for the Indians in the land of their birth was hanging by a thread; it gave credence to private fears that independence would be fraught with uncertainties, and the Indians might not be totally secure under the constitution as planned by Britain.

The disinformation and indoctrination relentlessly drilled into the Fijians for more than ninety years bore fruit seventeen years after independence. All the pre-independence colonial, anti-Indian rhetoric surfaced and changed the course of Fiji's history through violence.

Ratu Sir Kamisese Mara was prime minister for the first seventeen years of independence in 1970, and it appears that he expected to continue as leader and prime minister for the rest of his life. During this period, he continued with many colonial policies and biases. He was defeated in the 1987 elections by a fellow Fijian, the founder of the Fiji Labour Party, Dr Timoci Bavadra. Dr Bavadra forged a coalition with the National Federation Party, a mainly Indian political party, and formed his government.

Dr Bavadra's failure to allocate more senior posts to Fijians, instead of to Indians and others, was a red flag that seemed to be a first step in the Indians' strategy to take over. This was anathema to the traditional chiefs. So, within a month of Dr Bavadra's forming a government, the Dominion of Fiji's

---

[12] A. Ravuvu, *The Façade of Democracy: Fijian Struggles for Political Control 1830–1987* (Reader Publishing House, 1991), p. 49.

politicised military forces removed him from office by force, despite the fact that he was an elected *indigenous* Fijian prime minister.

With the march of Colonel Sitiveni Rabuka's battalion into the parliament building in 1987, Fiji's colonial past came to haunt the new nation, erasing its glorious label, the *"Paradise of the Pacific"* – forever.

Multiple coups followed and ended with the final military intervention in December 2006, which brought in a former naval officer, Commodore Josaia Voreqe "Frank" Bainimarama, who maintained a principled stand, changed the constitution that had plagued the nation, and introduced the long-awaited universal franchise in 2014.

The impact of the colonial racial fiction ran so deep that, even post-independence, Fijian intellectuals found it difficult to shake off. Sentiments such as those promoted by Dr Ravuvu discouraged close interracial cooperation. He urged other "cultures and people to contribute to Fiji and its way of life . . ." – a commendable appeal, but he warned that "their influence . . . [could] become a *threat* to Fijian traditions; *they should not* dominate *the Fijian way of life or supersede it*".[13]

It was a meaningless observation, if ever there were one. It was born out of a lack of confidence in oneself and the lack of conviction in one's traditions and institutions. The result of many years of isolation and its associated lack of observation and understanding of other cultures. The fear that other races would harm and destroy Fijian traditions and cultural values is unfair and out of synch with the aspirations of people around the globe.

***

To an outside observer, it might not be obvious that
1. There was a bias against the involvement of local talent in high administrative posts. Fijians were the least likely candidates for such appointments.

---

[13] Ravuvu, *The Façade of Democracy*, p. 92, *emphasis added*.

2. Little effort was made to set up schools in villages to encourage indigenous and other children's education to achieve higher secondary school grades; when it came, it was too little, too late.

3. The colonial political infrastructure trapped the population in a racially oriented system, which accentuated and perpetuated communal divisions.

4. The administration created an elite brigade of traditional chiefs and selected commoners to support its regressive policies.

Apartheid was a political and social evil in South Africa, but it had its derivatives in the British colonies; Fiji was no different. If blame were to be apportioned for the practice of racism, even in shades of grey, the chiefs must accept their lack of vision as a root cause of their people's backwardness.

Throughout their colonial history, Fijians wholly depended on the British for their security, welfare, and development. They were largely within their rights to expect it. In return, they offered total loyalty to the Crown.

That respect ran deep and never wavered, and the Fijians never failed to respond when called by the Crown to serve. However, throughout the colonial period, the British never repaid that trust as honourably as the chiefs offered it on behalf of the people. But that does not absolve the Fijian leaders of the fact that they washed their hands of their responsibilities towards their own people who according to Sir Lala Sukuna, had to prove themselves first.

The colonisers, however, betrayed that trust in a more sinister manner: the attempted genocide through a measles epidemic in the aftermath of the Cession to Britain. *European settlers* were isolated from the infected peoples, but the Surgeon-General decided not to impose a quarantine on the rest of the public. The general welfare and protection of the citizens was fundamental but absent, and many thousands succumbed to the disease.

Like many Indian immigrant families, the Charitra family had their moments of tears and frustrations. However, they never gave up hope or stopped trying for better days.

Ram Charitra rose from among those immigrants to become a teacher, chief law clerk, accountant, tax consultant, property developer, and senior assessor in the Inland Revenue Department.

Ram never sought to become a civil servant; but his experiences within that distinct environment expose an ugly side of British colonialism that defies logic.

Gustave Flaubert, the nineteenth-century French novelist and thinker, expressed the values expected of a sane and civilised society:

> "I'm no more modern than ancient, no more French than Chinese, and the idea of a native country, that is to say, the imperative to live on one bit of ground marked red or blue on the map and to hate the other bits in green or black, has always seemed to me narrow-minded, blinkered and profoundly stupid. I am a soul brother to everything that lives, to the giraffe and to the crocodile as much as to man."

1

The First Fijians

The community stagnates without the impulse of the individual; the impulse dies away without the sympathy of the community.[1]

Fiji is a group of hundreds of islands in the South Pacific, some of which are inhabited, while others are too small or rugged to support human life. Fijians comprise disparate groups, whose origins are uncertain and about which no definitive theory has been established. One hypothesis maintains that, about two and a half thousand years ago, a group left an area around Lake Tanganyika in Africa and reached the shores of Fiji via the Timor Straits, New Caledonia, and New Guinea. The other theory suggests that the settlers had similar origins but got to Taiwan and then arrived at Vuda Point – between today's Nadi International Airport and Lautoka City - about two thousand years ago. Both groups would have followed a route much the same as the earlier one via Melanesia, picking up local inhabitants as they went. Consequently, the indigenous peoples of Fiji are not a homogeneous race, with uniform and harmonised cultural origins and history.

Upon arrival, the people remained close to where they had landed and preserved their original heritage, as well as the traditions they had acquired during their journeys.

Each group had a chief or warlord, who guarded his territory and people with appropriate tenacity, and formed alliances with other groups to establish "confederacies". In time, three such alliances evolved and survived the violence of the period: the *Kabuna*, *Burebasaga*, and *Tovata* Confederacies.

---

[1] William James, quoted in Dale C. Godby. "*Group Therapy: A Group-Analytic Approach* by Nick Barwick and Martin Weegman", *International Journal of Group Psychotherapy*, vol. 70, no. 3 (22 October 2019), pp. 475–9, https://doi.org/10.1080/00207284.2019.1676644.

The First Fijians

Today, the indigenous peoples are collectively known as *iTaukei*, which also generally applies to those from more recent migrations, including Rotumans, Rabi Islanders (also known as Banabans), Solomon Islanders, and Kioa Islanders. Rotuma was annexed by the British in 1881 and absorbed into the colony of Fiji. Rotumans have Tongan and Samoan influences. Rabi Islanders (also known as Banabans) are Micronesians who arrived in Fiji following the devastation of their islands by Australian companies mining guano, a byproduct of bird manure. The companies virtually stripped the island of its resources, making it uninhabitable. After the Second World War ended, they were resettled on Rabi Island, Fiji. Solomon Islanders arrived after Fiji's annexation by the British in 1874 to work on sugar plantations. Their descendants settled around Suva, Deuba, and the Ovalau Island group. The Kioa Islanders originally came from the islands of Tuvalu, which had become overcrowded. Following the Second World War, the Kioans purchased Kioa Island in Fiji and resettled there.

The Approach to Annexation

The people of Fiji at the time the Deed of Cession – the treaty that transferred sovereignty to Britain, was signed, were "a mixture of Melanesians and Polynesians . . . Fiji was not politically united; it consisted of fourteen chiefdoms, separate political entities with differing dialects.[2] These groups materialised into the three confederacies. The two pre-eminent entities were the Kabuna, led by the Vunivalu of Bau, Ratu Seru Cakobau, and Tovata, led by the influential Tongan chief Enele Ma'afu, who was Cakobau's nemesis.

Ma'afu was sent by the Tongan king to maintain good relations with the locals and ensure the expatriate Tongan community's safety and welfare following the murder of a Tongan preacher. He was an influential and powerful warlord who soon became entangled in local partisan politics, and with

---

[2] Helen Goodwill Tavola, *Secondary Education in Fiji: A Key to the Future* (Institute of Pacific Studies of the University of the South Pacific, 1991).

Perspectives of British Colonial Rule in the Fiji Islands

his power base in Fiji intact, he was included in the final stages of the annexation of Fiji.

Cakobau inherited the title Tui Vunivalu or King of Bau from his father, Chief Tanoa, who had defeated the powerful Burebasaga Confederacy with the help of the Swedish beachcomber, Charlie Savage.

The institutions of government, in the modern sense, were made up of settlers, mostly Australians, with the Tui Viti as the head of the government. In June 1871, John Bates Thurston, an adventurer and businessman and the British honorary consul, persuaded most of the high chiefs, including Ma'afu, to accept a monarchy with Cakobau as *the King* of all Fiji.

With the encouragement of the settler members of his government, Cakobau assumed the style of Tui Viti – King of Fiji – and he let it be understood that he held sway over *all* of Fiji, which to some chieftains was an invitation to war. Still, none dared to declare war because of the mercenaries lined up against them. Thus encouraged, Cakobau held no prior consultation with the remaining confederate chieftains and proceeded with the advice of his cabinet to open negotiations with London.

What "constitutional monarchy" meant in translation is debatable, and some chiefs thought they were betrayed, but it seems that Cakobau was not concerned with such minutiae as concerned other chiefs. A formal representation was made to London to annexe the islands without preconditions. The title "King of Fiji" suited London: it signified and legitimised the transfer of the entire archipelago to Great Britain under the terms of the Deed signed on 10 October 1874.

The transfer was made without the consent and authority of *all* the confederate chiefs. Cakobau's fiat was limited in scope; however, he had become a powerful warlord, with the support of the settlers and the constabulary, who were able to sideline the dissenting elements.

Had all the chiefs signed the Deed of Cession, they would have acknowledged Cakobau as their "king" and overlord. It begs the question of whether the Deed of Cession was a legitimate document because it had just thirteen signatories, three of whom were from Cakobau's clan.

The First Fijians

The successful annexation of Fiji signalled the settlers' hijacking of the indigenous people's legal position. Fiji's future was in the hands of some characters with dubious credentials. Some had seen commercial opportunities on the islands and deliberated on the possibilities of increasing their control in the administration to deprive the indigenous Fijians of most of their rights under the Deed, effectively changing their status and bringing in laws similar to Australia's management of its indigenous peoples.

The settlers looked forward to adding Fiji to the empire's list of territories and aimed to marginalise and eventually ostracise the Fijians.

The euphoric *Fiji Times* reflected views held by the majority of settlers in 1873:

> Cakobau feels the power of the white race and must bow to it. Already, the Anglo-Saxon has firmly planted his foot here, and so certainly must he remain. The whites can do without the natives, but Fiji can never again be free of the white man. Her destiny is sealed, and as sure as the American Indians, the New Zealanders, and Australians have had to give way to the superior race, so surely must the Fijian. *Fiji* must now become the home of a white race; its original inhabitants are no doubt doomed . . .[3]

The settlers had serious intentions and considered it their patriotic duty to expand the empire and establish greater control over the Pacific region, with Fiji playing the central role. It would become a British bastion in the South Seas, a proper British colony run in the interests of Englishmen and the Empire.[4]

---

[3] Emphasis added. For implementation of policy on a wider scale generally, see Martin J. Wiener, *An Empire on Trial: Race, Murder and Justice under British Rule, 1875–1935* (Cambridge University Press, 2009).

[4] Timothy J. Macnaught, *The Fijian Colonial Experience: A Study of the Neotraditional Order under British Colonial Rule Prior to World War II* (Australian National University, 1982).

Perspectives of British Colonial Rule in the Fiji Islands

Sir Hercules Robinson departed soon after the treaty was signed and sealed and his permanent replacement Sir Arthur Hamilton-Gordon arrived in 1875; it was a fortuitous choice: a dedicated and committed Christian, he had extensive experience overseeing the oppressed in the colonies and interpreted the recently executed deed to favour the Fijian traditions and customs as much as he could to get maximum advantage to his causes and to extract maximum cooperation from the still powerful chiefs.

The proposition was thwarted by J. B. Thurston, Cakobau's putative prime minister. The choice of Sir Arthur Hamilton-Gordon was fortuitous: a dedicated and committed Christian, his extensive experience overseeing the oppressed in the colonies heralded a sympathetic outcome for the Fijians. Aware of the plans and previous intrigues, he made it plain that the needs of some 140,000 Fijians and their expectations of being governed righteously and in accordance with native usages and customs were not to be subordinated to the contrary expectations of some 1,500 European settlers and resident adventurers.

The Chiefs of Fiji - *Turaga Bose Levu* **("Great Council of Chiefs")**

Following the cession, the high chiefs had no real power, but the reverential aspects of customary deference and regard continued. The people's attachment to their leaders was a welcome feature of the native culture and endured throughout British rule. The chiefs and the administration enjoyed the stability that augmented total control over their lives, but only after the Governor extracted their allegiance to the Crown.

Their leverage over the commoners was by the Governor's grace, and the chiefs were now presented and appeared to the people as rulers, which was a satisfactory outcome for all concerned.

The "Great Council of Chiefs" (GCC) was established as an advisory body to the Governor; it was viewed by the commoners as an important institution where their chiefs convened to discuss significant issues and as a source of *their* government.

The First Fijians

For nearly a century, the attachment to the Executive Council, the GCC, became a powerful adjunct to streamline and devise policies suitable for governing the indigenous Fijians peacefully and successfully. Despite the warmth of the bond, the chiefs could not individually or collectively influence many aspects of government policy that demanded greater integration of the Fijians into the mainstream. Policies that might enrich people's lives regarding social and health issues did not get the attention they deserved.

Consequently, as the twenty-first century dawned, the Fijians continued to struggle with modern commercial practices and entrepreneurial skills. After more than a century of the treaty with Great Britain and fifty years following independence, no *Fijian* commercial outfit of any significance serves the nation.

Politically, people's perception that Britain had brought peace to the land and that the chiefs were involved in the new regime brought comfort and a measure of certainty to both the people and the administration. Peace was a bonus, and the almost seamless continuity helped to consolidate the new era of colonialism in the Pacific.

Time had stood still, suspended as if the chiefs were soon to bestow the magical means to equalise people's expectations. After decades of colonial rule, the people continued to acknowledge that only the chiefs knew what was best for them. Professor Ford quotes an interview with a villager. It gives a revealing insight into the people's consciousness, and the understanding the British had of the people:

> "Whatever the chief says shall be carried out. He knows what is best for us. Who would want to destroy the Tui? . . . he is the leader of our community, and no one could take his place. If he were not here, we would be lost." [5]

---

[5] Professor Clellan S. Ford. The Role of A Fijian Chiefs. American Sociological Review. Vol. 3. No. 4. Aug.1938. pp. 541 – 550. Yale University. 550. https://doi.org/3773421

Perspectives of British Colonial Rule in the Fiji Islands

The British, being totally aware of this attachment, kept the chiefs close.

Under Gordon's administration, residual, inconsequential powers were vested in the native authority of traditional rulers, as constituted under the aegis of the GCC's ordinance. The effectiveness of indirect rule rested on the total commitment and collaboration of the chiefs, as well as their close bond with the people.

After independence, during the calamitous period of the mid-1980s, the Fijian leaders were emboldened, without Britain's restraining influence, to act more in line with ancient traditional indifference to other rights and privileges. This collection of individuals, with inflated egos, came out on their own and displayed their grip on the nation during this period. Their latent political conditioning sprang into action.

In May 1988, almost a year after the first coup, Ratu Sir Penaia Ganilau, GCMG, KCVO, KBE, DSO, the Governor-General of Fiji, reminded the GCC that "the leadership, the source of life, the future of Fiji, is in your hands"! He did not order the troops to return to their barracks; rather, the tone and action of Her Majesty's representative led to unqualified support for the rebellion.

In the twentieth century, in a post-colonial, multicultural nation, the voice of the unelected Ratu Sir Penaia was heard after the military coup as he addressed his fellow chiefs: "The future is in your hands". Instead of seeking solutions based on modern democratic principles as a permanent solution, he exhorted them to return to the prehistoric era of colonial rule. A period when the elite enjoyed patronage and the high life. The endowment of the selected few was preserved in the institutionalised Council of Chiefs, to which he now referred to bring stability to the nation.

Even after what Oxford and distinguished institutions had given them, that was the extent of his intellectual prowess in resolving the national turmoil and instability gusting across the former British colony.

This one-time army officer and committed colonialist was knighted for his personal service to the Queen and for his role in perpetuating the special relationship between Fiji and the

The First Fijians

throne. As the Governor-General, he pardoned and promoted Rabuka, the coup leader, and installed him as head of the government. He further declared that Rabuka was immune from prosecution.[6] Colonel Rabuka later removed the monarch and declared Fiji a republic!

The GCC, as an advisory body to the colonial Governor, had outlived its usefulness by the time of Fiji's independence. Like Sir Penaia and others, the chiefs had derived strength and support from the colonial Executive Council and the GCC. Under the new constitution of an independent nation and the expanded bicameral parliament, the work of the GCC was redundant. It had served the colonial masters with great honour and dedication.

The GCC's most significant influence and actions were during and after the revolutions of 1987. It backed the coup leaders against all logic and prudence. During this chaos, it collectively seemed to celebrate the outcome of an illegal and unconstitutional act of a military leader.

The GCC had assumed a political role that was not intended when it was established in the early days of colonisation. Surprisingly, however, even inexplicably, in their chaotic mental state, the military dictator removed the monarch as the nation's head of state, declared Fiji a republic, and subsequently it was expelled Fiji from the Commonwealth.

The new constitution entrenched the age-old phobias and biases of the colonial era and polarised and institutionalised racism.

---

[6] Daryl Tarte, *Ratu Penaia Ganilau in 20th century Fiji: People Who Shaped the Nation* (University of the South Pacific, 2001), p. 177. For the nepotism and double standards practised by the chiefs during this period of crisis, see Kenneth Bain, "Obituary: Ratu Sir Penaia Ganilau", *The Independent*, 17 December 1993, www.independent.co.uk/news/people/obituary-ratu-sir-penaia-ganilau-1467936.html, accessed 12 February 2025.

Perspectives of British Colonial Rule in the Fiji Islands

During negotiations for constitutional changes prior to independence, the Fijians sought reassurance that the bond between the Fijian people and the Crown would remain intact.[7]

The events themselves proved that the chiefs were playing games with the British to extract maximum rewards for their allegiance to the administration and to the Crown. With the ease and the lack of remorse or even shame, they ditched the monarchy; it would not be unreasonable to suggest that their loyalty was skin-deep and opportunistic.

Advent of Commodore Bainimarama.

Before Commodore Frank Bainimarama appeared on the political scene in 2006 and reset and recalibrated Fiji's ethnic components, the chiefs were virtual directors of the people's destiny.

The chiefs required the nation's constitutional arrangement to recognise indigenous Fijians as rulers, without giving any rights, entitlements, and privileges to other races, especially the Indians, a major factor in Fiji's prosperity. The immigrants' basic requirements were political assurances that would ensure political stability, so necessary to foster a good economic environment.

The commodore sought to overturn the existing racist concepts that had persisted in previous constitutions. As a farsighted leader, he understood that there were no credible and realistic alternatives except to remove the regressive elements that had dogged the nation for over a century. To achieve a lasting and stable future for the new nation, a drastic change was needed, but without a systematic overhaul. The political system established by the colonial administration served its specific objectives of embedding discord among the races, which ultimately bore fruit in the multiple coups of the new nation.

---

[7] Brij V. Lal, Ed. *A Timebomb Lies Buried: Fiji's Road to Independence, 1960–1970.* Australian National University. Ch. 4. Fiji's Constitutional Conference, 1965.

Bainimarama acted decisively and irrevocably to -

"lead us into peace and prosperity and mend the ever-widening racial divide that currently besets our multicultural nation."[8]

Following his ultimatum to the sitting Prime Minister Laisenia Qarase, who was brought in following the coup of George Speight in 2000, was finally removed after a period of stagnation and further regressive policies, by Commodore Bainimarama in the coup of 2006.

Finally, now at the helm, he undertook and reversed the many causes of the nation's unhappiness that had been fostered over many years, as well as the destabilising and futile coups of the past decades.

He established the Fiji First Party and, as prime minister in 2014, undertook a comprehensive review that was necessary for a permanent resolution, instituting the long-awaited universal suffrage.

In his address to the UN in September 2007, he said:

> "In 1970, Fiji started its journey as a young nation on a rather shaky foundation, with a race-based Constitution, one which rigidly compartmentalised our communities. The "democracy" which came to be practised in Fiji was marked by divisive, adversarial, inward-looking, race-based politics. The legacy of leadership, at both community and national levels, was a fractured nation. Fiji's people were not allowed to share a common national identity.
>
> Of the two major communities, indigenous Fijians were instilled with fear of dominance and dispossession by Indo-Fijians, and they desired protection of their status as

---

[8] https://en.wikipedia.org/wiki/Frank_Bainimarama. "Commander RFMF: Public Declaration of Military Takeover", archived 15 September 2009 at the Wayback Machine, Fiji Government, 5 December 2006.

the Indigenous people. Indo-Fijians, on the other hand, felt alienated and marginalised, as second-class citizens in their own country, the country of their birth, Fiji."[9]

The reactions in chiefly circles were mostly unsympathetic. The antagonists displayed no understanding or sympathy for Bainimarama's changes. Their perennial concerns were that Indians had no rights in the colony, and the law should reflect this position.

The new constitution, which had far-reaching consequences for the future, was put to the general electorate, ratified, and enacted in 2014, seventy years after it was first mooted by the then Indian lawmakers.

Ratu Sukuna, KBE, KCMG: A Social Reformer?

To whom much is given, much will be required.[10]

Dignity does not consist in possessing honours, but in the consciousness that we deserve them.[11]

A burden was lifted from the chiefs with the transfer of sovereignty to the British in 1874. However, they were transformed instantly from the dreaded warriors and cannibals of the South Pacific to more moderate pursuits, and within decades, had successfully produced a leader worthy of admiration by the British Empire.

Gordon lost no time in corralling the former adversaries into a cohesive group. The higher-ranking chiefs were assigned duties to maintain and manage control in villages according to the governor's edicts and advice.

---

[9] From a statement by Commodore Josaia Voreqe Bainimarama, Prime Minister of the Republic of the Fiji Islands, 62nd Session of the UN General Assembly, New York, 28 September 2007; PDF available at www.un.org/webcast/ga/62/2007/pdfs/fiji-en.pdf, accessed 27 February 2025.

[10] Luke 12:48.

[11] Aristotle.

The First Fijians

The rise of Ratu Sukuna – a chief of high rank, a descendant of the King of Fiji - was timely and a stabilising conduit throughout the layers of Fijian tribes and hierarchy.

Today, he looks down from his lofty plinths erected by a grateful nation.

The lion's share of his active life revolved around broader issues of colonial administrative matters and Fijian organisational policies. As a member of the Executive Council, he had no executive powers or authority in his own right. What influence he exercised at the top table for his people's advancement and transformation into the modern age is a moot point.

The government never exactly pampered the Fijians with social or economic support. Schools and amenities were basic and never intended or designed to intensify the community's reach into the twentieth century.

In his time, he was a highly decorated individual; his presence boosted confidence among his people, assuring them that all was well. But aligning this great accolade with his declared aspirations for his people, who lived and survived the daily grind of unvarying village life, will not be easy, as the two aspects cannot be shown to be morally equivalent.

Emitai Boladuadua (Fiji Times 4.6.2023) supported the colonial view of Sir Lala that he had -

> "laid the *basis of economic development* of the colony at the back of the sugar and related agro-based industries. This he did when he made possible the opening of Indigenous Fijian traditional land for all those [Indian] farmers who needed land." *[emphasis added]*

By the time Ratu Sukuna entered the Fijian political scene, sugar production was a well-established industry, producing both the raw material and profits for the government and investors, operating as a well-oiled machine. Leasing land to farmers was a controllable process, although it needed adjustments and simplification. This could have been accomplished by the GCC through an Executive Council order or by legislation. To make a big deal that Ratu Sukuna's

Perspectives of British Colonial Rule in the Fiji Islands

contributions led to the success of the sugar industry is taking his praises to a level that would embarrass the great man to tears.

The colonial power was less concerned about the minutiae of the Fijians' land leasing process, which it had left to the clans and the chiefs. It was happy to keep away from it as it directly concerned the Fijians' communal land as vested in the *mataqali*. The land was in high demand from expanding sugar cane farmers. The government had devolved the issue to villages to arrange directly with the farmers on a commercial basis.

Sir Lala was aware of the system's irregularities, and he played a key role in streamlining it and implementing uniform rules across the colony. The expanding economy's demands had to be met with a better system of land distribution. He displayed leadership as he set up the Native Land Trust Board – the NLTB[12] and he devoted his energies to convincing the clans, many holding contrary views, to agree to common terms on which to assign the leases. This brought uniformity and predictability to the process, giving confidence to the farmers who now had to settle the length of the lease, rather than the entire terms and conditions.

Delaying or denying land to the growers would defeat the purpose of the high cost of importing foreign labour. It was in the interests of the colony that a streamlined and efficient system of leasing was instituted for better management and consistency of sugar production.

Ratu Sukuna was born on 22 April 1888, after Gordon and Thurston laid the foundations of the industry, and after the immigrants were loaded on cargo ships in Calcutta and arrived in Fiji in 1879.

As head of the *iTaukei*, his influence in the GCC counted. Ratu Sukuna was a charismatic leader and guiding light for his community. He indeed worked to maintain cordial relations with all citizens of the colony, and one cannot recall disparaging remarks he made against any community.

---

[12] Emitai Boladuadua. Fiji Times. 4/6/2023. "Life and Legacy". "The Life and Legacy of Ratu Sir Lala Sukuna", *Fiji Times* (4 June 2023)

"…as a leader and statesman who was the first to recognize and accept that Fiji belongs to all its peoples both as individuals and as communities, and that our well-being and prosperity as a country require our commitment to each other, in mutual trust and cooperation, to building a shared future.[13]

His preoccupations with mega projects and his role as a colonial administrator were impressive and struck a chord with the establishment, but left little time to direct his energies to primary societal projects he may have wished to pursue.

As a conscientious and resolute leader, he no doubt had concerns about his people's future, but it would have required superhuman efforts to serve two masters. The absence of a clear roadmap to improve the quality of their lives through education, for instance, has led to speculation about the Fijian leader's role and purpose in the lives of commoners. Helen Tavola suggests that "The lack of pressure for improved education [by the Chiefs] for Fijians resulted in the government's lack of interest and neglect."[14]

Colonial Fijians were disciplined and well organised and could be called upon at a moment's notice to do the chief's bidding. They, however, estimated that the people's future would be better served cushioned against the uncertainties and confusions of the outside world, which only they, the chiefs, could understand and deal with - on behalf of their people: the ethnic and political stresses, economic challenges and social and intercommunal issues. Magnanimity or madness?

The colonial government's lack of interest is understandable, as their primary motive was to maintain power with minimal effort. This was easily achieved with the ready and

---

[13] Jioji Kotobalavu on Ratu Sukuna's legacy at special symposium: Ratu Sir Lala Sukuna: Remembering his contribution to Fiji. Fiji Leaks. 24 April 2016. https//: fijileaks.com. accessed 12 March 2025.

[14] Tavola, "Secondary Education in Fiji", p. 21.

Perspectives of British Colonial Rule in the Fiji Islands

eager cooperation without exception of the hereditary chiefs. Most were highly decorated and educated but not enlightened individuals; cultured, perhaps, but remote and insulated from their poor and deprived kith and kin.

There would be no budding middle classes of the future to engineer further reforms and encourage others to follow them.

Historically, no *iTaukei* - Fijian leader of note stood up as a social crusader or activist. Among the chiefs, Ratu Sukuna believed his people were rather better off as farmers and artisans.[15] As far as he was concerned, the people were beyond liberation from their subsistence culture and existence, and he had more pressing commitments as an officer of the Crown. He was the establishment's voice, *not* the people's – people remained rudderless and suspended between the Neolithic Revolution (when humans transitioned from hunter-gatherers to settled agricultural pursuits) and the Middle Ages.

Ratu Sukuna's statement [16] recorded that his nation needed

> "boat-builders, men skilled in Indigenous handicrafts, girls with a practical knowledge of housecraft: home-cleaning, cooking, washing, sewing, nursing".

While he was aware of and understood the current conditions in his communities, his evaluation and proposals lacked confidence and determination to help the people transition into the modern enterprise culture.

It is doubtful that the leadership was collectively unaware of the existential problems at the core and the best solutions to remedy the deficit, but were unwilling to seek help. This was a delicate issue – this would have meant a confrontation with the authorities. The government of the day, however one may wish

---

[15] Helen Goodwill Tavola, "Secondary Education in Fiji: An Investigation into School Effectiveness in a Changing Society", Quoting her PhD thesis, University of London, 1990, p. 21

[16] Ibid

to describe it, was never in sympathy with or ever encouraged or planned higher educational development in any non-white British citizen with facilities to match. They did not need engineers, doctors, accountants, lawyers, entrepreneurs, architects, and the like.

The writing was writ large on the wall long before independence. Ill-prepared at independence to face the pressures of the modern world in economic, technical, and scientific challenges, people came up with a solution of their own as soon as a scapegoat was identified. The period between then and 1987 was one of frustrating attempts on almost all fronts of economic activity to level up, but without much success under a government whose concerns for the indigenous population were on par with those of the former colonial administration. As then *"A commoner never has had to think for himself, for his work has always been directed under the communal system."* Dr Brij Lal observed that leading figures, such as Ratu Sir Lala Sukuna and later his successor, Ratu Sir Kamisese Mara, considered that the people, individually and collectively, would benefit from continuing with the traditional occupations of village life. The view was very much endorsed by the government. This was demonstrably an error of judgement and foresight.

As a legislator – a member of the executive branch – Ratu Sukuna was aware of how other communities, particularly Indian immigrants, had acclimated to their unfamiliar environment and improved their outlook for the future through self-help. They had elevated their lifestyles within a few decades, with no concessions or support from the government. Ratu Sukuna was also aware of the immigrants' preoccupations with and proactivity in certain matters and directly addressed and raised the issue:

> "Let us not ignore the fact that there is another community settled in our midst. I refer to the Indians. They have increased more rapidly than we. They have become producers on our soil. They are continuously striving to better themselves. Although they are of a different race, yet we are each a unit in

the British Empire. They have shouldered many burdens that have helped Fiji onward [17]"

The issue is not known to have inspired many to emulate the actions of the immigrants. No committee was known to have been set up to investigate the matter and seek help, advisory or financial, to formulate plans and ideas for a comprehensive overhaul of the Fijian educational system, from primary to secondary to tertiary levels – nothing less.

Ratu Sukuna possessed many attributes, including an unparalleled personal experience and erudition unmatched by any indigenous leader in Melanesia, Micronesia, or Polynesia. The last governor of the colony was quite pointed in his remarks about the opportunities the chiefs missed during the British hegemony.

Education for Fijians

Within twenty years of the annexation in 1874, the government set up rudimentary primary schools, and most indigenous children were taught the Fijian language. The limited scope of the vernacular limited their learning horizons, but the Church, as the primary source of education, had its reasons. Their primary objective was to civilise the heathens in readiness to introduce the teachings of Christ.

The Methodist Church chose the vernacular as its medium. Improving people's vocational potential and inter-communal relationships-predicated on speaking a common language, to allow them to come together for any common purpose, was not among their concerns. Heavily dependent on missionaries, the Fijian education scheme, approved by the government, has been described as *"irrelevant to the progress of Fiji"*.[18] With that level of erudition, the people were never well-positioned to compete for scarce resources within the context of the new social order and emerging enterprise culture.

---

[17] Sir Lala's speech during Great Council of Chief's meeting in 1939.

[18] K.L. Gillion, quoted in Tavola, "Secondary Education in Fiji", p. 13.

The First Fijians

The colonial government had declared on many occasions that it was responsible for seeing that everyone in every village was well-provided for and resourced to have a fighting chance of catching up with the twentieth century.

Sir Robert Foster, the last colonial governor of Fiji, had a different view: in 1970, he sagely observed in his last despatch to the Colonial Office:

> "Yet another sensitive subject is that of employment generally. When jobs are scarce, members of each community are always liable to resent losing an opportunity for work to someone of another race. Fijians also now realise how much they have missed by failing to start businesses of their own. *Their reaction is to blame everyone else for their lack of the necessary capital and training, and to ignore the fact that with greater effort and resolution they could have done much to help themselves.* A reconstituted and (hopefully) revitalized Ministry of Fijian Affairs is to be charged with particular responsibility for securing for them a fairer slice of the economic cake, probably by providing them with special assistance.[19]"

The plans of Sir Arthur Gordon – later Lord Stanmore - for the Fijians' literary and intellectual development fell short of a comprehensive and focused introduction to the modern world's economic and technological future. The Fijian leadership never prompted him to develop this proposition further. The Governor insisted that he wished to *preserve* their traditions, decreeing that -

> the Fijian people should be freed from the pressures of commercial employment and allowed to progress at their own

---

[19] Brij V. Lal, *A Time Bomb Lies Buried: Fiji's Road to Independence, 1960–1970* (ANU Press, 2008) *p.* 103; Appendix 2. Fiji Final Dispatch (8 Oct. 1970). PDF available at https://library.oapen.org/viewer/web/viewer.html?file=/bitstream/handle/20.500.12657/33611/459739.pdf?sequence=1&isAllowed=y, accessed 13 February 2025.

pace in their traditional surroundings, paying tax in kind rather than cash, and tending to their subsistence lifestyle in their age-old fashion.[20]

This was a significant error of judgement that was never corrected, despite the fact that many Fijian *leaders* returned with degrees paid for by the British government. These "leaders" today are held in high esteem by the people, thanks to the Public Relations Department of the colonial administration.

A decade before Fiji gained its independence, Sir Alan Burns was appointed to investigate the country's land and population issues. The Commission of Inquiry (the Burns Commission)[21] recommended reforms to bring Indigenous Fijians up to date with modern life.

The chiefs rejected the recommendations in favour of continuing communal systems, customs, and associated traditions.

---

[20] Brij V. Lal, *Islands of Turmoil* (ANU Press, 2020). p 3.
[21] Commission of Inquiry to Investigate Land and Population Problems in Fiji. The National Archives, Kew. Reference: CO 1036/811.

2

Events Leading to Colonisation

It will be the high task of all My Governments to superintend and assist the development of these countries, according to their varying degrees of advancement, for the benefit of the inhabitants and the general welfare of mankind.[1]

Abel Tasman was the first European to sight the Fiji Islands and sail in Fijian waters. He crossed the northeast fringe of the group in 1643; Captain James Cook followed in 1774; and Captain Bligh was chased out of Fiji waters by the ferocious Fijians in their quick war canoes in 1789. After the mutiny on the *Bounty*, Captain Bligh returned in 1792 to map the area known today as Bligh Waters.

Until the treaty that transferred the islands to British sovereignty, the settlers were preoccupied with the slave trade. The Hansard Report of 13 June 1873 records details of slave traders perpetrating the horrors of the bloodstained ship 'Carl', and the murders which had been committed on the natives who had been caught and imprisoned in the hold and fired upon; a Member of the Government (Cakobau's) being the consignee of the cargo and having disposed of the survivors at a commission of 5%.[2]

It was not usually acknowledged nor observed by Fijian historians and other commentators that members of the

---

[1] George V. His Majesty's Speech. House of Lords. 23 December 1920 Hansard.vol 39 cc950-4

[2] Parl. Deb. vol. 216, cols. 934–59 (13 June 1873). The resolution debated was that "the Chiefs of Fiji and the White residents therein have signified their desire that Great Britain should assume the protectorate or sovereignty of those islands". The resolution was moved by Mr M'Arthur.

government, under the leadership of Thurston, were slave owners plying the vast Pacific area, safe from the attention of British warships. One member of that government, Mr Smith, owned the notorious slave ship, the *Nukulau*. The trade was centred in Fiji and had brought such reproach on the British name that annexation was considered the only way to put a stop to it. [3]

Members of the then so-called White Government of Fiji enjoyed the patronage of Tui Vunivalu, the Chief of Bau. The government was in debt to the Americans, and the cotton industry was in a free fall. J. B. Thurston, the "prime minister", pleaded with the Colonial Office to transfer the sovereignty of Fiji to Great Britain to save it from bankruptcy. This request was highlighted in the Resolution of the House of Commons: "The Chiefs of Fiji and the white settlers therein have signified their desire that Great Britain should assume the protectorate or sovereignty of those Islands."[4]

European Settlers: What Brought Them to Fiji

The discovery of gold in Australia attracted fortune seekers and adventurers from Europe. Thousands of gold hunters and opportunists created a fierce and crowded environment, leading many to seek richer pastures elsewhere in the Pacific. Fiji conveniently loomed on the horizon. Returning seafarers seemed to see almost limitless possibilities in the islands, from cheap and fertile land to trading in *bêche-de-mer* (sea cucumber), a delicacy in the Far East, and the possibilities of abundance of sandalwood.

Taxation was unheard of in Fiji. No law governed the sale and purchase of land during the Cakobau–Thurston period of government. Land was available and affordable, and its price was determined according to what the chiefs believed to be fair. Payment in kind ranged from trinkets to muskets and depended

---

[3] HC Deb 13 June 1873 vol 216 cc934-59
[4] Ibid.

Events Leading to Colonisation

on the status of the chief. The attractions were too great to ignore, and increasing numbers of settlers arrived.

They came in many guises: some were shipwrecked, there were "blackbirders",[5] beachcombers, adventurers, and those who had had enough of seafaring and pirating settled down with local wives. They exploited sandalwood from 1804 until it was depleted by 1809. Attention reverted to other commodities, helped by increased shipping traffic between Australia and the US. The ships replenished supplies at local ports, traded *bêche-de-mer*,[6] and exchanged other goods until it was impossible to source them in profitable quantities. Fiji was an open territory. Many found refuge, freedom, and profit in the wilds of this tropical paradise.

A new agricultural industry with great commercial possibilities was cotton, which some found alluring and set forth to establish on an industrial scale. However, the nascent enterprise needed a predictable and reliable local labour force. Some were recruited from other Pacific Islands: an arrangement that worked for a short term. The endurance of the Pacific Islanders had its limits, and many soon succumbed to the malaise that had afflicted most Melanesians. A disciplined way of life was not for them, especially if this meant uprooting trees, digging and hoeing all day for days.

The American Civil War (1861–5) interrupted the supply of cotton to the world market. Cotton grew wild in Fiji, and as the global appetite for this raw material increased, the prospect of farming cotton on the islands attracted persons with grand ambitions, but they lacked knowledge of the varieties of cotton best suited for the locations. The island of Taveuni, in the northeast of the archipelago near Vanua Levu, had the ideal land for this developing industry.

---

[5] People kidnapped or deceived into working as slaves. The perpetrators, usually captains, owners of ships based in Australian and other parts of the Pacific, were called "blackbirders"

[6] Jay Narayan, *The Political Economy of Fiji* (University of the South Pacific, 1984), p. 15.

Perspectives of British Colonial Rule in the Fiji Islands

Incorrect decisions and a lack of government support cost the industry significant monetary loss. After a decade of growing the wrong variety of cotton, the discovery of the Sea Island cotton raised hopes of a better outcome. The new variety was introduced and proved a success. It received widespread international acclaim for its high quality and established Fiji as a leading producer of high-grade cotton on the global stage. However, this success was brief, as Fiji's perennial labour problems and worsening world prices led to the industry's final and sad demise, despite holding much promise. The producers' grief stemmed from a lack of adequate consideration for its propagation.

Settlers Seek a Settlement with Great Britain

Settlements on the islands continued to grow with speculators and adventurers from nearby islands occupied by Germans – in Samoa, and French in New Caledonia and Tahiti - and Americans, among parties in search of richer pastures but none were more interested in Fiji than the Anglo-Saxons from Great Britain, Australia, and New Zealand who formed the largest group in the archipelago and eventually put together a government with the local warlord and administered large sections of the Fiji Islands.

To the ambitious and politically inclined European immigrants, the islands seemed stable and ready for a political settlement with London. However, a more menacing problem arose, which initially seemed minor but grew to threaten Fiji's existence as a free nation.

3

The Americans and Fiji's Future

A small group of Americans resided on the island of Levuka (which later became Fiji's capital in 1874). On 4 July 1858, American Independence Day, the American consul's store caught fire accidentally after a shell fired by the consul landed near it and damaged the building. A local group of Fijians took advantage, looted the shop, and caused further loss to the building.

The American government claimed damages from the chief responsible for the villagers who resided in the local confederacy. The legitimate authority to claim compensation from was Cakobau, the *"Tui Vunivalu* of Bau" – the paramount chief of Bau, who claimed suzerainty over the rest of Fiji. This was sufficient for the Americans to direct their claims for damages to this self-styled king of Fiji. Needless to say, the other chiefs would have nothing to do with this claim – to them, Cakobau was at best "first among equals".

The cost of reparation claimed by the American consul was estimated at $5,000 for the damage to the store. Worse was to follow for Cakobau. Shortly after the disaster in Levuka, Ratu Cakobau's subjects set fire to the American consul's establishment on the island of Nukulau, just off the Suva Peninsula. The American government's claim escalated to $50,000—a sum beyond the impoverished and hapless Chief.

When the Americans saw no movement from Cakobau, a warship was dispatched to persuade him to satisfy the Americans' claim, or they would carry out their threat to annihilate or annexe the islands. Neither of these prospects appealed to him nor to the settler communities. With the increased traffic between the US and Australasia, the Americans would have happily annexed the islands to have a dedicated base at this important crossroad in the central South Pacific.

Perspectives of British Colonial Rule in the Fiji Islands

The Cakobau government was not constituted in the conventional Western political structure. It did not have departments responsible for foreign affairs, internal matters, taxation, and finance. Under the circumstances, the American liability was beyond the Paramount Chief's resources, and he was at wits' end to find a way out of this gargantuan impasse.

With the help of his British advisers, he made a formal approach to Queen Victoria for aid, but it was rejected. Without industries or natural resources to exploit or act as collateral, Britain saw neither immediate gain nor the possibility of future commercialisation and profit from the islands. On balance, the island's sizeable liability outweighed its assets and prospects.

The British government's reluctance to accept liability caused trepidation at the heart of the government. The Americans' threats to blow up Levuka were becoming real. Cakobau's advisers resolved to take matters into their own hands. They counselled the Chief, saying that the only practical strategy left to them was to sell some real estate in a remote area to entrepreneurs who wished to engage in sugar cane production, turning a possible disaster into a potential win-win situation for the Tui Vunivalu. A large chunk of Suva, approximately 200,000 acres, was sold, and sufficient funds were raised to settle the debt.

The influence of foreign advisers in this "government" gained ascendancy. Australians who knew the country well were well-organised and able, and assumed major influence under the astute leadership of J. B. Thurston.

For the island's future security and progress, they advised the Chief to seek transfer of sovereignty to Britain. Thurston was ready to facilitate an application to the Colonial Office for the unconditional annexation of the islands. No other foreign power had as great a presence and level of influence in the archipelago as the British.

Since the first fire accident and the subsequent settlement with the Americans, the cotton industry had shown promise; however, the issues faced were now linked to fluctuations in global cotton prices.

With political and financial stability set to improve, and the Americans' demands satisfied, a treaty was now a real possibility. A glimmer of hope spread among the settlers for a profitable development of this newfound real estate that could be an idyllic setting for the well-healed and adventurous from the nearby dominions.

Great Britain accepted the new terms and conditions, and despatched Sir Hercules Robinson, the Governor of New South Wales, as emissary to Fiji to complete the formalities as the Queen's representative. The King of Fiji and the confederate chiefs, including Chief Ma'afu of Tonga, who were persuaded to be parties to the deal, set their seals on the document on 10 October 1874.

Commercialisation and Expansion

The incoming Governor, Sir Arthur Hamilton-Gordon, had a packed in-tray. It was an unenviable task, which he managed with skill. He formed a government *from scratch, launched a new industry, began subduing the still-warring* and anti-Cession factions, and moderated traditional and cultural excesses that often led to conflicts. Political stability and regulatory frameworks were essential to effect the government's remit to maintain peace and order across the colony, and all these priorities needed urgent attention.

Dependencies, however, had to be self-financing and *not dependent on Britain*.[1] The cotton industry had its difficulties and drawbacks. However, it had given some hope that industrial-scale cultivation of commercial agriculture was possible despite some intractable problems, and a replacement crop was sought. Time was not on the new Governor's side; he had a full in-tray: to secure economic recovery and ensure political stability and peace in some areas.

The new treaty with Britain, in itself, did not resolve the perennial problems that had vexed the cotton industry for two decades: labour supply and the unpredictable fluctuations in cotton prices. The cotton days were over: the American Civil

---

[1] John T. Ducker, *Beyond Empire: The End of Britain's Colonial Encounter* (Bloomsbury, 2020), p. 2.

Perspectives of British Colonial Rule in the Fiji Islands

War (1861–5) and then the Franco-Prussian War (1870) had put paid to thoughts of its reconsideration.

Fiji's Future: Sugar?

Fiji's future was in the balance. There were no natural resources to exploit, and failed agricultural enterprises that were heavily dependent on manual labour were still raw in the settlers' minds. They also weighed heavily on the Governor's calculations. He turned to an industry familiar to him from his postings in other colonies. His experiences on the island of Mauritius (from 1871 to 1874) proved to be an important factor as he set about establishing the sugar industry in Fiji.

Gordon's initiatives and the concessions granted to the investors and millers sweetened the wallets of the Colonial Sugar Refining Company and the investors J C Smith, who had

> "experimented sugar production in 1874-76 and it was probably he, along with Sahl, who in 1878 asked CSR to build a mill in Rewa."

In 1880, CSR entered the market after coming to a mutual agreement with the Government. This would later prove to be one of the most fruitful decisions in the case of sustaining the sugar industry in Fiji. [2]

The sugar industry was a work-in-progress, and its future success was very much in the hands of the chiefs and the *mataqali* to allocate land to the farmers.

Gordon's objective, primarily, was to arrange a continuous supply of dependable labour that would be its mainstay and a permanent fix for the economy. The Governor's calculations excluded the use of Fijian labour in sugar-cane work.

"Free" economy works on the basic principle of demand and supply of men and materials at a cost. All factors are weighted and evaluated against financial considerations, which are valued against time. For this reason, it was impractical to expand valuable

---

[2] Shayal Devi in an article "Forging Fiji's sweet success The struggle, triumph of the early sugar industry". The Fiji Times. 28.08.2023.

time in coaching and guiding the Fijians in labour for which they could see no immediate benefit to the clan.

Europe and America's economic and political situation stabilised, and sugar was in greater demand as prosperity across the industrialised world exponentially grew. The Governor's experience and knowledge of industrial-scale operations were essential to establishing a solid foundation for long-term financial recovery. Imported immigrant Chinese and Indian labourers were used in the Caribbean colonies by the British, French and Dutch to set up

The Governor's experiences in Mauritius and Trinidad had convinced him of the feasibility of employing Indian labourers; he was also aware that this was a delicate issue with the Indian government, which was concerned about the ill-treatment of labourers in other colonies. The mistreatment led the Indian authorities to tighten regulations and the indenture agreement to curb abuses. Even so, now that slavery was outlawed, indentured servitude was an answer to the labour shortage in sugar-cane plantations.

The Governor applied to the government of India and agreed with the terms that would ensure humane treatment of the labourers by the plantation and mill owners, on whose behalf the colony accepted the terms.

The die-hard former slavers oversaw the workers as if they were dealing with slaves. Although slow to act, the Governor worked positively to enact regulations to protect the labourers against brutal overseers and violent settlers. Gordon was criticised for this from within the growers' circle and from London. He was a considerate and sensitive human being. The reactions to his humane acts only reflected the colonial attitudes towards non-European workers. His subsequent reticence limited his ability to address grievances from the labourers as effectively as he would have wished.

However, by 1916, the government of India, disappointed at the continuing hardships faced by Indians in Fiji, ceased the seemingly endless supply of cheap labour after its frequent warnings about Fiji's behaviour towards the workers were disregarded. The last shipload of labourers arrived on the cargo ship SS *Sutlej* at Suva harbour on 2 November 1916.

4

Europeans Create a New World Order

European expansion and exploitation began in the fifteenth century, when the Portuguese sought new trade routes. Land routes to the East had become perilous, and competition compelled nations to seek alternative sources and markets for spices and luxury goods.

In 1415, the Portuguese conquered Ceuta in North Africa and acquired its land and resources. Their success encouraged other European nations to follow suit; they founded colonies to exploit, trade in, and settle. After looting and pillaging, empire-building became an art. The British Empire, the Portuguese Empire, the Spanish Empire, the German Empire, the Dutch Empire, and the French Empire denuded non-European peoples of gold, natural resources, valuable artefacts, and much more. In exchange, they bequeathed Christianity, currency, disease, and "democracy"; Western values displaced ancient cultural mores.

The tenacity of the Europeans' advances and their lethal activities caused people and languages to die out. By the beginning of the twentieth century, the British had murdered Indigenous Tasmanians in their entirety and had stolen their land. Forced to learn English, many Native Americans gradually lost touch with their ancient cultures and languages. The concept of federalism was first encountered among these prehistoric peoples' settlements and adopted by the Americans as they emerged from the heavy-handedness of colonialism.

By the end of the nineteenth century, with its burgeoning wealth and military prowess, Europe was a continent virtually unrecognisable from its pre-industrial days. Their unparalleled capacity to absorb their ill-gotten gains created a dynamism that

Perspectives of British Colonial Rule in the Fiji Islands

led to many wars within Europe and the emergence of great powers, such as Spain, France, Germany, and, of course, Great Britain, which acquired the most extensive collection of colonies in history.

Britain's Industrial Revolution began with India's de-industrialisation and the destruction of its textile industries by the East India Company. By 1947, India's economy had fallen sixfold since the 19th century.

Europeans sought new areas to exploit, to forage for profit, and gratify their cravings for exotic produce and products. They departed in unsuitable and cramped wooden-hulled sailing ships to traverse uncharted waters. Undeterred, they sailed on, often baffled by their location on the high seas, with only the stars to guide them. They were unaware of the risks of the unknown ahead – the elements, the strange seas, and the final mystery of making landfall – hopefully in India.

Colonisation was not the primary consideration when they first set out; it was the inevitable consequence of their discoveries. The people they encountered were hospitable and mostly welcoming, the land fertile and abundantly endowed with exotic plants, herbs and vegetables. The flora and fauna later enriched the palates of Europe's great and good.

The subsequent violent encroachment of territorial rights left the conquered bewildered and lost. The creeping domination proved a disaster for indigenous peoples, many of whom suffered persecution, diseases, and genocide.

These daring, reckless adventurers viewed other people as chattels; local produce and valuables were theirs to seize, and land and people were no exceptions. A century later, the new world order had become a functioning reality, with the full force and might of Western technologies and cultures. The world had not witnessed such a pervasive force, at once insidious and culturally enlightened, as well as technologically advanced.

Within decades of their arrival in other lands, they had managed to eliminate local hierarchies, confiscate wealth, and set the people on the road to deprivation and misery: lives, cultures, and families in tatters; land and tribes subdivided arbitrarily to satisfy the overwhelming greed of the superpowers of the day.

Transmutation of Slavery into the Indenture System

The cost of labour in any industry is a significant recurring expenditure.

Much of Europe, now enriched from its exploits, was set to compete for scarce resources and greater glory. Wars were inevitable among the more tenacious, determined and dominant nations, such as France and England. Both derived their wealth and power from the colonies and were determined not to be outdone.

The Bank of England was founded in 1694. After its defeat by the French in 1690, England's navy was in tatters. The English were almost on their knees and low on resources to build up their navy to be among the best, and King William III turned to the Bank of England to finance the project.

Slavery was an ideal solution to labour problems in the new colonies, and further access to regular finance was a vital means to ensure that a steady supply of ships and slaves kept the cotton plantations of the Americas flourishing.

Slave voyages were financed by the Lloyds of London and Barclays during the 18th and 19th centuries in the Atlantic slave trade. Similarly engrossed in the slave trade with huge rewards were J.P. Morgan and the predecessors of Citibank, Bank of America and Wells Fargo.

Such was the deep-rooted dependency on slaves for many nations' financial well-being that it seemed it would endure till the end of time. Even so, the writing was on the wall. Slavery was beginning to disturb the minds of conscientious, humanitarian public figures, including Thomas Clarkson, Granville Sharp, William Wilberforce, Olaudah Equiano, also known as 'Gustavus Vaasa' and Josiah Wedgewood, among many others. Many of these were dedicated and practising Christians, as were many of the slave traders!

As Eric Williams puts it:

> "Perhaps the greatest shame of the Atlantic slave trade was that it inspired no shame at all. In their own time, Britain's

slave traders were men of distinction: "worthy men, fathers of families and excellent citizens."[1]

If a novel approach could circumvent this moral dilemma and keep the industries growing and flourishing, that would relieve their consciences of the burden. In their heyday, the slave traders were the leading "humanitarians" of their age: they instituted schools, hospitals, and libraries in some areas. The accolades that followed these great and the good overlooked the pain that preceded the profits.

An enslaved person is a human being owned by another human being as a chattel. As defined by the law, slaves were the property of the free person and were deprived of most of the rights of choice and movement.

The West enjoyed for six centuries the fruits of its peoples' collective callousness and inhumanity to other humans. The moral issues of the day reflected the tensions between Western greed and the Christian doctrine that all men are equal.

The rise of capitalism in Britain and America coincided with the expansion of the slave trade and global trade. Some who agonised over its moral predicament were also found sitting on the fence. Premier financiers such as David Barclay, whose role at the time was described as "ambivalent" as he worked to stop the slave trade while extending credit to slave traders.

The Indenture System

The intensifying anti-slavery sentiments were a growing threat, but not in danger of an immediate cessation of the practice. The indenture agreement previously used in the American colonies found its way into the arsenal of former slave owners, now trading as sugar cane planters. The agreement was a convenient arrangement that placed the burden and duties of carrying out their contractual obligations on the labourers, without putting pressure on the millers and plantation owners to honour their part of the contract.

---

[1] Eric Williams, *Capitalism and Slavery* (Penguin, 2022).

Europeans Create a New World Order

This agreement was a primary contract between the plantation owners and the hired labourers. In effect, it was a get-out-of-jail document for owners, perceived as evidence that the labourers were not enslaved.

Only the means of procuring labourers had altered, not their treatment, which in most cases continued without change.

The transformation was undertaken with great reluctance and foot-dragging. From the abolitionists of the trade movement of the 1770s, the British Empire moved to abolish it in 1807 which ended the buying and selling of people as slaves, when it passed Abolition of the Slave Trade Act; but it took thirty years in the colonies before the practice ceased in 1838, and not before the *enslavers* were compensated for their loss of slave labour.

However, the recruitment process was an exercise in trickery and half-truths. When the ships disgorged their human cargoes in the West Indies, Fiji, or Mauritius, the plantations quickly adopted old slavery methods of controlling the labourers. The simple document prevailed over the constraints imposed by the Emancipation Act of 1838. The terms did not include provisions for fair treatment or methods of dispute resolution. Labourers signified their agreement by their thumbprint on a document which they could neither read nor understand.

The sugar mill owners enthusiastically adopted the indenture system and were reluctant to release the labourers when their terms expired; retaining them saved recruiting and transport costs. The millers and the government ignored reports of ill-treatment, which was rife in all the sugar-cane areas. Government officers, expatriate workers, and their compatriot settlers were of a similar mind, so the old habits of ill-treating plantation workers did not disappear with slavery.

The new device that replaced slavery came to be known as the "indenture system" at the behest and instigation of John Gladstone, and the first shipload of labourers, bound by their indenture contract, left for British Guyana in 1837. But it did not take long before Lord Russell, in 1840, had to write: *"I am not prepared to encounter the responsibility of a measure which may lead to a dreadful loss of life on the one hand, or, on the other, to a new system of slavery".*[2]

The story of the indentured labour system is among the more gut-wrenching tales of the nineteenth century. It was the defining feature of plantations during this period and allowed Western agricultural capitalism a "soft landing" as it struggled to cope with the end of the slave trade, due to the popular mood turning against this most exploitative of all labour practices.[3]

---

[2] National Archives. *Russell to Governor Light, 15 February 1840. Parliamentary Papers. Volume XVI (No56)*
[3] Karthik Venkatesh, "Totaram Sanadhya, an Indian in Fiji: A Life Defined by the Indentured Labour System and the Fight Against It", Firstpost (12 January 2020), www.firstpost.com/india /totaram-sanadhya-an-indian-in-fiji-a-life-defined-by-the-indentured-labour-system-and-the-fight-against-it-7872921.html, accessed 26 August 2020.

5

A New Colony Is Shaped

Omnia mutantur, et nos mutamur in illis.
"All things change, and we change with them."[1]

It is one of the guiding principles in my life, which serves as a reminder that in order to move forward and grow, I must be flexible and willing to change.[2]

Sir Hercules Robinson arrived on 23 September 1874, as *interim* Governor to execute the Deed of Cession on behalf of the Queen. Sir Arthur Hamilton-Gordon arrived in June 1875 as the first full-time Governor of Fiji. He established significant institutions and incorporated customs and traditions that were in harmony with the colony's hierarchy to win the support of the Chiefs, such as granting them chiefly privileges, including rights to the prime produce of the village. Gordon reacted in this way as he viewed the dispossession of Māori lands in Aotearoa (New Zealand) with dismay. He protected Fijian customs and recognised and secured land in perpetuity to the clans as was the wish of the Chiefs. His actions profoundly affected the daily lives of Fijians for nearly a century. He orchestrated the high chiefs, gave them purpose and responsibility, and established their rights and privileges, which they accepted with everlasting gratitude.

Gordon was born in 1829 to aristocratic parents, graduated from Oxford, and joined his father, George Hamilton-Gordon, when the latter was the British Prime Minister, as his private secretary.

He served as a governor of Trinidad and, subsequently, of Mauritius. In 1874, he landed in Fiji to accept the governorship

---

[1] Ovid, *Metamorphoses*.
[2] Lothair I (795–855), Holy Roman Emperor.

Perspectives of British Colonial Rule in the Fiji Islands

there. Sir Arthur succeeded Sir Hercules Robinson, the Governor of New South Wales, and the representative of Queen Victoria, at the signing of the Deed of Cession that transferred sovereignty to Britain. He served the colony well and with sensitivity to the indigenous people's customs and traditions.

His well-meaning policies, however, removed the commoners from the daily discourse of the colony's changing landscape. The consequences of this ultimately spilt over into the political dialogue and the chaos of 1987.

Gordon reorganised the country into regions and districts. He appointed district officers and district commissioners, who oversaw his dispatches and briefs on the conduct of the chiefs and *bulis* of the villages.

The colony was effectively split into two seamless areas of operation. The Fijians were organised into one administrative zone under the chiefs and the *bulis*.[3] Everyone else was overseen by the central government. The transformation was speedily achieved; the *tauvanua* accepted the changes and remained loyal to their chiefs, who now collected taxes and appeared to dispense law and justice in their villages.

This new framework controlled the warlords and tribal chiefs, engaging them in ways that prevented them from seeking revenge for past confrontations. Gordon also recognised their heritage and importance within their constituent units and devolved minor powers accordingly; according to them, civic responsibilities elevated their status. It gave them the esteem they expected by right and justified recognition by the government of their titles and positions within their communities.

Some other outstanding business now demanded the Governor's attention. During the pre-Cession negotiations, an

---

[3] Fijians played a minor part in the economic life of the colony. The official policy was to keep them within their villages under a separate system of administration, which was reorganized in 1944 as the Fijian Administration. It was virtually to be a state within a state, but the government's resources were too limited to introduce welfare measures or to promote development on any great scale. A good deal depended on the missions and other private organizations. See Francis James West and Sophie Foster, "Pacific Islands", *Encyclopaedia Britannica*, (9 September 2024), www.britannica.com/place/Pacific-Islands, accessed 10 November 2024.

A New Colony Is Shaped

unholy alliance of some warring factions was formed to cobble together a quorum, enabling the legal transfer of sovereignty from Fiji to Britain. The other factions had opposed Cakobau's deal and were potential threats. It now fell to Gordon to prevent possible friction from arising among the former Confederate warlords.

The opposition was minor, but if the warlords' presence had been ignored, their antagonism could have developed and become a significant threat to the Queen's peace. Containment and then elimination of rebellious and destabilising elements from various groups was necessary, as they were still unconvinced by the government's recognition of the crucial roles their chiefs would play in the new administration. The detractors viewed the action as a quid pro quo for the land taken from their villages by the settlers, who were considered usurpers, and they sought the return of their land. They favoured the former traditional village system and the rule of the confederate chiefs. The days of violence, warmongering and feasts of captured enemies were, however, now a distant memory.

The Chiefs – the now defunct warlords - looked on the European settlers as usurpers who wanted to take away their land, and as people with whom they could not compete, for they [Fijians] would have to work too hard.[4]

Fijian Land Ownership

The controls and rules Gordon imposed finally put to rest doubts about Fiji's future. The land issue was resolved, with the Europeans retaining, through dubious means, the more significant portion of the disputed prime areas. The residue, which formed a considerable part of the land traditionally held by the indigenous collectives, was retained by the chiefs in trust for the benefit of the people.

The Great Council of Chiefs was established with wide-ranging responsibilities regarding the use and transmission of

---

[4] John Wesley Coulter, *The Drama of Fiji: A Contemporary History* (Paul Flesch & Co., 1967), p. 21.

Perspectives of British Colonial Rule in the Fiji Islands

"native land". It assured the people that their land was secure and held in trust for them, in perpetuity, by their chiefs.

The administration registered and regulated land sales and purchases. This process conserved all land in their hands and ensured that irregular private dealings were no longer possible. Land would now be leased for specific periods, and sales of native land would no longer be permitted.

By 1940, all non-freehold land was transferred to the Native Land Trust Board (NLTB), which now administered all regions defined as native land. Most of the other non-native land was held by the Europeans, with the remaining land owned by the government and designated Crown property.

Land under the NLTB's oversight amounted to about 91% of Fiji's total land mass. It was the custodian who now acted on behalf of Fijian communal landowners. The NLTB has now been renamed the *iTaukei Land Trust Board (TLTB)*.

6

Rebellion Crushed

Governor Gordon's main concern was the fundamental issue of security and managing indigenous dissidents. Without immediate, direct, and robust action, dissent would become a deep-seated problem. The colony was not without organised resistance. However, the Colo War (1876), the Tuka Movement (1878–91), the Seaqaqa War (1894), the Movement for Federation with New Zealand (which ended without resolution in 1893), and the Viti Kabani Movement (1913) had all been successfully pacified.

As a priority, the new administration eradicated remnants of the anti-British rebellion in the North-western Viti Levu, known as the Colo, and the people *as "kai colo"* - from Colo. The King of Fiji short-changed some chiefs by excluding them from negotiations, and the message about the impending changes was not effectively conveyed or communicated to certain parts of the land. This irked the people of the "Colo areas" of the interior of the largest island, Viti Levu. Gordon secured a satisfactory outcome with the help of his nephew, A. J. L. Gordon.

From 1876, the Governor continued consolidating British rule. By 1913, with the help of the chiefs, vestiges of Apolosi's rebellion[1] had evaporated. The pay-off for the chiefs

---

[1] Apolosi Nawai founded and led the Viti Trading Company in 1915 that first aimed to capture the profits of trading in Fijian village produce for its mainly Fijian shareholders. The trading company was seen by the European settlers as a challenge to their influence, and the colonial authorities and courts were encouraged to suppress it.

In 1917, Apolosi was reported to have told supporters:

"I alone am the chief of Fiji: it is the will of God. These other chiefs only work for themselves; they don't spare a thought for you or your welfare."

That year, 1917, Governor Bickham Sweet-Escott issued a Confining Order exiling Apolosi to Rotuma. – a remote island in the northern Fijian archipelago.

Perspectives of British Colonial Rule in the Fiji Islands

was that they gained ultimate and indisputable charge of the villages, with the governor's blessings.

Discipline among the chiefs was an essential requirement for British rule. It was achieved through patronage, vigilance, and sensitive guidance by the District Commissioners and the District Officers, and was a novel experience for them. The disciplined official routine was a constraint on their previous incarnation as free-ranging warlords. Each high-ranking chief was given a role in the administration, without substantive executive powers, that commanded esteem and reverence among the people. To the chiefs' credit, they accepted and adapted to the new system of peaceful coexistence with former adversaries.

The Great Council of Chiefs was a significant tool in the Governor's armoury to set an agenda for the villages and the people's lives. The *tauvanua* were administered ostensibly by their own leaders, which, it was hoped, would ensure that, in time, peace and a more settled life would bring about a change in their outlook and perception of the order, values, and culture that were now upon them.

Gordon organised the former warlords and resolved the long-standing land issues. Now he had to set about fixing the economy and deliberate on the best course of action to lead Fijians out of their primaeval existence into the comforts of the modern world. He had to find the means and measures to regenerate the economy to replenish the empty Treasury.

Pre-Cession, Fiji was an independent, sovereign kingdom under Cakobau and governed by the General Assembly from 1860 until its collapse in 1867. European ministers comprised the

---

In 1924 Apolosi's first exile came to an end. His persistent anti-British sentiments – he hoped for the fall of the British Empire – and in 1930 he was exiled for a second time.

In 1940 Apolosi was allowed to return from exile, but the authorities' fear that he would lead a quasi-religious movement meant that he was exiled again just weeks later, this time to New Zealand. In 1946 he was brought back to Yacata to die. Wikipedia. Accessed: 3 March 2025.

Also: Timothy Mac naught, *The Fijian Colonial Experience,* Australian National University Press, 1982 p 89, 90.

Rebellion Crushed

government; there were institutions to sustain the administration, and tax-collecting powers had been given to the chiefs. The chiefs failed to collect taxes, with serious consequences for the nation. Thus, Gordon faced a significant challenge, which was further exacerbated by the demise of the short-lived and chaotic cotton industry. However, he was determined to resolve this dilemma with perseverance, patience, and all the experience he could muster.

Coaching Fijians

Before the new government's intervention, local Fijians were employed in the cotton fields. Later, they were coached on preparing the ground for planting sugar cane. They continued to show little aptitude for farming and even less for disciplined and regulated agricultural work.

Overseers in the cane fields would give specific instructions and demonstrations on how to do the work, followed by distributing premium-quality seeds to the groups of labourers, including their bulis, and then leaving them to it. When the overseers returned, they found the workers and the *bulis* had absconded.[2]

---

[2] During the governorship of Sir George T. M. O'Brien, efforts to develop a culture of disciplined agrarian methods among the Fijians repeatedly failed. "Growing cane is a nightmare to the natives and to the inspectors," wrote Mr McOwen from Nauva, "until absenteeism can be quashed." In another instance, the colonial secretary, W. L. Allardyce supervised the work during his visit to the Serua province. That effort kept the local mill in Deuba uninterruptedly supplied with cane. There were not many of this calibre to sustain that impetus with the Fijians. In Labasa, the CSR company [Colonial Sugar Refining Company] officers provided "£60 of first-class cane tops for planting. Mr Chalmers laid the tops out on the field and showed the *buli* and his men how to cut the tops, lay them in sets, and space them in the rows. The weather was exceptionally dry, so he instructed them to tread down about 6 inches of soil over each set. With the planting under way, he left the *buli* in charge and returned to his office. The next day he heard that all 48 acres had been completed. He rode out to inspect the work. The cane tops had been thrown anywhere into the furrows, uncut, and with a foot or two exposed to the scorching sun. He galloped to the *buli's* house and demanded that the entire field be replanted immediately. This time he supervised the work for a

Perspectives of British Colonial Rule in the Fiji Islands

The confidence of the plantation managers in the indigenous people as labourers soon eroded, and with it, any hope of their involvement in the agricultural industry or any other commercial activity. The village leaders – the chiefs and the *bulis* - were stubborn, unreceptive, and not likely to succeed in any enterprise that required self-discipline and resolve. They understood very little of the challenges and changes taking place outside the sphere of their villages. The transition from a traditional, subsistence-based economy to a modern, commercial one posed a significant challenge for the Fijians; their limited understanding and experience in this new system hindered their progress.

By the time of the Second World War, Fiji had endured sixty-five years of British rule; yet, the Fijians were no more acquainted with entrepreneurial culture than they had been soon after the Deed of Cession was signed. Maybe the administration should not have left it to the chiefs to unshackle their people. Note these telling comments and observations of Cyril Belshaw – a Canadian professor of Anthropology at the University of British Columbia – they are hard to ignore:

> The effects of Fijian Administration on the economic growth of the Fijian people have been little short of disastrous, and the source of much difficulty lies within *the structure and philosophy* of the Administration as a political unit.[3]

---

few hours, but the moment he was on his way back to Labasa to hold a court the cane was 'shoved in anyhow' with the result that not one set in 500 vegetated." (Timothy J. Macnaught, *The Fijian Colonial Experience: A Study of the Neotraditional Order under British Colonial Rule before World War II* (Australian National University, 2016), https://press.anu.edu.au/ publications/fijian-colonial-experience, accessed 20 April 2021.

[3] Timothy J. Macnaught, *The Fijian Colonial Experience: A Study of the Neotraditional Order under British Colonial Rule Prior to World War II* (Australian National University, 2016), p. 157.

Rebellion Crushed

The Colonial Office had assumed that it was impossible to instruct the Fijians in the workings of the modern economy; the effort would not benefit the people, as the *"Fijians inherently had poor reasoning faculties"*.[4] This incorrect hypothesis led them to make decisions that were ultimately detrimental to their subjects in the long term.

Preconceived sentiments and views based on racial profiling prevailed during the nineteenth century, and no doubt influenced the decisions of local colonial executives and administrators. These attitudes were no doubt hardened or made worse by the eugenicist beliefs popularised by Sir Francis Galton (a close relative of Charles Darwin) in the 1860s, damaging the long-term prospects of non-white races worldwide.

These sentiments resonated throughout Europe, but by the twentieth century, the notion was discredited. However, for many, they remained a "fact". They had become deeply ingrained in the consciousness of generations of governors, in government policies, and in decisions about Fiji, resulting in profound consequences for the people. This ideology undoubtedly played a significant role in the socio-economic and political development of the indigenous people, resulting in the disparities and challenges faced by the Fijians, who struggled to adopt and adapt to the modern economic systems and commercial activities introduced by British colonial rule.

The millers, whose efforts resulted in time and money being lost, mostly gave up trying to train Fijians, more out of desperation and frustration. It was clear that industrial agriculture could not rely on Fijian labour, and there seemed to be no realistic alternative on the horizon.

The Governor now had a blank slate to seek and establish a different foundation for an economy that would endure and sustain the colony's needs, both present and future.

Sugar cane was successfully grown on a small scale, but it was an unproven commodity from Fijian industrial production

---

[4] Helen Goodwill Tavola, *Secondary Education in Fiji: A Key to the Future* (Institute of Pacific Studies of the University of the South Pacific, 1991), p. 19.

perspectives: existential issues bedevilled the agriculture industry. The fertile, lush land of Viti Levu and Vanua Levu was ideal for sugar.

Wakaya Island was the original home of the sugar industry in Fiji. David Whippy, an American naval commander familiar with the stuff from his hometown, produced sugar for local consumption. His project and enterprise failed, mostly because of his inability to increase production with the facilities and resources at his disposal.

Providentially, the Governor's understanding of the industry from his previous postings proved timely. He had seen firsthand that sugar was a commodity with great commercial potential. With suitable resources, production could be ramped up within a few short years to plug the deficit in Fiji's finances.

7

Origins of the Sugar Industry and Indentured Labour

It is the hearing of the ear, the thought of the thinking faculty, the spoken word of speech, the breathing of the breath and the sight of the eyes.[1]

A new approach to identifying a suitable and profitable agricultural product was a priority. The economy of Britain's latest colony was on life support, and investors and speculators were deserting or going bankrupt, leaving the government in an unpredictable and lamentable situation.

Sugar cane was on the horizon and reckoned to be a serious alternative to cotton, but could the perennial problems plaguing the cotton industry return and blight its successor?

Although physiologically suited to the challenging agricultural work, the Fijians preferred living and working in small communal gardens in familiar surroundings. Their familiar lifestyle and the habits of millennia were almost impossible to overcome within the short period required to set right Fiji's balance sheet.

It seemed that John Gladstone's initial reaction to source labourers from India would be the "go-to" place to resolve Gordon's problems.

Britain had reorganised its industrial base in India at the expense of some major industries. Following the 1857 Great Rebellion (also known as the "Indian Mutiny"), major changes were on the way. The East India Company, which literally had the run of the mill since the 1600s, was dissolved in 1874.

---

[1] Kena Upanishad 1.2. Extract from the Vedas, ancient Sanskrit texts composed from about 900 BC to the 1st Millenium, A.D.

Perspectives of British Colonial Rule in the Fiji Islands

Britain relocated the manufacture of cotton goods to Manchester, Birmingham, and Glasgow, and accelerated its own economic growth.

The empire's expansion at this point was without parallel in history, but it created an industrial void in one of the world's most densely populated countries. The unskilled hands, the middle management, machinists, and all the others in between were on the streets of Bombay, Calcutta, Madras, and other manufacturing centres, desperate for work. University graduates were often employed in menial jobs or struggled to find work on the streets, and bazaars and marketplaces teemed with pathetic faces in search of employment. The government that created the situation was silent and blind to their plight.

Closing those mills and factories was a massive disaster for all communities and social groups. Disasters, natural and man-made, through neglect of the means of production, soon blighted the Indian Empire. The Indian government continued to export wheat to England during the famine of 1876 - 1878.[2] Lord Robert Bulwer-Lytton oversaw the export of a record 6.4 million hundredweight (320,000 tons) of grain to England, which made the region more vulnerable.[3] These disasters of the 1860s and 1870s led many to seek refuge elsewhere, often ending up in hazardous situations and unfamiliar territories.

Factories in Britain accelerated industrialisation, but the repercussions and the social and financial impact of mass unemployment in India continued to worsen but British overseas territories expanded and needed cheaper labour, and India was now ideally placed to meet the demand from the colonies.

Recruiting agents for labourers were active in various parts of India, including Bihar, Uttar Pradesh, Bengal, Madras

---

[2] The Great Famine was caused by an intense drought resulting in crop failure in the Deccan Plateau and across India and China. But that did not prevent the Viceroy from exporting grains from India to Great Britain.

[3] "Great Famine of 1876–1878", Bharatpedia (updated 6 May 2022), https://en.bharatpedia.org/wiki/ Great_Famine_of_1876–1878, accessed 27 February 2025.

(now Chennai), and later, in other districts. They were aware of Indian workers' ambitions; they upped the ante and hyped the work description, saying that workers could go to other colonies, make their fortunes, and soon return home loaded with riches. The recruiters gave the impression that the journey to Fiji was just a short distance down the Hooghly River. Satisfied with the work description that "they were going there to clean, sift and pack sugar" [4], many registered for the unknown and the unpredictable.

The agents read out the agreement that formed the basis of their employment terms and transportation to the destination for the prospective immigrants, who were presumed to have understood the legal terms and their implications.

Many who were recruited were illiterate, and what they understood or misunderstood did not matter to the recruiting agents. They had a document with the workers' thumbprints that legalised labour for hire in the Fijian cane fields. Some workers who had doubts about the agents' honesty tried to escape. Those caught were isolated and forced onto a ship, which usually sailed out during the night to conceal the direction in which it was heading.

No one who agreed to be sent to Fiji anticipated the pain of the long journey, the diseases, and suicides caused by the distress of travelling in overcrowded ships or agonising over how they had allowed themselves to be misled.

The Final Decision

Before Governor Sir Arthur Gordon's final decision to introduce labourers from India, he had sought a supply of workers from various parts of the world, including Pacific Islanders and others. This experiment failed for several reasons, including a lack of the temperament to persist in the rugged

---

[4] Thakur Ranjit Singh, "The Legacy of Rajasthani Girmitiya", Girmit.org (n.d.), https://girmitiya.girmit.org/new/index.php/articles/thakur-ranjit-singh/thakur-bansi-chauhan, accessed 30 December 2021.

terrain, as well as the discipline and motivation needed to endure harsh conditions imposed by both man and nature.

Following this experiment, the first Indians were imported from Trinidad on trial. The success of this first load of labourers encouraged the governor to seek a regular supply, which continued until 1916.

Fortunately, Gordon's powers of persuasion allowed him to finalise a deal that would put Fiji on the map of the sugar-producing world. His prompt application to the government of India was successful, and the terms of the new labour supply were finalised. The settlers and millers were satisfied with both governments' decisions. The terms of the indenture contract by which the workers would be engaged were a new set of guidelines for the plantations. However, the safeguards and working conditions were non-existent, allowing the managers to treat the labourers inhumanely.

For the Indians, the gulf between the hype and reality regarding the destination and their prospects in the sugar plantations became apparent upon their arrival. Even as they landed, they saw that their new situation did not seem to match the rhetoric. Hustled and jostled into compounds, they soon became disillusioned and disheartened. However, they were now in a hostile environment, six thousand miles from home. The people they encountered differed markedly from them; they were not at all like those they might expect to meet "down the Hooghly". Additionally, the land allocated to them did not match the description given in Bengal and Madras. Life was tough in the villages of Behar and United Provinces, but in Fiji, they were beaten, harassed, and continually lied to. They had landed in hell.

The First Shipload Leaves India

The first shipload of labourers left the port of Calcutta in 1878. With this last piece of the jigsaw in place, Fiji was now on its way to a future that would see a prosperous and stable outcome for its citizens.

The consequence of introducing this new dimension was more profound and longer-lasting. The new immigrants established a new life with their unique traditions, cultures, and aspirations for a better life, which all had a lasting impact on the colony's future.

Fiji began to develop economically without interruption or periodic concerns about labour. The Treasury was now in better shape than when Gordon had arrived. He had successfully transformed the islands from a bankrupt backwater into a viable, productive colony: one recognised for its potential to produce and export sugar and other products of the quality and quantity the market demanded.

The new arrivals from India were first quarantined on Nukulau Island, just off the Suva peninsula. The Surgeon-General assessed the health of those who had survived the arduous journey, confirmed the number who had perished on board, and identified those suffering from cholera and other infectious illnesses. After the required procedures were completed, the able-bodied workers were released to the sugar companies' housing compounds – lines of basic construction buildings containing rooms approximately three square meters in size – and then assigned to work at various locations.

Commercial factors were attractive, and success and profitability would be assured if the value of sugar grew in tandem with greater demand in Europe and elsewhere. World prices stabilised, and many colonies became established as going concerns based on the sugar industry and imported labour.

The "Agreement" and the Work

The "agreement" was essentially a marketing ploy and a means to circumvent slavery legislation. Slavery in the colonies was abolished in 1838, so a novel method of hiring labour was devised that allowed those who hired labourers much latitude and freedom in dealing with their workers, without fear of infringing the slavery law.

Removing the obvious elements of slavery made the indenture agreement seem less inhumane. The contract was for a fixed five-year term. After this initial period, the indentured workers could return to India at their own expense. A further extension of five years would entitle them to claim return fares. The terms stated the hours and days to be worked (nine hours every day of the week, excluding Sunday). Wages were paid on Saturdays: adult males were to earn not less than one shilling and adult females not less than nine pence; children below the age of fifteen would get wages proportionate to the work done. The pay included food rations, dwellings, and medical supplies.

The remuneration agreed was not always paid as a matter of course; in practice, the labourers were often subjected to "task"-related assignments or *ticca* rates. They were assigned specified jobs and paid only when the task was completed: a decision made subjectively by the managers. This arrangement was not in the labourers' contracts, but the labourers tended not to object or mention their contract's terms for fear of violent repercussions from supervisors.

The Indians had various languages, dialects, religions, customs, and traditions, so although communication (or its lack) within the indentured community was a problem, it was an advantage for the millers. The labourers were unlikely to plan and organise protests about their treatment, which gave the bosses a free hand to intimidate and bully them. Despite being so disadvantaged – and without friends or family for comfort and reassurance – the workers' fortitude pulled them through the quagmire of the inhuman practices of the plantations. Of course, many wished to return to India – but as each exhausting day turned into weeks, months, and years, the thought of making the journey across the *"kala pani"* – the black sea, became less likely. The heart was willing, but the stamina was sapped out.

In the meantime, India reinvented itself as the font that nourished the expansion of the British Empire, from the South Pacific to the Caribbean. Prosperity and opulence for the British overlords followed the blood and tears. Still, no monuments exist in any corner of the British Empire that memorialise the sacrifices or recognise the contributions of those labourers.

In these notorious historical transfers of humans, India made significant contributions to the progress and prosperity of the new territories, as evident in Fiji in the South Pacific and the Caribbean. The group of workers, which comprised people from many cultures and experiences, all aspired to the common hope of improving their fortunes and comforts – a normal aspiration

Origins of the Sugar Industry and Indentured Labour

for any individual born on this earth. During their long and challenging journey, their inner strengths overcame much of their religious and caste differences – the taboos – and they became *jahaji bhais, a literal translation: the brotherhood of the boat,* a fellow traveller. The prohibitions of the caste system gave way to common-sense realities, helping to ease the discomforts and griefs suffered by all. Once these ancient and outmoded fears dissipated, their inner strengths thrust them to devote their energies to growing their wealth and contributing to the colony's welfare and prosperity.

The story of the lives of these workers spoke more about the character of the entrepreneurs who from their conduct and attitudes towards their workers left much to be desired; for many it was reminiscent of the days of slavery, than of the presumed changed attitudes of the sahib whose word, they believed was his bond, and his apparent fairness would not let them down.

The game was up when they barked their orders in broken Hindustani or sometimes in English, followed by a crack of the whip. No one was treated humanely, with courtesy, or with moderation. Even when the injustices they suffered were brought before the judges and magistrates, they were never given the benefit of doubt – the justices chose to accept the arguments spun out by the plantation managers and their legal representatives.

For obvious reasons, the uneducated, illiterate, and unqualified were preferred as indentured labourers. Uneducated working classes were the preferred candidates of the recruiting agents. These would be less likely to contradict or find reasons to complain about breaches of the agreement, which both parties had agreed to. Any means of manipulating the worker would do. Mr J. W. Burton, a missionary, went as far as to forbid the "coolies" from converting to Christianity. He feared they would acquire the absurd idea that *all* men were brothers![5] And demand fair play and justice, perhaps?

---

[5] J. W. Burton, 1910. Girmitiya.org.

Perspectives of British Colonial Rule in the Fiji Islands

His Christian beliefs were founded on stony ground. From his experiences, he knew the labourers lived a wretched existence. Although he expressed his views graphically, he failed to show concern and act to improve their situation. As a missionary, he was unconcerned about their spiritual well-being, and even less about their material well-being and safety. As a committed Christian, his services would have been better served in England.

From his experiences, he knew the labourers lived a wretched existence:

> "The life on the plantation as an indentured labourer is not of a very inviting character. The difference between this state and absolute slavery is merely in the name and the term of years. The coolies themselves frankly call it *narak* (hell). The wages are low, and the cost of living is comparatively high. The accommodation appears to us very wretched. There are some lines where the coolies are herded together like so many penned cattle amid the most insanitary conditions and indescribable filth." [6]

Although Burton expressed his views so graphically, he failed to act to remove those very filth and insanitary conditions he described.

Women and Mortality Rates

A ratio of only forty women for every hundred men were permitted to board the ship to Fiji. More work could be extracted from men, both individually and collectively, than from women. This decision was based on the false premise that women would impede and distract the men. The women who arrived worked just as hard and conscientiously, with responsibilities continuing after they got home after an arduous day in the tropical sun and the whip of the plantation manager.

---

[6] J. W. Burton, *Our Work in Fiji. 1909. See also Girmit.org: Discussing the Living Conditions of the Indians Emigrants (1879 – 1916).*

Origins of the Sugar Industry and Indentured Labour

Deaths from suicides and sickness during the journey on the high seas, and the effects of the harsh conditions on the farms, reduced the ratio further.

The result was that tensions caused by dramatic changes in their lives, living under conditions that were not prepared for nor expected, and the social issues, all of which disrupted the rhythm and pace of daily living; and their inabilities to practice cultural or traditional routine or observation of religious customs, which may have brought some relief, led to the inevitable disquiet and disharmony and tensions.

Maternity leave was unheard of in the coolie lines: women had to return to work soon after giving birth; little regard was given to the health of, or caring for, the children or mothers.

Women also suffered at the hands of plantation managers who took advantage of their vulnerability.

The story is told of a young woman, Kunti, who escaped the clutches of Mr Cobcroft on 10 April 1913. She ran off towards the Wainibokasi River and threw herself in. She was rescued by a young man, Jagdeo, who pulled her into his small canoe. Her story and her escape gained widespread attention in India and were reported by the press. The British Indian government went into overdrive to discredit the story and stop the growth of anti-emigration sentiments, which might have adversely affected recruitment to the colonies.[7]

Rajendra Prasad relates an instance of inhumanity that severely challenges most sane people's beliefs in humanity to understand how such barbarity could be committed by a "civilised" person, and the equally abhorrent response of the colonial judge.

On 22 August 1910, a Girmitiya (indentured) woman named Naraini was given the task of breaking stones with a hammer on the Sigatoka tramline six days after childbirth. She

---

[7] Brij V. Lal, Chalo *Jahaji: On a Journey through Indenture in Fiji* (ANU E Press, 2012). p. 196

was unable to cope with the task. In response, an overseer, Harold Blomfield, held her by her hair and bashed her face on the stones. Naraini was grievously wounded and later became insane; she was repatriated to India. Blomfield was charged but escaped punishment.[8]

In 1912, Miss Hannah Dudley[9] of the Methodist Mission was pained to say of the Indian women:

> They arrived in the country, timid, fearful, not knowing where they are to be sent. They are allotted to the plantations like so many dumb animals. If they do not perform the work given to them satisfactorily, they are struck, fined or even sent to jail. The life of the plantations alters their demeanour and even their very faces. Some looked crushed and broken-hearted, others sullen, others hard and evil. I shall never forget the first time I saw indentured women when they were returning from their day's work. The look on those women's faces haunts me.[10]

Within a few decades, the cultural and religious practices that had separated and prevented or discouraged communication or interaction among the labourers soon dissipated. The realities and practicalities of living and survival, this was the only choice these wretched human beings could take for mutual help's sake.

Human survival and ingenuity advanced rapidly, and in a short time, the heterogeneous indentured community transitioned almost seamlessly into a nearly homogeneous one. Their tribulations united them to confront adversity. In the blink

---

[8] Rajendra Prasad, "Banished and Excluded: The Girmit of Fiji", Himal Southasian (2 January 2015), www.himalmag.com/comment/girmit-fiji, accessed 28 September 2023.

[9] Hannah Dudley fluent in Urdu and Tamil from her mission work in India, arrived in Fiji after recuperating from illness, from Australia on August 24, 1897, and began a mission which lasted 13 years. From Toorak in Suva, where she founded the Dudley Girls School in Amy Street, Miss Dudley's work reached out towards Nausori as she taught the young and ministered to the sick.

[10] Fiji Times. Poems of Indenture Period. 16 May 2016.

of an eye, they shared festivals and traditional feasts; they shared pain and grief; and celebrated marriages and births, and in grief, all lent a hand to alleviate the pain. These times were relief and respite from the toil.

Still, the relentless severity of the work and the cold insensitivity of the millers and their managers caused many to take their own lives. They would usually end their suffering between 3 and 4 a.m. – when the managers arrived and banged tin drums to rouse the workers – rather than face another day of pain, they sought peace and relief forever.

Many of the workers chose to return to India upon completion of their contracts. There, they raised the Indian public's awareness of the appalling conditions in the sugar-cane plantations. Public figures and politicians began a campaign to warn people to keep their distance from the recruiters. Associations arose to crusade and lobby against the lax rules and the worthless indenture contracts that attracted unsuspecting, innocent applicants.

Others stayed; they saw opportunities and, when the time was right, they diversified into other enterprises, such as farming green crops and animals, including cows, chickens, and pigs. With these mini-commercial activities, they managed to supply their neighbours with fresh food for cash and soon left the "barracks" or "lines" where they had been settled since their arrival, never to return. Others moved into trades such as carpentry, setting up small businesses and contributing to the growing commerce in the colony.

The continuity of the labour supply was essential to sustain the development of the sugar industry. There were no alternative sources to replace Indian labour. Recruiting new workers took time and effort. Encouraging those already in the colony and on the plantations to remain made economic sense.

They were almost indispensable; they had proved their usefulness and effectiveness to the industry as labourers, but now as independent workers, their roles changed to take a more active role in growing the economy. Those who left, and particularly the remainers, deserve the credit for Fiji's development and continued prosperity.

Perspectives of British Colonial Rule in the Fiji Islands

Dr Gillion observed:

The Colonial Sugar Refining Company suggested that the right to return passages should be limited, with a view to retaining Indians in Fiji and settling them on the land as small cane farmers.[11]

Had the government been more sympathetic and attentive to the workers' needs, many more would have remained. However, they had no voice, no justice, barely any access to medical attention, and no government assistance in social care. They were considered disposable commodities that had served their usefulness.[12]

Margery Perham expressed the deep feelings of hurt, injustice, and the lack of social progress that the labourers experienced, despite the legal signatures on the indenture agreements:

It almost seems as if, having brought them here, the government has resented their presence and feared to educate them.[13]

---

[11] Dr Gillion, PhD thesis, *A History of Indian Immigration & Settlement in Fiji*. Australian National University, 1958. p. 380.

[12] John Edward Jenkins, *The Coolie: His Rights and Wrongs* (George Routledge & Sons, 1871), quoted in "The Agreement and the Girmitiya", *Harvard Law Review*, vol. 134, no. 5 (March 2021), https://harvardlawreview.org/2021/03/the-agreement-and-the-girmitiya, accessed 7 January 2022.

[13] Margery Perham, *Pacific Prelude: A Journey to Samoa and Australia, 1929* (Peter Owen, 1988), p. 116.

8

Social Workers from India: Self-emancipation

Whoever complies nobly with necessity, we count as wise and expert in the ways of the gods.[1]

The immigrants who decided to remain and settle in Fiji were an unhappy lot. The stress and exertions of the labourers, as they struggled to earn a living in conditions not conducive to an economic situation that had yet to put down tangible roots of supply and demand.

Other concerns faced by the migrants needed government help. Complaints were not welcomed, nor were the interventions of the activists and advisors among them, whose good intentions only incurred the wrath of the government. There were real problems with the availability of good land for immediate use by freed labourers and to construct a reasonable structure for living. The government was at arm's length, which was detrimental to the colony's real economic growth. Seeds and animals for farms could not be sourced easily, and the administration's lack of concern put an end to many who decided to seek employment in the mills, regardless of the available situation. The colonial administration was least concerned with the farmers' wants and needs.

The future well-being of the labourers depended on the efforts of their "leaders" and activists, whom the government neither acknowledged nor accepted as representatives of the sugar-cane labourers' fraternity.

However, these workers were indispensable, and the administration was desperate to retain them. The plantations and

---

[1] Epictetus, *Handbook* 53.

the government, under pressure to be proactive in ensuring continued economic growth, worked to lease land for fixed terms and to provide the basic necessities for survival.

The labourers' patience and their positive actions of setting up self-groups or rudimentary *panchayats* [2] to discuss locally important issues and their determination to survive through the dark days of their indentured servitude helped them through despite all the rejections from the British. Those rejections were impediments to the farmers' aspirations.

Gordon was sympathetic, but his brief fell short of the demands of the Indian farmers. He was nonetheless aware of their basic but essential needs. Napoleon Bonaparte noted: *"The wickedness of the wicked does not ruin the world but the weakness of the good."*[3]

Time to Act

The plight of the immigrant labourers reached the authorities in India and drew the attention of institutions, the press, and Mohandas K. Gandhi. Soon, educators, social workers, and investigators, such as Rev. C. F. Andrews, Manilal Maganlal Doctor (also known as "Doctor"), and Vashist Muni, arrived to look into and advise the labourers and support them in their demands for a just and equitable outcome. None were welcome to the authorities, especially Manilal and Muni. Both were expelled. Both sought solutions through negotiations and peaceful protests.

Encouraged by the visitors' suggestions and recommendations, the indentured labourers absorbed every word eagerly as each was delivered. But the visitors' warnings that hopes must not be raised prematurely tempered their anger and frustrations. The government was not inclined to improve their

---

[2] "panchayats" (*panch* meaning five; *ayat* meaning assembly) in its original format in India consisted usually of five local wise and respected elders to resolve local issues.

[3] https://azquotes.com/author/1621-Napoleon_Bonaparte

Social Workers from India: Self-emancipation

lives or provide the community with material benefits as demanded. Their patience would be tested.

The visiting investigators' stay in Fiji was short-lived. In some cases, it was even shorter when the British observed notable changes in the labourers' communal reorganisation and their approach to social and political problems.

This measurable progress was considered a distraction from the business of sugar production and was unacceptable to the plantation managers. The administration claimed that the investigators were "interfering" with the government's work.

* * *

Manilal Doctor arrived in Fiji in August 1912. Doctor knew enough of Gandhi's experiences in South Africa to suspect that the colonial government's sympathies would lie with the settlers and plantation owners rather than with the labourers.

The colonial administration was none too pleased with his turning up on the islands. For his part in the Veeraswamy affair, it began to suspect that he was an "agent" of Gandhi.

Veeraswamy, a Madras University graduate, was despatched to work as a postal officer in Fiji in October 1911. Instead, he was redirected to the telephone exchange as an operator at the Colonial Sugar Refining Company (CSR). This breached his original agreement with the Indian government and the colonial administration in Fiji. He voiced legitimate concerns and complained about the breach. In a fit of pique, the CSR sent him to work in the cane fields with the indentured labourers.

Manilal Doctor took up his case and forwarded the matter to the Anti-Slavery Society in London. With the subsequent intervention of the Colonial Office, Veeraswamy found freedom and employment outside the indenture system. It was a rare instance of success for an Indian lawyer over the colonial government's high-handedness.

The administration, rather than chastise the Company for its highhandedness, expressed its displeasure at Manilal. He was now a marked man.

The administration now sought ways to remove Manilal from the colony, and any excuse would do.

Perspectives of British Colonial Rule in the Fiji Islands

Manilal set to work. He was disturbed at the worsening conditions of the workers in Fiji and wrote to Gandhi. Rev C.F. Andrews and W.W. Pearson were sent to investigate.

Optimism rose, and working groups were organised. He established the Indian Settler newspaper and organised the Arya Samaj – a casteless and modernising religious and social entity within the Hindu community. Over time, it established institutions that ensured education was accessible to children of all races and creeds.

Until 1912, the colonial administration paid scant attention to the plight of the labourers. Manilal's active promotion of agitation, such as organising strike action by the sugar-cane workers, soon rattled the authorities. He wrote in the *Bombay Chronicle*:

> As a result of [the] tyrannical and cruel treatment of the Indian population by the whites, a reign of terror exists in Fiji, and the free Indian is taught a lesson which he can never forget. Whether under "indenture" or not, the Indians of Fiji must remain a means to the end of the white capitalists . . . Conditions in India in the darkest days of the Moghul rule were not worse than [those] which exist in the Fiji Islands today.[4]

In 1920, Manilal directed his attention to advise the workers of the Public Works Department who went on strike when their working hours were extended from 40 hours to 45 hours. The peaceful meetings he conducted drew praise from the Inspector General of Constabulary.

A subsequent meeting organised by Mrs Jayunkvar, Manilal and the wives of the workers was broken up violently by the police. The European constabulary arrived with fixed

---

[4] Om Marathe, "Explained: Who was Manilal Doctor?" *The Indian Express* (updated 10 January 2020), https://indianexpress.com/article/explained/explained-manilal-doctor-mahatma-gandhi-overseas-work-6208393/#:~:text=Doctor%20organised%20the%20Indian%20community,to%20bonded%20workers%20in%20need., accessed 1 April 2020.

Social Workers from India: Self-emancipation

bayonets and confronted the ladies on the Rewa Bridge in Nausori. Telephone wires between Suva and Nausori were cut, and the strikers dispersed. The next day, on 12 February, a New Zealand force of 60 soldiers with machine guns arrived, and a warship docked at the Suva harbour from England. On 13 February, the police and army held up a group of Indians at Samabula Bridge. With such force confronting them, they stood their ground and refused to disperse. In the ensuing struggle between strikers armed with sticks and stones, three Indians were hit by firearms, leading to one death.

Manilal exposed government policies towards the workers in a very public manner. The plight of the farmers was now in the public domain in India. The Fijian colonial autocracy was not going to tolerate such a brazen outburst; the harassment continued with restrictions in New Zealand, where he was stopped from practising law. He sent newspaper cuttings about Fiji to Rev Andrews. This letter was intercepted, and the British government deregistered his bar credentials; as a result, he was unable to practice law in Australia or India. Rev. Andrews contacted Gandhi, whose reaction was unequivocal:

> "An Empire that requires such calculated persecution of a man, without even trying to prove anything against him, deserves to be dissolved."[5]

The voices of former indentured returnees from Fiji and other territories were heard in India, prompting the leaders to act. Other social workers landed in Fiji to assess the gravity of the exploitation and oppression.

A further report on the mistreatment of indentured labourers came from Totaram Sanadhya, another victim of indentured servitude, now freed from his ordeal; he determined to bring his experiences to a broader audience.

---

[5] Om Marathe. "Explained: Who Was Manilal Doctor" Indian Express. New Delhi. Updated: January 10, 2020

Perspectives of British Colonial Rule in the Fiji Islands

After his release from indenture, he turned his hand to farming, successfully grew cane, and supplied the millers with his produce for twenty-one years before returning to India. He related his experiences as a labourer and as a freeman.

During his tenure in Fiji as an indentured labourer, Totaram survived "starvation and backbreaking work". [6] His experience was typical: the people were weighed down by an excessive burden that only a human with courage and patience could survive.

He travelled widely among his former indentured colleagues and listened to their experiences following their arrival in Fiji: their fight for survival and the injustices suffered. He recorded their dealings with the millers and the plantation owners. He hoped that someone among the bosses would listen. The truth, however, was that he was talking to the workers' archenemies, and no one needed an introduction to the tribulations of the workers.

On his return to India in 1914, Totaram voiced his opinions as he related his experiences during and after indenture. He recorded his experiences of the colony in the book *Fiji Dweep Me Mere Ikkis Varsh*: a powerful work that influenced Mr Gandhi.

The publication revealed at first hand the extent of the exploitation suffered by the Indians in Fiji.

Totaram requested that Gandhi dispatch an English-speaking lawyer to Fiji to investigate the conditions and organise the farmers into focus groups that could effectively raise their concerns with the government. Gandhi published the letter in *Indian Opinion*, which came to Manilal's notice. He then left with Gandhi's blessings, arriving in Fiji from Mauritius, with fares collected and paid for by contributors from Fiji.

Totaram was a caring person and determined that future generations of sugar-cane workers should not be subjected to the horrors that he and many of his compatriots had suffered. His

---

[6]Lala Totaram Sanadhya, *"Fiji Dweep Me Mere Ikkis Varsh", My Twenty-One Years in the Fiji Islands and the Story of the Haunted Line*, tr. and ed. John Dunham Kelly and Uttra Kumari Singh (Fiji Museum, 1991, repr. 2003).

conscience guided his judgment, and doing nothing was not an option.

From time to time, as other groups returned home, they added their thoughts on recruitment and their semi-subsistence lifestyle in Fiji. A group of returnees lectured under the auspices of the Indentured Cooly Protection Society. Their collective experiences profoundly mobilised and solidified public opinion, causing the Indian government to act.

Gandhi was gravely concerned. He sent the Revd C. F. Andrews on a fact-finding mission; he arrived in Fiji in 1915. Andrews' report and Totaram's account were enough to convince the Indian government to call a stop to the recruitment and transportation of unskilled labourers to the cane fields of Fiji.

Vashist Muni arrived in Fiji in May 1920. Known as the *Sadhu* ("holy man"), he settled among the cane farmers. He patiently gathered groups of them, encouraging and inspiring them to be self-reliant, peaceful, and patient. He argued that fiery language or threats would be counterproductive. He set about with what he believed to be a priority – education – and started a school in Ba, followed by another in Naitonitoni, Navua, in 1920. Ram Charitra's prospects of becoming a tax expert might have been negligible without the Sadhu's initiatives.

Vashist Muni's efforts, along with the work of other reformers, were beginning to result in a more relaxed and revitalised community. Within a few short years, literacy and numeracy began making their mark on the young. The more thoughtful and ambitious men, those who were not keen on farming, ventured out from the cane fields and sought opportunities in other areas of employment. Without those first hard-won initiatives, Fiji today would be a pale imitation of itself: there might still be distressed communities begging for crumbs.

This progress was a visible testament to Muni's achievements during his short stay in Fiji; so, he became another casualty of the administration's wrath and was deported in March 1921. Indian children were viewed by the white settlers as a natural increase in the labour force: preoccupation with or distractions from anything other than sugar production could not be tolerated.

Labourers' Indomitable Spirit

When recruited, both literate and illiterate individuals were handed legal contracts to which they acquiesced by placing their thumbprints in the designated area. They "accepted" the terms without so much as a glance at the document.

The workers were pitted against a well-oiled and resourced plantation management that was supported by the colonial administration. They soon worked out that they had not been sent to Fiji to pick lemons and oranges. Rather, they were herded into groups, transported to forested areas, and dumped into "barracks".

Those who understood the ignominy of their situation were powerless to object or to claim their contractual rights. If they had understood the "agreement" they had "signed", they would have realised that they had no rights to the comforts they were used to, even in their impoverished situations back home.

Even so, they were politically and socially perceptive; they understood that, without persistently demanding improvements and political safeguards, no colonial government ran a proactive policy of social advancement of black or brown peoples. Martin Luther King spoke of a dream which today remains unfulfilled 62 years later.

Therefore, they could not afford to remain passive and submissive. The plantation managers had no constituency and no responsibilities towards indentured workers. No pressure would persuade them to listen to the labourers' queries or grievances.

From Manilal, Vashist Muni, and Rev. Andrews, the clear message was to resort to peaceful means. All followed Gandhi's principles of non-violent methods. Yet the colonial government removed Manilal and Muni because they were "agents of Gandhi".

The collective impatience of the people generated the impetus to accelerate social improvements. The community was prepared to take what action it could to begin the long haul to better days. Without the support and intervention of the visiting social workers, who had set the tone and instilled courage and patience in their efforts to improve their health, wealth, and social well-being, their prospects might have remained bleak. However, without any official blessing, the transition was gradual and, at times, painful.

***

The work of Badri Maharaj, another former indentured labourer and farmer who became a philanthropist and politician, attracted attention and brought him widespread recognition, but not popularity, among his community. When a modicum of legislative representation was extended to Indians in 1916, the Governor selected Maharaj to represent them. He served two terms as a nominated member of the Legislative Council, in 1916 and 1926.

The school he had established – the first for Indian children in Wairuku, Rakiraki, in 1898 – was a success, and he encouraged others to emulate the model. Maharaj was ambitious; he ingratiated himself with the government by opposing the popular social worker Manilal Doctor's presence in Fiji. He also provided information to the government about the movements and meetings of another visitor from India, Vashist Muni.

Badri was an opportunist and worked to succeed as a businessman and political activist; he was not keen on cooperating or working with people who had similar commercial objectives, as noted in his declared opposition to Manilal. However, his altruistic motives cannot be questioned: his efforts paved the way for others, and his accomplishments in the hostile environment of the colonial era served as a beacon of hope.

Steadily and almost imperceptibly, by the 1950s, Indians could finance and organise primary and secondary schools, with places available to all boys and girls regardless of race or religion. It must be noted that, with little support or encouragement from the government, the descendants' determined efforts, which focused on matters most concerning to them, paid dividends.

9

First Sugar Mill Established

Before the first full-scale industrial milling operations were established at Nausori with government approval and involvement, the first privately owned mill was built in Suva by Mr Brewster and Mr Joske in 1872. Other mills followed, with varying degrees of success, until a government delegation, with Thurston's blessings, travelled to Brisbane and convinced CSR to set up an operation in Fiji.

The dreams of many previous growers were realised when the mill was located on the banks of the Rewa River, on the edge of Nausori township in 1882. The jigsaw for an industrial base in Fiji was coming together: land, capital, and labour, all now in equilibrium, boded well for the future of commercial sugarcane production.

However, by the mid-twentieth century, the mills' cost-benefit ratio had become untenable. The wet and humid conditions of the Rewa hinterland were not the ideal place for growing cane of high sugar content and in the quantities needed to feed the voracious crushers. After seventy-seven years, it suffered the same fate as the Navua mill, with all operations ceasing in 1959. The announcement of the Nausori mill's closure came as a surprise to many, including Ram's relatives, friends, and clients.

Although disheartened by the closure, Indian farmers were not discouraged; they had overcome more challenging hurdles. They sought practical ways to make ends meet and keep family, body, and soul together. Community support played an essential part again; in a few short years, the desperation caused by the mill's loss was just another ordeal faced and overcome.

The more resourceful individuals and those with other skills within the community either left the town or opted to commute daily by bus or car, a distance of twelve miles to Suva

First Sugar Mill Established

City. There they searched for opportunities to work as labourers, taxi drivers or builders' hands. These were undoubtedly difficult times for some, and they adapted to the available possibilities. Many feared that Nausori was in danger of becoming a ghost town. Undeterred, the former farmers and mill workers who remained stoical reinvented themselves as small-business market traders and smallholding farmers, some of whom tried their hand at animal husbandry; they kept the township from financial collapse. In time, with imagination and initiative, the town recovered and expanded. Today, Nausori is a bustling, thriving town that serves the Rewa district and the capital.

The CSR company continued to prosper; it was a monopoly, and with the assured labour supply, the company performed well, although much of its success or otherwise depended on world sugar prices and demand. It maintained its mills at Lautoka – Fiji's largest; the Rarawai mill in Ba District, the Penang mill in Rakiraki and the Labasa mill on the island of Vanua Levu continued until it ceased operations in 1973. Its future as an operator in Fiji had become untenable. The farmer's complaints to the company and the government over many years failed to find a resolution to the question of the formula for dividing the proceeds between the miller and the growers. When the contract came up for renewal in 1970, no agreement was reached, and an arbitration commission was appointed under Lord Denning, who found in favour of the growers:

> The growers had, over the years, disputed the share of the proceeds accruing to them. Lord Denning, after a lengthy arbitration, decided that the growers would receive 65 per cent of the sugar and molasses proceeds with a minimum price of F$7.75 per tonne, and the miller would receive 35 per cent, or less. This was a major victory for the growers. They saw the award as redressing a longstanding grievance.

The company was disappointed and decided to leave Fiji in March 1973 after nearly a century in the islands.

10

Political Security

No one is born a good citizen; no nation is born a democracy. Rather, both are processes that continue to evolve over a lifetime. Young people must be included from birth.[1]

Forty years after their arrival in Fiji, it had become apparent to the immigrants that a common franchise was an essential political mechanism that the government had to establish to give a sound basis for the Indians' continued faith in the colony's potential. Their services were needed, now more than before, as they had set essential professional and commercial roots.

During the late 1940s, the Indian community began to pressure the administration for universal suffrage, seeking greater integration, transparency, and clarity, and accepting all citizens as equals. The expected integration would help reduce economic and social disparities and prevent or mitigate political tensions inherent in the current colonial setup.

The immigrants were now established as citizens, and the country was on a path to growth and prosperity. An imaginative and compelling extension for future political stability. The Europeans believed their position in the colony needed to be protected, against whom or what we were not privy; perhaps this was a smokescreen to preserve the undemocratic state of affairs. They held themselves out as guardians of the indigenous peoples' rights and privileges. Ironically and historically, the Fijians were in greater danger from the European settlers. Until Governor Gordon "settled" the issue of land sales, the most fertile land remained in the hands of the settlers, despite the stress and unhappiness of the outcome for the Fijians.

---

[1] Kofi Annan, UN Secretary General, 8 August 1998.

Political Security

Without cause, the Europeans projected an image of Indians as greedy and having ulterior motives.

They had arrived penniless; now they were counting their hard-earned pounds. The growing middle class of Indians was becoming a significant contributor to the Treasury and a visible presence with the trappings of modern living. On the other hand, aware that the administration would continue with its narrow political agenda, they were quite naturally demanding changes to reflect the growing investments of the immigrants in the colony's future prosperity. The indentured document that brought them to Fiji was their "passport", which notably did not define their status; nor did it bestow any rights or privileges.

The immigrants reminded the administration that recognising their presence as permanent residents of the colony was due, and that inclusive and non-discriminatory universal suffrage would be an appropriate vehicle by which to secure rights in common with others born in the colony as British subjects.

Lord Salisbury, the Secretary of State for India, said in his Despatch Note of March 1875, that those Indians who wished to remain in Fiji after their agreements expired:

> "…above all things we must confidently expect, as an indispensable condition of the proposed arrangements, … the Colonial laws and their administration will be such that Indian settlers who have completed their terms of service to which they are agreed as return for the expense of bringing them to the Colonies, will be in all respects free men, with privileges no whit inferior to those of any other class of Her Majesty's subjects resident in the colonies".

The fly in the ointment was the usual cynics bent on maintaining an immovable stance on political change. The exception from this large group was perhaps Ratu Sir Lala Sukuna, who appeared more open and reasonable in inter-racial issues; the rest, Ratu Sir Edward and Ratu Sir George Cakobau, Ratu Sir Penaia Ganilau and Ratu Sir Kamisese Mara, among

Perspectives of British Colonial Rule in the Fiji Islands

others, all opposed the integration and typically favoured the settlers' posture. Colonial machinery worked overtime to maintain a volume of insinuations of anti-Indian rhetoric that impacted commoners like Semesa Sikivou and Ravuama Vunivalu. The latter, with his particularly virulent outbursts, represented the impact colonial disinformation had on a significant section of Fijian intellectuals. They bear a heavy burden for the events of 1987–2006 and their consequences.

Although the leading proponents of change in the political system were Indian politicians, there were other progressive minorities, such as some Europeans and Fijians who had grasped the significance of the movement's future adverse impact on the colony but were mostly silent on the issue for fear of seeming to tilt the balance in favour of the Indian and thus incurring the wrath and possible consequent repercussions from others.

The majority of the European settlers deflected the universal franchise argument with the bogus contention that providing everyone with the vote would give Indians the opportunity to take over the colony and remove the British as rulers, with serious implications for the Fijians. This flagrant mischaracterisation of the Indians' demands did not dampen the chiefs' vigour and enthusiasm for the status quo. Ratu Sukuna was, and is still, held in high esteem, but his words about the immigrants fell on deaf ears. He was unequivocal during his speech to the Great Council of Chiefs in 1939 about the settled status of the Indians in Fiji within the empire. They deserved it as of right. To their credit, they had fulfilled their contracts and returned the country in better condition than they had found it a hundred or so years ago, despite so much being sacrificed along the way.

***

The Governor, Sir Arthur Gordon, and, later, his successor, J. B. Thurston, laid down a charm offensive to retain the favour of the chiefs and nurtured and enthused them to do the administration's every bidding, without question.

The Indians were brought in to work and their success was recognised in that 1939 speech, but others viewed them as

Political Security

dispensable with little thought of the consequences. The Fijians were ill-prepared, even fifty years after the annexation, to replace the immigrants in the sugar industry or in the professions. Yet no Fijian intellectual of the day dared to speak out on the lack of progress within the indigenous community. To follow the herd instincts was fashionable than to be critical of the government's lack of investment in Fijian youths' education.

Where Fijians and Indians co-existed as neighbours in closely settled parts such as Rewa, Navua and Ba, the hospitality of each community needed no encouragement, the Indians soon acquired a fair knowledge of Fijian language, and the Fijians were equally willing to learn some Hindustani pleasantries and even join in Indian festivals or sporting events. Individuals might share a bowl of "grog" *(yagona or kava)* on occasion, borrow tools, barter foodstuffs, or simply engage in talanoa in the markets, but there was almost no intermarriage, and Indian children were not admitted to Fijian schools. Each community, then, adjusted to a pattern of quite cordial but reserved relationships, neither seeking nor being educated into truly common bonds of citizenship.[2]

The political setup ensured that the people of both communities engaged at an arm's length. Fijian and Indian were driven hard to remain separate. Dr Gillion alludes to the fear that the Fiji Indians were a challenge to the Europeans [3].

---

[2] Timothy J. MacNaught, *The Fijian Colonial Experience: A Study of the Neotraditional Order under British Colonial Rule before World War II* (Australian National University, 2016), p. 113, https://press.anu.edu.au/ publications/fijian-colonial-experience, accessed 20 April 2021.

[3] K.L Gillion. *The Fiji Indians Challenge to European Domination.* Australian National University. p.16. 1977.
European dominance was expressed in many ways: political, through the exclusion of Indians from any voice in central or local government; economic, through the power of Australian companies, notably the CSR, the exclusion of Indians from many non-manual posts, and differential wage-rates; educational, through separate schools and inadequate provision for Indian education; social, through racial discrimination in social life, in associations, and in public places; and ideological, through the upholding of British culture as the model and the downgrading of Indian culture. Correspondingly, the challenge to European dominance was to take many forms: political organisation, agitation, and boycott, economic striving and occupational diversification, educational initiatives, and the search for an Indian identity.

Perspectives of British Colonial Rule in the Fiji Islands

As for the Fijians, throughout the entirety of British colonial rule, the chiefs saw what the settlers wanted them to see, believed what the settlers wanted them to believe, and said the right things that matched the colonial viewpoint.

That loyalty came at the expense of freedom of movement and a lack of investment in social transformations for the indigenous commoners. It would not be an exaggeration to describe the relationship as that of puppeteers and puppets: the Fijians' energies were dissipated by gestures and ceremonial flourishes that portrayed the highest chiefs as being in charge and busy ruling the country.

Democracy

In a democracy, a government's exercise of its powers is tempered by the will of the people. These "powers" are renewed, usually at intervals of four or five years. Principles of a modern democracy tend to include human rights, equality of opportunity for all and the freedom of the press, which are held to be guardians of freedom.

Other forms of government are dictatorships, autocracies, and oligarchies. In dictatorships and autocracies, one person rules, usually employing force to maintain law and order. An oligarchy is a group of persons who have control of a country and are run by a President with the support of the military.

A colony is governed by an imperial power, often remotely, through a governor who has wide-ranging powers and authority akin to those of an autocrat.

The typical democratic characteristics of freedom of the press, human rights, and equal opportunities for all citizens are curtailed and controlled to serve the ultimate goals of the imperial power or the emperor.

Colonialism was practised by the ancient civilisations around the Mediterranean, including the Phoenicians, Greeks, and Romans. It was not the *raison d'être* of exploration but its consequence. As powerful nations conquered and subjugated weaker ones, they imposed laws, taxes, and exploited resources.

Indirectly, colonialism benefited the less developed peoples in the long term. However, no coloniser arrived with

Political Security

altruistic motives. With some minor exceptions, most people were colonised by force and exploited at will. Exploitation was the imperialists' primary objective, although the missionaries and social workers who typically followed in the wake of the explorers contributed to the uplift of the local inhabitants. Imperialism was incompatible with the democratic ideals of the twentieth century, undermining the openness and freedoms that democracy represented.

Demands for Change

However, the clamour for change in Fiji began during the 1940s and continued intermittently without success until its enforced introduction at a much later date after independence.

The Hon. Vishnu Deo, OBE, a member of the Legislative Council from 1929 to 1959, and later Mr A. D. Patel, a notable and well-respected community member – a politician and lawyer, respectively - added their voices to its demand.

The European Electors' Association, a minority pressure group, had pre-empted Messrs Deo and Patel by decades. They had petitioned the Secretary of State for the Colonies for universal suffrage. Most European settlers and Fijians were not as enlightened as this small group. Mr Creech Jones, MP, said in the House of Commons that giving equal representation to the three communities in Fiji had been considered, but he could not accept the suggestion that this change reflected the wishes of *all European* electors:

> I am aware that representations were made by the European Electors' Association in 1945 and again last year advocating measures for constitutional reform, including the creation of an unofficial majority in the Legislative Council, and the introduction of universal adult suffrage on a common roll, but these and other proposals were not accepted because neither my predecessor nor I considered that such changes would at

present be of advantage to the community at large or would receive the support of the Fijians.[4]

The divide-and-rule ideology of a century was now coming home to roost. With just a decade to independence, neither the government nor the chiefs could envisage a way to unite all the peoples to form the new nation. The gulf that separated the peoples, creating political, social, and economic problems, did not narrow because the chiefs continued to be overconfident about, and underprepared for, the colony's future.

The British have also been criticised for condoning, if not actively encouraging, communal or racially segregated schooling. The practice, common in multi-racial communities like those found in Kenya, Tanganyika, Malaya, and Fiji, had been condemned on the grounds that it exacerbated racial distinctions and animosities and was inimical to the development of a sense of national identity. Some writers have even suggested that communal schools were part of *a deliberate policy to "divide and rule"*.[5]

Subtle Segregation

Segregation was inhuman and demeaning. Outside Europe, its use was widespread among the black and brown races to curb movements and aspirations. But discrimination was also practised within and among the white communities, where slums and ghettos confirmed the presence of the underprivileged and destitute people marginalised by the rapidly upwardly mobile classes.

For the colonial powers, this became an art form and the central pillar in their armoury of people control.

---

[4] Hansard, HC vol. 438, cols 184–5 (4 June 1947): self-government was debated in response to a question from Mr George Jeger about whether the Secretary of State had considered the representations from the European Electors' Association on the question of a greater measure of self-government for the Colony and the issue of the "common roll".

[5] Clive Whitehead, "Education in British Colonial Dependencies, 1919–39: A Reappraisal", *Comparative Education*, vol. 17, no. 1 (March 1981), pp. 71–80 (emphasis added), www.jstor.org/stable/3098767, accessed 10 February 2025.

Political Security

The power and influence of companies operating within this setting benefited from government support, thus restricting commerce to monopolies that were both able and willing to cooperate with its political agenda. The Shell and Vacuum Oil companies significantly reduced their offer of wage settlement to the workers when the government, under Ratu Sir Kamisese Mara, intervened in their dispute in 1959 and coerced the indigenous union leader to step away from the strike.

Education was not spared from political interventions. The approach in education was markedly different from the official claims that it treated all races as equals. In reality, schools were partially segregated: Chinese, Fijians, Indians and other races coming together under one roof, and European children were taught under a different regime where no other race could also be present.

Marist Brothers is an example. It was forced *to not* accept European children in its new secondary school, where non-Europeans were taught.

In the civil service, no less, higher positions were reserved for expatriates from Britain, Australia, and New Zealand; and membership of social and sporting clubs was similarly expected to be organised along racial lines. There were no laws that demanded segregation, which made it even more deceptive and led people to believe that racism did not exist in Fiji.

***

The administration had completely misread the country's general mood; it was politically ready for change. Late as it was, a bold approach would have set the pace and the agenda towards peaceful coexistence following its independence. It may have avoided the disaster that struck the new nation in the 1980s.

11

Impact of the Second World War on Fiji's Economy

Fiji was an important outpost. Its location in the central South Pacific – on a direct route between the US, Australia, and New Zealand – made it a vital and strategic place to protect the supply routes to Britain's southern dominions. Soon after war was declared, New Zealand and American forces dashed to Fiji and set up defences between 1940 and 1941.

Goods and dollars flooded in, which excited the locals, who seized the opportunity to supply services and consumables to the servicemen. The Americans built roads and telecommunications primarily for their needs, but Fiji's infrastructure benefited. The new infrastructure accelerated the transportation of goods across the colony. An early project was the road connecting Walu Bay, Suva, to Samabula via Edinburgh Drive. This made the journey to Nausori and Suva International Airport quicker. The upgraded airport, located within a fifteen-mile radius of the capital, Suva, is a boon to international travellers with its fast connection to Fiji's main international gateway, the Nadi International Airport.

Of particular interest was the Americans' plan to build a road from Suva through the middle of Viti Levu, connecting with the airport at Nadi. If completed, this project would have opened up Viti Levu. The administration of the day rejected the proposal on the presumed grounds that villages in the interior would be fragmented or destroyed. That seemed a perverse assumption. The villages might have benefited from relocation closer to better communications, commerce, and modern amenities. For other communities, the war years were marked by numerous opportunities.

Impact of the Second World War on Fiji's Economy

This period saw fledgling and small businesses grow, such as G. B. Hari & Co. and Narsey's in Suva; P. S. B. Singh in Nausori; and A. J. C. Patel Bros in Ba, northwest Viti Levu. New transportation firms emerged, easing the movements of men and materials so essential in the economic environment. Expatriate firms – such as Burns Philp, W. R. Carpenter, Morris Hedstrom Millers Ltd, and Walter Horne – expanded and were wholesalers to these prospering local firms.

The commercial sectors of the colony were well-positioned to supply a good amount of the provisions and other amenities needed by the visiting armed forces. Many businesses in Suva expanded during the wars, and within a decade, in October 1952, it was declared a city. One such example, among many others, was Munna Lal Maharaj & Co., which traded as Universal Motor Parts and operated as a small, family-owned business. It specialised in trading used spare parts bought from the American garrison's surplus stores. Similarly, Harm Nam, the butcher's, and Kwong Tiy, the general store selling a variety of commodities, flourished in Cumming Street, all taking advantage of and benefiting from the supply and demand of their new clientele.

The colony awoke from its imperial slumber at a moment's notice to supply the demands of its visitors. By the end of the war, the country had gained new thoroughfares and telecommunication systems, and an improved economy that had transformed many businesses and ignited start-up ventures throughout the colony.

During the occupation years, many young people received training in electronics, engineering, and mechanical work. Although some were Fijians, the majority were Indians who were able to fill the vacancies.

Immigrant artisans, farmers, and skilled people, such as motor mechanics – predominantly self-taught – met the increased demands by the armed forces for provisions and services. The foreign military presence created a mini-economic boom: a much-needed shake-up to rejuvenate an otherwise flaccid economy. The fundamentals of enterprise raced to meet the

Perspectives of British Colonial Rule in the Fiji Islands

needs of supply and demand. Fortunately, Fiji was up to the task and grasped the opportunities offered.

The troops with disposable cash provided a unique, once-in-a-lifetime chance for Fijians of all ethnicities to supply services and materials for the military's day-to-day maintenance and sustenance. Liberally endowed with materials and cash, the Americans easily related to people, made friends, and exchanged and bartered various commodities. Many start-up hopefuls began here and reinvented themselves as providers of essentials to a voracious army. Provided no enemy landed on the Fiji Islands, many would take up the challenges coming their way.

The contribution of the Fijians to the local economy was minimal and primarily limited to the supply of manual labour and fresh produce from the villages. This arrangement lasted throughout the war. The benefits to them were short-term and transitory; but, more importantly, many of them collectively experienced rare micro-cash transactions:

> Many Melanesians found they had access to more rewarding forms of labour with the armed forces compared to plantation labour, until then their only entry into the cash economy.[1]

Before the war, most European homes had the convenience and advantages of a telephone. The rest of the colony was mainly without. After peace was declared, a limited number of phones were made available to the general public. The Suva telephone exchange was located on Thompson Street, a stone's throw from the post office, and still stands as a monument to colonial enterprise.

Ram's application for a telephone line was approved, and the Posts & Telegraph Department installed the equipment at Amy Street in 1945. The imposing polished wood and metal phone was mounted on the wall in the front room, part of which was sectioned off as "office" during the war. It was an Art Deco-

---

[1] Douglas Ngaire, *They Came for Savages: 100 years of Tourism in Melanesia* (Southern Cross Press, 1996).

Impact of the Second World War on Fiji's Economy

style device: on the right-hand side was the cranking handle, and on the left hung the handset.

An outside call was initiated by one forward turn of the handle. A lady at the exchange would respond and ask: "Number, please?" The caller would give her the telephone number he wished to reach. Subscribers were distinguished by the number of times the bell rang: Ram's telephone number was "269 – 3 rings".

A shortage in the telephone exchange's capacity caused lines (known as "party lines") to be shared between subscribers, who were identified by the number of times the bell rang. The number (in this case "269") identified the "party" or group of subscribers; the number of rings (here, "3") identified the subscriber in the group. If the bell rang twice, the handset was not answered, as the call was intended for another subscriber. We shared our line with Mr Hargovind's No. 7 Laundry on Toorak Road, which had the number "269 – 2 rings". It was convenient because it was our family laundry; a couple of cranks of the handle called the laundry directly as an internal call. It was very easy for us to find out about our laundry deliveries and collections.

The war's impact on Fiji's economy was strong. It was also a voyage of discovery for the descendants of indentured labourers, who now sought relief and change from arduous toil with little return and an unsympathetic government. By the mid-1920s, most labourers had been freed from their contracts; those who chose to remain in Fiji relocated to other areas, away from the cane fields and farming, in search of greater financial rewards.

From the desperate days of the 1870s to the 1940s, Fiji's economic landscape underwent significant changes; it had evolved into a modern, sustainable agro-industrial colony. However, sustaining its growing population required much more investment and human resources. Britain was nearly bankrupt and would struggle to aid Fiji's growing needs. Yet Fiji depended on only half of its population, as the other half was confined to their *koros* (Fijian villages) under colonial regulations.

Fiji was spared the ravages of war. Fijian battalions fought the Japanese in the Solomon Islands and executed their duties with bravery and honour.

For some reason, best known to the Fijian chiefs, they sensed that the Fijians had to prove themselves worthy of recognition by the British; otherwise, "Fijians [would] never be recognised unless our blood is first shed".[2]

Indians in Fiji had mixed reactions to participation in the Second World War. Some had memories of the First World War[3] when their parents had served in active duty in Europe and the Middle East. For the 1.5 million Indians who fought for the British, their bravery and sacrifices were repaid with brutality and prejudice.[4] Awards for gallantry among these troops were among the highest in the British armed forces.

This war reignited an old irritation among the immigrants. Mindful of their recent experiences of discrimination and ill-treatment during their indenture days, they were not emotionally connected to Europe's war; they were engaged in a struggle to survive. The European volunteers were on a different pay scale, which was not available to others. This contradicted the general assumption that all people were equal, and the Indians decided to remain detached unless it became mandatory to join the armed forces.

In 1934, Governor Fletcher established an Indian platoon, which drew considerable attention. Once again, the race bias worked into the armed forces and the Indians were denied the same amount of pay as European volunteers. The Indian platoon was disbanded to prevent demands for parity spreading to Fijian servicemen. The chiefs had already accepted a lower rate of pay on their behalf.

What Next?

Until the fateful five years of the war, Fiji was an untouched outpost of the British Empire; at the cessation of

---

[2] Ratu Sir Lala Sukuna. https://justpdflab.com

[3] Gandhi actively supported recruitment of volunteers for active service during the First World War. As a man of peace, he was criticised for this, by Rev C.F. Andrews, a close associate of Gandhi.

[4] *The Guardian* (27 October 2018).

hostilities, it emerged as a more mature and confident colony, ready and able to step into a larger configuration of commercial pursuits for twentieth-century entrepreneurs.

Individuals and businesses continued to develop their services, as they had throughout the war and scaled up products and production. Those more aware of the opportunities available raised their profiles during the period and established their presence in their community. Increased demands for expert opinion led to further expansion of professional classes, with many professionals taking the opportunity to pursue degrees and diplomas in New Zealand and Australia.

Ram Charitra had a day job at the offices of Ellis, Munro, Warren & Leys, a firm of solicitors, in Suva. He supplemented his income with private accounting and taxation work. His income doubled during the war period, as he worked late into the night; the curtains were drawn, all the lights switched off, with just the table lamps' shades skewed and carefully directed onto the working area. At a safe distance from important documents, candles were used sparingly, placed on dinner plates and serving dishes, with a small quantity of water around them as a further precaution against hot, dripping wax. Tablecloths were repurposed as curtains to ensure total darkness during curfew.

During those darkened nights, the household routine underwent a change. Life and businesses continued, with modified schedules. Dinner and bedtime were earlier. In Amy Street, an office was set up in a corner of the front room, which had been rearranged to accommodate a table and a couple of chairs for clients, with space left for socialising and for the children to use.

Fiji's national revenue increased, resulting in a surge of funds into the Treasury coffers, prompting the Inland Revenue Department to seek additional staff. In 1945, the department was small and had only one tax inspector. It now faced challenges. These were welcome challenges of economic growth and prosperity.

The unexpected inward investment in infrastructure contributed by foreign military presence was a factor, and increased demands for goods and services spurring many to enter new businesses.

The people's increasing purchasing power and a greater variety of goods in the shops stimulated the national appetite for more consumer goods. The financial profile of the colony changed, and it continued to expand at a greater rate.

***

Many citizens of Britain, Australia and New Zealand did not return from the war, creating staffing issues for Fiji's colonial administration, which had to find civil servants elsewhere.

The colony's pool of administrative professionals was bare, and the Inland Revenue Department recruited from the nearby dominions for readily available expertise.

Accounting professionals were primarily found among the local Chinese and Indian communities. However, these were confined to local and family enterprises with limited experience in the wider context of taxation law and technical know-how.

The usual practice of engaging expatriates was a shortsighted policy in a colony that was growing and expanding in many directions. The government, confident as ever in its own projections and policies, was found wanting. We can infer from the shortage of expertise in the Income Tax department that similar problems existed in other parts of the government.

The key to technical excellence and expertise, as required in many sections of the civil service, was educating and training local talents with appropriate on-site experience. Unlike the private sector, the state's responsibilities are manifold, not least to ensure that its operations are continuous at all levels of management and supervision.

Until the 1940s, Fiji's economy expanded across all sectors, from farming to retail and wholesale businesses. The war altered the dynamics and changed people's motives and attitudes toward work. Encouraged by greater rewards, many from the farms drifted into larger commercial conurbations.

Fiji was spared the violence and interruption; the government continued with its normal policies quite oblivious to the enterprising start-ups now proliferating around the islands. Fiji was turning the corner from an obscure, failed economy at the time of transfer of sovereignty to a vibrant one within half a century.

When the hostilities ended, the curfew days were over, and the heavy drapes came down, the government's pre-war policies continued. No new measures or moves to institute social reforms. The pre-war attitudes continued at pace, and although Fiji was less financially dependent on Britain now, it was in no hurry to match the people's enthusiasm for modernisation.

At this stage, in the latter half of the 1940s, the colony's independence was just a generation away, making it an ideal time to begin a programme to educate, train, and establish a cadre of trainees as future leaders in administration. It was perhaps the last call for the government to adjust its policies and rectify the deficits in the localisation programme.

By the mid-1960s, constitutional changes made it clear what the future of Fiji might look like. Some were concerned about the lack of preparation in political and practical administrative matters, including Ram. He called me in London in 1969 to inform me about independence being planned for 1970. *"I am not sure if this is the right time. A country even this size cannot be prepared for freedom in five years. Politics and politicians are all over the place. Fijians don't want it! And there are no experienced administrators; unless we rely on expatriates for their continued services, Fiji can go to the dogs very quickly"*

> "the whole process was so compressed that nowhere was there sufficient time to create and establish a well-staffed public service with the necessary experience and detachment to run the countries satisfactorily after independence." [5]

---

[5] John T. Ducker. Beyond Empire. *The End of Britain's Colonial Encounter.* (Bloomsbury. 2020). p 198.

12

Fiji's New Era and New Problems

Besides the several evident causes of destruction, there appears to be some more mysterious agency generally at work. Wherever the Europeans have trod, death seems to pursue the Aboriginals. We may look to the wide extent of the Americas, Polynesia, the Cape of Good Hope, and Australia and find the same result.[1]

Governor Gordon's able subordinate and experienced adviser, J. B. Thurston, had played a key role in colonising Fiji. He weaved through the intrigues of local settlers, American threats, the cotton industry debacle, and the warring Confederate rulers, roping in Chief Ma'afu to advise and manoeuvre them into handing over the islands to Britain.

The people were now at liberty to pursue their peaceful occupations after generations of violence and instability. A more settled life and frequent contacts with the outside world, one hoped, would accelerate the modernisation process.

Gordon was also mindful that the people were recovering from the ravages of recent measles and smallpox outbreaks and had barely survived as a race.[2] Suspicion was rife in some circles that this was deliberate. Europeans were

---

[1] Charles Darwin, *The Voyage of the Beagle* (1839), ch.19.

[2] At Sir Hercules Robinson's invitation, Ratu Cakobau, along with his two sons and other chiefs, was invited to Sydney for celebratory festivities. The party succumbed to smallpox, but the ship, HMS *Dido*, returned the group to Fiji. They were not quarantined despite the fact that the dangers of the disease and its prevention were well known to the then medication fraternity; but the government decided to take no action to stop the infected members from travelling to the far-flung villages and spreading the disease among the population. Forty thousand people died as a result.

unaffected and kept isolated, on the advice of the Surgeon-General present. The colonisers may have betrayed the trust to protect them from attempted genocide of the natives through the measles epidemic soon after the Cession was signed. The settlers were isolated from the natives, but the Surgeon-General's decision not to quarantine the affected population from the rest was a gross act of negligence. The general welfare of the natives was fundamental, but absent, and many thousands succumbed to the disease.

The Governor's next task was closer to home. His immediate attention was drawn to the problems within the settler community and their increasingly acrimonious relationship with the chiefs. The questionable methods of land acquisition in prime locations had to be addressed if the Governor were to have any reasonable expectation of continuing cooperation with the former overlords.

As guarantor and protector, he had some serious obligations towards the welfare of the people and their primary and only asset – land, which was all communally owned. He required an understanding of, and sensitivity to, the needs and concerns of both sides.

The settler community appeared to have a degree of collective deceitfulness as they acquired land in exchange for trinkets and muskets. They effectively deceived local chiefs into giving away large tracts of the best and most productive land in locations of their choice. The responsibility now fell to the Governor to arbitrate fairly to restore confidence of both parties. Under the dubious transactions, the "sale and purchase" was a travesty. But it was difficult for him to ignore the demands of the settlers to settle in their favour.

He restored the chiefs' positions and titles to most of the land but left some disputed areas unresolved. The Governor favoured the settlers in instances where prime land was beneficial to the planters. Both parties were left with outstanding grievances. The Fijians thought Gordon had given away too much for little compensation, and the Europeans complained that too much was returned to the chiefs.

Perspectives of British Colonial Rule in the Fiji Islands

Managing Education

Britain had accepted responsibilities to prepare the colony for the new reality that was on the horizon. But as it had distanced itself from direct involvement in Fijian affairs, it had in fact reneged on that duty.

So far, the Fijians had no input into the government's decisions; their chiefs could not influence a programme of building schools and staffing them with qualified and experienced teachers. Even such a systematic and sustained approach would still mean that it would take people generations to achieve a degree of proficiency in subjects like language and numeracy, and develop the skills necessary to advance in modern society.

The government's education policy was based on false ideological and dogmatic beliefs that Fijians did not need education. Governor Gordon had declared that traditional values and their traditional village environment were best for them, and that unskilled workers did not need to be educated. He presumed that the ordinary men and women of the future would not aspire to anything other than menial work.

The colonial administration applied this false narrative to the indigenous communities and, to a certain extent, to the Indians. The latter, however, never took "no" for an answer and took steps to bring education to its people. The Chiefs, as representatives of the people, however, relied on the government's plans and generosity, as well as the efforts of the missionaries.

The missionaries continued their evangelising work while accepting the segregated traditional village format. They were unsuccessful in producing future professionals and administrators. The indigenous Fijians were pigeon-holed, tribally profiled, and mainly retained in *koros* under chiefs, who defined the parameters of comfort, privilege, and power of the people.

The imparting of knowledge was measured and controlled. Only those deserving to be educated got the best that existed – and that came at a price.

Did Britain depart Fiji, leaving a legacy of harmony and mutual social responsibility firmly rooted in the hearts and minds of all its citizens? The obvious answer to this must be negative.

Fiji's New Era and New Problems

On his departure from Fiji for the last time, Sir Kenneth Maddocks summarised the colony's social and political state of affairs, and in his final report before he left Fiji, he laid the blame squarely on the shoulders of the Fijian leaders and people:

Sir Kenneth's major concerns throughout his years in office were twofold: to address the imbalance between the two main races in the public service and to forge an appropriate path for the orderly constitutional development of the colony. Fijians were not only underrepresented in the professions but also greatly outnumbered in the higher echelons of the civil service.

This under-representation had several causes. Among them was the *"reluctance of traditional leaders, including Ratu Sukuna, to encourage academic education for their people whose appropriate place, they felt, was in the villages."*[3]

He was blissfully unaware that it was his government's responsibility *"to superintend and assist the development of these countries for the benefit of the inhabitants and the general welfare of humankind"*.[4]

In 1958 – 84 years after Cakobau's treaty with Great Britain, for instance, there was no professionally qualified Fijian lawyer; there was only one dentist and one medical doctor. In contrast, the Indian immigrants produced thirty-eight lawyers, twelve medical doctors, and eight dentists. According to the governor, the chiefs viewed the gap as someone else's fault.

The issue of education for the Fijians was a matter of *discretion* for the government. They spared no expense to educate a few select Fijians, mostly the chiefs. A handful of chosen commoners were selected for academic courses, but the majority of Fijians never gained meaningful access to good government schools, which limited their opportunities for pursuing further education and vocational qualifications.

---

[3] Brij V. Lal, A Time Bomb Lies Buried: Fiji's Road to Independence, 1960 – 1970. Australian National University Press. 2008. Pp. 25 – 48.

[4] George VI, quoted in the Kenya National Assembly Hansard, 14 June 1928, p. 313.

Perspectives of British Colonial Rule in the Fiji Islands

Ratu Sir Lala Sukuna received his primary education at an Indian school and completed his secondary education at Wanganui College in New Zealand, before being dispatched to Wadham College, Oxford. Semesa Sikivou, a commoner and therefore an exception, was educated at the University of Auckland and later acquired a postgraduate degree at the London School of Economics and Political Science. Before his appointment to the civil service, he taught at a Methodist primary school in Suva. Ratu Sir Kamisese Mara (the first prime minister of an independent Fiji) spent his first five years at Otago University, New Zealand, as a medical student, then transferred to Wadham College for political indoctrination, and was awarded an MA. Dr Ratu Jione Antonio Rabici and "Tom" Doviverata, OBE (Ratu Dovi), a brother of Ratu Sukuna, received his medical training at Otago University, but served as a colonial administrator rather than working among his community in the villages and elsewhere. These were the chosen few, and quite rightly, they were grateful for the privilege.

Aloof and isolated, these leaders never stood as role models, nor did they inspire many to emulate them as individuals to venture forth to carve out a place for themselves as professionals.

To the people, the chiefs embodied and symbolised authority. They did not influence or advocate changes to the constitution that could revolutionise and expedite Fijians' journey towards converging with other communities' aspirations for material betterment in personal comforts, and reducing or removing disparities and conflicts.

As a figurehead leader, Sir Lala followed his convictions. A faithful and dedicated servant, he prepared his people to serve the empire in perpetuity. The words "independence", "freedom", "self-determination", and "liberty" never crossed his lips. His political philosophy remained constant despite movements around the world that despaired at and challenged colonialism and all that it stood for.

As we have seen, good-quality education was limited to carefully chosen candidates; schools were established, but the imported teachers in them were well-versed in maintaining the status quo:

> The development of self-government is not one of the objectives of education, but one of its inevitable consequences. We cannot educate the people of a colony without expecting them to ask for self-government. Conversely, we cannot confer self-government unless we develop educational institutions.[5]

Essentials of Political Process Denied to Fijians: Implications

The colonial administration's appointments of "nominated members" to the legislature were a great honour of significant importance to the individuals and their community.

With an official majority, they helped to get the government's policies on indigenous affairs through without so much as a murmur. These members were also the eyes and ears of the government, tasked with detecting dissenting voices and ensuring that villagers understood government policies in the intended manner.

The colony had reached a stage by the late 1950s when it was becoming imperative to move forward in a new political direction. The government was understandably constrained by serious doubts about the differences of attitude, political demands, financial standing, and social disparities of the races.

The administration had based its policies on some dubious "science" that had consequences for Fijians' overall intellectual and emotional development. The underlying sentiment was based on perceptions about "native" peoples and their "genetically inherited racial characteristics" [6].

---

[5] Sir W. Ivor Jennings, *The Approach to Self-Government* (Cambridge University Press, 1958), p. 138.

[6] Helen Tavola. 1991. p.19.

Perspectives of British Colonial Rule in the Fiji Islands

The London Advisory Committee on Education in the Colonies espoused an approach that concluded that the Fijians could not cope with advanced education. The views held by the Chiefs may have endorsed this view – note Ratu Sukuna's statement about the "boat-builders" whom he presumed were incapable of "advanced education". This policy followed the Hadow Report on the education of Africans.[7] He may have been aware of their conclusion that "the Fijians are an agricultural people. There is, therefore, nothing in the racial composition of the Fijians to warrant their education in European schools either in or out of Fiji".[8] Tavola continues:

It was acceptable at this time to form social and economic policy on the basis of allegedly genetically inherited racial characteristics. The London Advisory Committee on Education in the Colonies endorsed this stance, proposing that secondary education for Fijians should be non-academic education. The Committee was opposed to allowing a pre-university external examination for Fijians, as it had learned from experience in other colonies that academic education would become more preferred over agricultural education.[9]

An absurd commentary on native peoples everywhere, but one which, paradoxically, Ratu Sir Lala Sukuna might have found sympathy.

Apollos Nwauwa reminds us that similar sentiments prevailed in Nigeria, but for different reasons. Europeans who were there for the long haul knew that if they intensified the

---

[7] Ibid

[8] From a despatch from the Governor to the Secretary of State for the Colonies, CO83/225/8, in Helen Goodwill Tavola, "Secondary Education in Fiji: An Investigation into School Effectiveness in a Changing Society", PhD thesis, University of London, 1990, p. 19.

[9] Tavola, "Secondary Education in Fiji", 1991. p. 19.

education of Nigerians, they would hasten the end of the occupation. Education was thus rationed and drip-fed to maintain their hegemony for centuries.[10]

The Impact of Immigration: New Challenges on the Horizon

Policies differed for other races, who were proactive, motivated, and direct in terms of their future prospects and financial security. They built and maintained their schools, with some grudging support from the administration. In time, improved living standards were the result, and greater self-reliance helped them make further inroads into the professions and commerce.

The schools were not well-resourced. However, these rudimentary beginnings were indispensable in initiating the transition to knowledge-based occupations; the schools enabled young men to grasp the essentials necessary to achieve better technical abilities in various vocations and trades.

The Marist Brothers, a Roman Catholic religious community, operated St Columba's School and St Felix College. The former admitted all races, except Europeans and those of mixed European descent. Brother Claudius noted in his letter of 14 September 1909 on the subject of the Indian Question at the Marist Brothers Indian School. 1897 – 1936. *pdf*:

> "The policy of the Colonial Government of the day was to have separate racial schools for the Europeans and the Fijians"

and

> "On account of the colonial government's racial policy, the Brothers were debarred from admitting them into their Suva school that had been registered for children of European descent only"

---

[10] Uduaroh Okeke, quoted in Appolos O. Nwauwa, *Imperialism, Academe and Nationalism: Britain and University Education for Africans, 1860–1960* (F. Cass, 1997), p. xiv.

Perspectives of British Colonial Rule in the Fiji Islands

In 1936, the Brothers announced that boys from both schools would be accepted for higher studies at their secondary school. A conflict broke out between St Columba's and the Education Department. St Felix College was registered as a European school; Segregation rules applied to primary and secondary schools.

Marist schools were funded privately, but that made no difference to the government's desire to keep the races from mingling; the government issued orders to disband the school.

Following representations from the Indian community, the school reassembled as a segregated institution, which began life as Marist Brothers High School in Suva. St Columba's continued in the same compound, at its Spring Street site, as a multiracial primary school that admitted Fijians, Indians, Chinese, and others.

After passing the entrance examination for the secondary schools, European children from St Felix migrated to the European-only Suva Grammar School for further studies. Occasionally, the odd European would find his way into the Marist Brothers High School.

The foresight and dedication of the Marist Brothers led immigrants to achieve professional status. Many leading politicians, social workers, entrepreneurs, and others emerged to drive Fiji's economic development, including John Grant (an Indian businessman and owner of the Lilac Theatre and other enterprises), Mr Kupsami (a businessman), Pandit Ram Dayal Sharma (a newspaper editor), and many others.

Before 1939, the progress of education depended on the *attitudes of the Governor, his advisers, and the Director of Education.* If the latter had been prepared to be forceful, he might have succeeded in getting more money for schools and teachers. On the other hand, everything finally depended on the Colonial Treasurer's advice to the Governor and his subsequent evaluation. It was not till after 1945 that education was accorded a higher priority by the government.[11]

---

[11] C. Whitehead, *Education in Fiji: Problems and Progress in Primary and Secondary Education, 1939–1973*, Pacific Research Monograph 6: Education in Fiji (Australian National University, 1981), p. 7.

13

The Future Is Here

You can't cross the sea merely by standing and staring at the water.[1]

The days of Cakobau Rex and J. B. Thurston were long gone.

The success of Governor Gordon's master plans was to be judged by the overall state of the colony in the decades to come: how would the sugar industry stand up to the novices experimenting with a new industry? Would the new Colonial Sugar Refining company last the distance or pack up with another failure in the quality of labour? How would the new racial element, with its unfamiliar attributes and habits, relate to the hostile panorama before them?

Testing Times ahead.

It seemed almost inevitable that the colony would at some stage face violent reactions to the presence of the immigrants. The British colonial experience in India's quest for freedom had repercussions on the Indians in Fiji. The anti-Indian sentiments generated in Fiji had no basis in fact but were widely parroted by the Chiefs and others. To their credit, the Indians ignored the most virulent comments, persevered and continued to build on their forefathers' successes. However, it appears that those comments had a sting in their tail, and the quiet build-up of ill-will towards the Indians was welling up in the dim corridors of Fiji's military barracks.

Time for reckoning - the future is here.

Just seventeen years after its freedom in 1970, Fiji lost its treasured designation of *"the Paradise of the Pacific"*.

---

[1] Sir Rabindranath Tagore.

The Future Is Here

Did the British feel a sense of achievement in granting independence to Fiji? The British may claim that they left the colony a better place. "A better place" is a relative term, and the truth lies somewhere between visible facts and the unsaid ambiguities, particularly about sensitive issues of race and politics. Britain had redesigned the nation over its ninety-six years of rule; the new edifice would tell its own story as the legacies of the past unfolded to reveal the future.

The old colony was ill-prepared; its leaders were never known to question the government's inflexibilities in relation to their reluctance to invest in indigenous matters, except in the most basic forms, which caused more harm than good. Their inadequacies led the youth to frustrations at their inability to match the skills and know-how of other races. Groomed to perfection, they could only govern within the limits of the guidelines, strategies, and ideologies laid down during the colonial period.

Independence or Dependence?

After independence, Fiji faced the reality that it lacked sufficient locally trained administrative officers in higher posts.

As might be expected, many permanent secretaries and others in the higher echelons of the civil service departed from Fiji before the ink was dry on the treaty of independence.

Finding itself on the back foot, the new government of a free Fiji sought the assistance of foreigners through advertisements in local and overseas journals or asked the incumbent expatriates to continue until locals were adequately trained to take over.

On 25 March 2016, forty-six years after independence, the *Fiji Sun* reported an unacceptably high turnover of expatriate chief executive officers (CEOs) and permanent secretaries. CEO salaries ranged between FJ$300,000 and FJ$500,000, and those of permanent secretaries between FJ$220,000 and FJ$260,000; the housing allowance for CEOs was a minimum of FJ$4,000 for three-year contracts. Other benefits included transport and travel allowances. The newspaper added:

Perspectives of British Colonial Rule in the Fiji Islands

> These expatriates have been recruited to lift levels of performance . . . but the lucrative packages don't seem to be working. So why, then, is there a high string of expatriate turnovers? [2]

Out of fourteen CEOs and permanent secretaries recruited overseas in 2016, only one permanent secretary was still at his post as of 25 March 2022.[3]

Fifty years after independence, the former colony continued in its quest for administrators experienced in the British governmental procedures and systems.

New dynamics required homegrown expertise, but this shortage compelled the government of a free and independent Fiji to continue to recruit new officers at a high cost.

---

[2] Ivamere Nataro, "Shine a Light: Our Locals Vs the Foreign Expats", *Fiji Sun*, 21 November 2021, https://fijisun.com.fj/2021/11/21/our-locals-vs-the-foreign-expats, accessed 18 February 2025.

[3] Fiji Sun. 21 November 2021

14

1963: A Watershed Year

The first steps toward a substantive political and legislative arrangement began in 1904. However, it was an insignificant process that failed to introduce the indigenous peoples to the *basics* of the political process.

In later years, the Legislative Council was expanded to include nineteen members. It had six Europeans who were all *elected* by the settlers; the remaining thirteen seats were selected–*nominated* by the governor on the advice of the Fijian chiefs. No group other than the Europeans was able to elect its own representatives to the legislature.

The chiefs' "advice" comprised a list of candidates prepared by them for the Governor, who exercised his discretion and chose those he believed would best serve the interests of the Crown. The candidates were picked at random, without the people's knowledge or involvement.

The nineteen members and the Governor formed the new Legislative Council, a basic model run as an advisory group to the Chief Executive. The indigenous members of the council had no portfolio. Their presence before the Speaker meant nothing to the administration or to the public. Their repertoire of interests consisted of support for the Executive Council's legislative agenda. The elected European members represented their constituencies and the vested interests of the settlers and plantation owners.

During these early days, the immigrant labourers were represented by the Agent-General for Immigration. His infrequent visits to his "constituents" hardly prepared him for his work for the labourers. This, for the people, was not a satisfactory arrangement, and they demanded direct *electoral* representation.

In 1916, a significant change occurred. The waiting and talking were over; the Governor announced that Indians would be represented on the council – *he* would select the individual. Although disappointed that their council member would be nominated by the Governor, the Indians nevertheless accepted the situation as a first step towards better representation and future constitutional change. They had to make the best of it. So long as the member brought *their* concerns to the chamber, they would be satisfied.

In addition, *seven* European members were now to be elected, which was out of all proportion to their numbers in the colony. Two Fijian chiefs were *selected* from the Great Council of Chiefs' members list. People's voices were not heard, and their concerns were dismissed as irrelevant, as only the chiefs were believed to know what was best for the people. The franchise would not be extended to the Fijians, and they would remain in the wilderness of political development until 1963, just seven years before Fiji gained independence. People who had never experienced the political process or understood the reasons why such representation was necessary, as well as the impact of the legislature's decisions on their lives, remained mystified as to what transpired in the corridors of power.

* * *

A *new* constitution was introduced in 1963. It had all the hallmarks of an incomplete scenario, a tentative arrangement to mollify the chiefs, but nothing that would or could lay the foundations of a stable political system. To the optimist, it was an improvement: the beginning of movement in the right direction. To the pessimist, it was a fudge with no direct or future benefits accruing to the colony.

To the chiefs, the new arrangements may have seemed a betrayal. It introduced a convoluted electoral system that included partial universal suffrage but retained race as the basis. An elector had to vote for a member of his race in addition to voting for a candidate of a different race. Going forward to independence, this ensured that race would remain at the core of Fijian politics.

Despite its minuscule departure from its usual immovable stance to introduce a common electoral roll, Britain's attempts to reshape the internal political landscape found deep resentment

1963: A Watershed Year

among the Fijians and the European settlers; they saw that the day may not be far off when the electoral system itself would fall victim to rational and prudent citizens. Compromises were fraught with difficulties, as the races were poles apart on such substantive issues; they were also complicated by demands that Fiji should be returned to the "Fijians".

European settlers considered themselves the "guardians" of the Fijian peoples and were there perpetually to guide and protect them. This belief impliedly supported the Hadow Report's idea that the Fijians were incapable of sustaining themselves. The few Fijian intellectuals who were there, such as Mosese Tuisawau, viewed such comments and attitudes as patronising and totally unacceptable, as denigrating a race that was capable of moving forward but had its hands tied.

Those small steps towards the middle ground were to be welcomed as a first step. It could be an exercise to demonstrate that voting for a candidate on the basis of merit alone had advantages for all people. The rights of the indigenous people were acknowledged and accepted as paramount, and the Indians had also accepted that the Treaty of 1874, which ceded the islands to Britain, was unalterable and not an issue. During discussions in the 1940s, the Hon. Vishnu Deo and Mr A. D. Patel concurred with these sentiments, which were later reaffirmed.

The continual opposition from the Europeans and the Fijians to independence appeared to contradict international opinion that as other island nations in the South Pacific had gained freedom, that Fiji must also be released to move forward as a member of the United Nations and contribute to and benefit from its association with the wider communities with similar social and economic issues.

The chiefs' regressive and repressive attitudes constantly held back progress: first, of their own people, and now by insisting that Britain had *moral* rights to return the colony to them. This reactionary notion was never going to take flight. Britain was realistic and too aware of world opinion to permit such a grossly retrograde move in the light of the demographic realities of the day. It could not ignore the demands of the United Nations'

Perspectives of British Colonial Rule in the Fiji Islands

Committee of Twenty-Four, an international group devoted to the issue of decolonisation.

The constitution, amended in the mid-1960s, embraced historic electoral changes, albeit flawed, it made some headway. This was an essential first step for all, but more so for the Fijians. It introduced them to a measure of democracy. Practical changes were afoot. Non-Europeans were now given higher civil service positions. To its credit, the administration pulled the right strings to edge the colony towards freedom, despite opposition. Some, of course, may argue that the changes were too little to make serious changes in people's attitudes and thinking.

> The whole process was so compressed that nowhere was there sufficient time to create and establish a well-staffed public service with necessary experience and detachment to run the countries satisfactorily after independence.[1]

These changes were significant and comprehensive and were unthinkable a few short years ago. The Executive Council was abolished, and the powers of the Legislative Council – the future parliament – were increased, with the elected members now forming the majority.

The elements of the elite who had proactively defended the government's policies for most of the colonial period now appeared bewildered as changes took place at a rapid pace. Could the British showcase Fiji as an example of foresight in economic development, societal enhancements and bestowing a stable and secure democratic political system?

Societal Changes

For many millennia, humankind moved across continents in search of better pastures. The exchange of ideas and materials that benefit humanity would not be possible without people's movements and interactions, at times in unpleasant circumstances or against their will. The idea of "better pastures"

---

[1] John.T. Ducker, *Beyond Empire: The End of Britain's Colonial Encounter* (Bloomsbury, 2020), p. 198.

1963: A Watershed Year

covers a multitude of sins, but primarily, people migrated to find richer sources of food. Later ages brought degrees of comfort, security, and societal enhancements, exciting innovation, and progress. The Greeks moved and settled and shared religion, language, and identity around the Mediterranean as "frogs around a pond", so said Plato in his *Phaedo*. The Romans, as they expanded, imparted knowledge of their legal system and improved their infrastructure. Western intellectual traditions may not be so advanced, and the locals richer for it, without the movement of peoples and ideas.

The journey into the unknown was hazardous and uncertain, and mostly at the mercy of not just the weather but of fellow humans whose treachery was limited only to their imagination.

Without all our forebears' courageous spirit and fortitude, the life-force of the modern world's material comforts would lie only in the realm of possibilities. Like seeds chosen for their qualities of resilience and scattered across inhospitable terrain and plains around the globe, they helped configure the modern world.

That the labourers' time-honoured conservative differences were put aside was the inevitable human reaction to adversity. Adversaries soon accommodated and linked up, and looked forward to cultural celebrations to soften their hardships and misery. Eid and Diwali became popular events shared among friends and locals, consolidating the villages and plantation units.

Deeper friendships developed across the divides as one community reached out to help another in times of stress and need. One example of a warm bond, formed during the hardships of the outward journey to Fiji, was my grandparents' friendship with a *jahaji*, a fellow passenger.

My *Nani's* - maternal grandmother's village was located on Vuci Road, Nausori. A simple conversation about the problems encountered during the journey to Fiji sparked an enduring connection between our family and the Bhatt family. Mr Bhatt was never in good health, and Nani and her family visited him often with food he enjoyed. An outsider would not have suspected that our families were not related; they weren't of the same faith either. My Nani - indeed, both our grandmothers often spoke of similarities in societies. Differences evaporated with familiarity over a short period of contact. No formalities. No transactions – just simple conversations on equal terms and an open mind usually triggered bonds across cultural and even racial divides. Tastes of exotic foods and materials added dimension and energy to new relationships.

In 1947, the ageing Mr Bhatt went on the hajj pilgrimage to Mecca. Before he boarded our cousin's bus, his last meal was with Nani and her family. That was the last meeting and farewell from an old friend. He never returned from the pilgrimage.

In the decades (that seemed centuries) since arriving in Fiji in 1879, the labourers who seemed an incongruous lot in tropical forests, eventually evolved from a near destitute and despairing underclass to creators of wealth. They moulded their abilities to the circumstances of the day and contributed to the welfare of the family and the nation. The new society forged under unimaginable circumstances justified the commitment undertaken by their forebears under the indenture agreement.[2]

---

[2] Lala Totaram Sanadhya, *My Twenty-One Years in the Fiji Islands and the Story of the Haunted Line*, tr. and ed. John Dunham Kelly and Uttra Kumari Singh (Fiji Museum, 1991, repr. 2003). Totaram was betrayed into travelling to Fiji in 1893. He worked out his contract, set up a small farm in the Nausori mill area. He worked as a Hindu priest to earn extra income and helped other farmers still under indenture. He learned the Fijian language, carpentry, metalwork, and photography. He wrote to Gandhi and others and appealed for teachers and lawyers to visit Fiji. The letters worked and, among others, Manilal Doctor and the Revd C. F. Andrews arrived to assess the situation and report to Gandhi and the Indian Government, which led to calling a halt to sending labourers to Fiji.

15

Political Development and the Role of Education

> In Cyprus – as in most colonial settings – "native" civil servants . . . were framed by rigid regulations and, more importantly, they could never reach the higher administrative jobs occupied by British officials.[1]

The Fijians' adult franchise came late, in fact, nearly eighty years after the European settlers, and about fifty years after the Indians started to have a say in the affairs of the colony.

The chiefs never seriously inconvenienced the administration with such considerations as franchise for their people, the *tauvanua*. They judged them to be beyond reconciliation with modern standards and best left to the customary routines of village life under the guidance of the local chief.

The chiefs knew best. The government occasionally tried to convince them that change was inevitable. Sir Ronald Garvey the governor of Fiji, 1952 to 1958, was desperate to move on from Gordon's protective village set-up; he wanted to introduce changes gradually to village administration and the policy on indigenous education. The chiefs had become so used to, and the people so dependent on, the old ways that it seemed almost impossible to introduce new ideas into their collective thinking.

---

[1] Alexis Rappas, "The Uncharted World of Cypriot Colonial Servants and the Ideological Foundations of British Rule", *Cyprus Review* (29 December 2017), p. 63. PDF available from www.cyprusreview.org/index.php/cr/article/view/156, accessed 10 February 2025.

Perspectives of British Colonial Rule in the Fiji Islands

The villages and the chiefs were on automatic pilot, and nothing seemed to alter that state.

> Sir Ronald counselled the chiefs that the
> "chiefly system on which so much depends should march with the times and should not ignore – for too long – the modern trend of democracy".[2]

And the Burns Report[3] rejected the system Governor Gordon had set up in 1876

> "to secure the continuance of the Fijian communal system and the customs and observances traditionally associated with it".[4]

It was not only the chiefs who wished to continue with Gordon's ordinance but also some lesser mortals – the *tauvanua*, the commoners – who supported the ideology. Some were chosen and sent abroad for education and returned, with gratitude oozing from their sinews for such a blessing. Semesa Sikivou and Ravuama Vunivalu may be included in this group. Both were intelligent men, good debaters, and significant government supporters, and they lived in their ivory towers happily ever after.

As ever, education *mattered*. We evolve through the learning process – friendly rivalries, competitions, and challenges take many shapes: from book learning to observations, benefits accrue for the individual and eventually the community benefits. In Fiji, however, education was dispensed in small, controlled portions, as if to make a statement about its authority, while being disingenuous about its generosity.

---

[2] Brij V. Lal. (ed.) A Time Bomb Lies Buried. Fiji's Road to Independence -1960 – 1970. 2 Paramountcy, Parity, Privilege.

[3] Sir Alan Burns, T.Y. Watson and Professor A.T. Peacock. Report of the Commission of Enquiry into the Natural Resources and Population Trends of the Colony of Fiji. 1959. Crown Agents. Legislative Council Paper No.1 of 1960.

[4] Brij V. Lal. (ed) above. 2 Paramountcy, Parity, Privilege.

Political Development and the Role of Education

Proactive parents educated their offspring, often at great personal cost. Many good secondary schools – mostly Indian – opened their doors with private contributions and institutions from the early 1950s: D. A. V. College, Mahatma Gandhi High School, Indian High School (now Jai Narayan College), Vivekananda High School, and others, all produced promising students who had high hopes of academic achievement but for the lack of tertiary facilities in Fiji. Marist Brothers schools set the benchmark for standards followed by one of the largest educational institutions in the Pacific – the Natabua High School, founded in 1930.

In 1963, the Ramakrishna Mission of Nadi, under the guidance of Swami Rudrananda and supported by the late Mr A. D. Patel, drew up plans for tertiary education in Fiji. The country was now at a crossroads: the growing population and economy and the political uncertainty all pointed to the need to remedy the shortages of professionals and those with technical expertise.

The proposed site for establishing a university was the mission's complex in Tailevu, Rewa. It would be funded by the mission and private enterprise. A. D. Patel, the Swamiji, and Ram Charitra attended the meeting. The project adviser was Professor Huddersfield from England. Ram oversaw the preparation of the financial aspects of the development and the institution's funding.

The colonial Director of Education agreed to attend this preliminary meeting, which was arranged to suit his convenience, at the proposed campus venue. On the appointed day, the Director did not present himself, and there was no prior apology for his absence. Later, he expressed regret and stated that it was "premature" to establish a university at that stage of Fiji's development!

As a member of the Executive Council, he was familiar with Fiji's growth and Britain's timetable for the colony's freedom. Education was the key to the momentous changes ahead, but the administration's colonial policy put a spanner in the works and wrecked the initiative, fearing that education might hasten demands for independence.

Perspectives of British Colonial Rule in the Fiji Islands

Time and events eventually caught up with the reluctant administration. A university – the first in the South Pacific – was now on the drawing board. Proposals for tertiary education had been mooted for nearly a decade, not least by Indian leaders, before the governments of Fiji, Australia, New Zealand, and other Pacific island countries coordinated their efforts and resources to inaugurate the University of the South Pacific, only two years before Fiji's independence.

16

Fijians & the Future

[In] Britain, ministers and permanent officials of the Colonial Office have been preoccupied with the problems of more importunate colonial peoples; and, although they have regarded it as necessary that Fiji should eventually become self-governing, they have shown only an intermittent and unimaginative concern with the process by which this change should be brought about. In the colony itself, senior officers of government have largely retained an attitude of benign, but outdated paternalism. To these men, there has seemed little need for change.[1]

The constitution adopted at the inception of colonial rule in Fiji preserved traditional Fijian values. It seemed a wise and practical solution, but, in fact, it deterred Fijian progress. It predetermined the future direction of their social and economic development. The ancient lifestyles and traditions survived incongruously into the twentieth century, living on and continuing to influence life as they had for centuries, but without the aggression and confrontational posturing of the warring factions. Visible signs of progress and modernisation included a stable environment, where peace reigned and cannibalism was a thing of the past. It was a seamless transition from a permanent state of war to a total absence of the fear of war that had preoccupied the Fijians' daily lives.

The framework to control people used to violence as part of daily life, and to lay the foundations of complete transformation, was never put in place when it was more opportune to do so. This was a period of peace, and King Cakobau had accepted the terms of the treaty written up by the

---

[1] J. W. Davidson, "Constitutional Changes in Fiji", *The Journal of Pacific History*, vol. 1 (1966), pp. 165–8.

Perspectives of British Colonial Rule in the Fiji Islands

Queen's representatives. There existed a rapport and acceptance of the governor's actions, which no Chief had repudiated.

Without hesitation, the chiefs moved on from Confederate politics to duties in the colonial services. The government's view of the village Fijians was based on antiquated beliefs and notions about so-called "backwards" races that have been largely discredited, but that was the basis of colonial policies for them throughout its hegemony that nothing approaching modernity could be applied to them "in the present state of development". Ahmed Ali observed that

> the circumstances affecting them were local rather than general. Fijians were governed along their traditional lines and, under the prevailing system, enjoyed a very large measure of self-government. It was officially observed that the voting system was "strange to native ideal" and based on qualifications which could not be made to apply to "native Fijians in the present state of development".[2]

Their foregone conclusions predetermined all colonial policies regardless of the state of "development" of people under their supervision and protection.

The development of a separate institution, which might have included a specialised department for training and introducing modern trends across the village complexes, was an opportunity missed.

Instead, the Council of Chiefs became a talking shop of the elders and cronies - a "government" within a government weakened Fiji by making it a two-tier nation: one entity was free to enjoy various liberties, such as freedom of movement and engaging in entrepreneurial activities; the other was constrained by regulatory controls and burdened by traditional occupations and pursuits. The responsibilities for overseeing the people's

---

[2] Ahmed Ali, "Fijian Chiefs and Constitutional Change, 1874–1937", ch. 6 in "Fiji and the Franchise: A History of Political Representation, 1900–1937", PhD thesis, Australian National University, 1973, p. 59.

Fijians & the Future

education and material progress were delegated to the local chiefs who were as much acquainted with present or future trends as was Rip van Winkle.

> The potentialities of the colonial peoples themselves for public service have not yet been anything like fully used. The future of each Colony rests ultimately in the hands of its own people, and substantial progress must depend upon the people themselves supplying the administrative and technical staffs which the needs of each territory demand.[3]

Universal suffrage, if introduced by the agreement of all parties during the colonial era, may have assuaged any conceivable flashpoints post-independence or prevented them.

The Hon. Vishnu Deo's propositions during the 1940s for "one man, one vote, one destiny" gained no traction with the administration. Like A. D. Patel, he sought to eliminate all race-based regulations in the interest of all citizens. Although this goal took a generation to achieve through small steps, Deo and Patel's persistence was rewarded, albeit posthumously, when the following small but significant changes to the electoral system were implemented in 1965 following the London conference.

Candidates from different races were included on the National Federation Party (NFP) ticket to the Senate: Isikeli Nadalo, Ratu Mosese Tuisawau, and Ratu Glanville Lalabalavu. In 1972, further integration led to the election of additional Fijians as NFP members to the House of Representatives, including Captain Atunaisa Maitoga, Apisai Tora, Isikeli Nadalo, and Edmund March. It was only a matter of time before the hard-nosed elements within some communities would welcome and establish permanent changes to the electoral system.

The limited changes introduced by the administration came about despite the Fijians' long-held reluctance to change. Some were unhappy to view it as a weakness in the government's

---

[3] Anthony Kirk-Greene, "Recruitment and Training: Improvement of Opportunities for Colonial Candidates", *On Crown Service: A History of HM Colonial and Overseas Civil Service, 1837–1997* (Bloomsbury, 1999), p. 203.

policy: if change was needed, then no half-measure would satisfy anyone. It was therefore not surprising that one high-ranking leader, the Bauan chief, Ratu Sir Edward Cakobau, who understood the meaning and the value of the *universal* suffrage, seemed exasperated – even mystified – that the government withheld its full implementation. He commented: "The *beauty of common roll* would be when it was accepted by all."

Were the Fijians going to be as intransigent on the common roll, as officials in London thought? A Colonial Office briefing summed up Governor Jakeway's talks with three pre-eminent Fijian leaders, Ratu Mara, Ratu Penaia Ganilau and Ratu Edward Cakobau: the governor reported

> that 'some gentle selling of the attractions of a limited common roll element in the next constitutional stage has been done with all three and does not appear to have fallen on entirely unreceptive ground'".[4]

In Sir Edward's quote, above, "all" was a euphemism for the European settlers of the colony. It referred obliquely to their fear of losing their pre-eminence as a pressure group, which was greater than their ability to see that the benefits the application of good electoral practice would offer the colony. Race as an instrument of control was built into the colonial electoral system. There was no logic or longer-term advantage to the colony except that it satisfied a vocal minority and xenophobic community that harped about the need to protect the Fijians.

As a prominent and significant member of the Fijian community, Ratu Sir Edward was careful not to tread on any sensitive toes; he chose his words with care. The introduction of crossvoting was a gesture to the Europeans as much as it was to the indigenous community. Some opposed it on the grounds that the next step would be universal franchise; others saw it as a compromise but reluctantly accepted the proposed changes.

---

[4] Dr. Brij V. Lal. A Time Bomb Lies Buried. 1960-1970. 4. 1965 Constitutional Conference.

The idiocy of this half-in, half-out approach became apparent when two diverse groups, the Europeans and the ethnic Chinese, became one racial group to accommodate the latter. If other races had been included in this group, the question of the universality of the electoral system would have been resolved.

This absurdity concerning electoral racial categorisation was further embroidered. A person of South Asian descent, who was, prima facie, the least likely person to be labelled as a European, was ruled by the colonial Electoral Commission to be a "European". Before this transformation, he was registered as an "Indian" voter and had exercised his rights as an Indian – until, that is, he was magically metamorphosed into a European. He proved he had Dutch ancestry and was permitted by the Electoral Commission to be included in the European/Chinese category.

The person in question was within his rights to pursue his electoral categorisation to its logical conclusion; in doing so, he exposed the absurd stance of the government and the European settlers, and how ridiculous the pursuit of such senseless policies in a multi-ethnic society was. The greater need, rather, was for unity in diversity. Under a functioning, full universal franchise, neither proof of race nor the lumping together of different groups for convenience would be necessary, as all citizens would be equally sovereign.

17

Early Years

Education is not the filling of a pail, but the lighting of a fire.
W. B. Yeats

Ram Charitra was born on 16 November 1912, in Nabukavesi, a small village on the outskirts of Navua Township. Navua was located at the southern tip of Viti Levu, struggling to grow sugar cane in commercial quantities. Ram's father, Algu Mahajan, passed away during Ram's early years, leaving his recollections of his father vague. Algu had suffered from weakness induced by long hours and injuries sustained during his days in the cane fields. Medical attention was non-existent and only available at plantations nearer the mill.

Algu had arrived in Fiji and settled in Navua township, where he first worked as a farmhand. When he was relieved from his indenture agreement, he was exhausted and unwell but happy to have reached the end of his contract.

He had left India a strong man, full of confidence and with expectations of a bright future. But now, a decade later, he was broken and disheartened. Pessimistic about his abilities to move forward, he begged to be returned to India; he longed to visit his village and family. He was due free passage, but the company procrastinated, which was usually its approach towards workers and labourers who wanted to return. Fiji was not a fit place for those labourers and their families who needed medical assistance. The government fell short of its commitment to care for people who had sacrificed their health and future to build the colony's financial infrastructure:

> Working and living conditions were so atrocious that Fiji had the highest rate of suicide in the world and the highest rate of

Early Years

infanticide among the colonies that deployed indentured labour.[1]

Despite his condition, Algu hired a shop space, and with the unflagging encouragement of his wife, Ram's mother (my grandmother, Mahadei), they managed to survive with their two children. Due to Algu's state of health, the shop became a burden to him, causing Ram's mother anxiety about the business's future. Ram was growing up, and she was conscious of his need for guidance and an education. She needed help and advice on how to supervise his journey through school and afterwards.

There were many boys of his age who were not in school, so she was concerned that he might end up in the wrong company – a possibility that greatly tormented her. Ram's future was in her hands. They had left farming, and the only option left was to move forward somehow, even with all the negativity and gloom around her. Ram became aware of the family's situation and asked to leave school and find a job, doing something, anything. Typically, he was firmly refused. The matter was never raised again.

My grandmother needed help. Algu had now passed on. She knew of a person from his work in the community and as a successful shopkeeper in his own right. After the first anniversary rituals for Grandfather Algu were over, she approached Bharti Maharaj and shared her concerns about the business and her children with him. She needed his help to oversee her son's education and to help him secure a comfortable future. Bharti Maharaj was a caring man; he took young Ram under his wing. They enjoyed a father–son relationship until Maharaj's departure from Fiji in 1948.

In late 1946, Maharaj was bedridden with a form of paralysis. He was nursed at the Charitra home on Amy Street, and attended by Dr C. M. Gopalan, until he recovered enough to

---

[1] Rajendra Prasad, *Tears in Paradise: Suffering and Struggles of Indians in Fiji, 1879–2004*. The author reproduced the quote in his blog on Girmit.org, https://girmitiya.girmit.org/new/index.php/2021/04/12/quotes-tears-in-paradise, accessed 10 February 2025.

travel to India in August 1948 on the *Orna*. He never returned and until 1952 there was no communication from him about his whereabouts.

In 1952 after the final protocol that cemented the partition of India was signed. Ram received a letter soon after from the government of India that revealed Bharti Maharaj's fate. He had fallen victim of the December 1948 Hindu–Muslim riots while travelling on a train from Meerut to Rajasthan, his destination. The letter confirmed his personal belongings could be reclaimed by producing appropriate identifications. The grief caused to the family by the disclosure ended its connections particularly as not being able to put an end to the matter in accordance with traditional rites he deserved – except for prayers that were held at home in his memory.

My one enduring memory of Bharti Maharaj, whom we affectionately called Dada (grandfather), is of him feeding grapes to Lalli (Manorama), Ram's second child and my sister. Seated in his usual chair, he peeled each grape and fed her, while she was snuggled between his legs; he occasionally put one in my mouth. While doing his grandfatherly duty, he continued his conversation with an old family friend, Mr Apa Bhai Patel (the founder of A. J. C. Patel Bros of Ba), whom we also addressed as Dada. Mr Patel usually came to our home with book-keeping documents to consult with Ram and, from time to time, to draw up final accounts for presentation to the Inland Revenue.

During the 1950s, when we were enroute to Deuba Beach, Ram would point out a large clump of trees among the surrounding vegetation. In a calm, measured voice, he told us, "We played under those trees after school. We kept a couple of cows there." He was happy there, as one could note from his tone of voice. There, under the shade and protection of the vast outstretched branches that drooped and formed a cosy, shady area below, his mind raced into the future as the cows chewed the cud, and the ocean breeze wafted through.

From conversations with my grandmother, I learned that Ram began his education as a pupil at the village's only school. There were more children than there was space available. He was fortunate to have a good start early in life. When a teacher was available, he and his classmates were taught the basics of arithmetic and the alphabet, first in Hindi and then later in English. He went on to attend a school in Navua, which was opened by Sadhu Vashist Muni.

These children were the first generation born to freed labourers, who were anxious for them to learn a trade or to aim for higher education, if or when it became available. The government had no plans to meet such requirements as the labourers needed. A leap to higher education would only encourage further demands, not in the best interests of colonial policies and outlook.

Education & Challenges

The immigrant labourers' focus on education led many to pursue worthy vocations, such as teaching. There was not much else available for ambitious and driven young people.

The Methodists had established a teaching institution, which was the primary professional attraction for progressive young men. Ram won a scholarship, and he grabbed the opportunity.

After graduating, he was employed by the Education Department as a Teacher at the Government Indian School, Samabula. He worked there from 30 June 1933 to 31 December 1934. A year was enough for him: he saw few prospects as a teacher and resigned.

Ram's mother continued to face many challenges. The medium of exchange in the colony was cash: pounds, shillings, pence, and gold sovereigns! [2] Barter was not uncommon among the smallholders just beginning to lay their foundations as freed farmers. The bartered items received were sold for money or exchanged for valuable objects that could be sold or put to good use. This no-nonsense approach required no

---

[2] The currency in the colony was sterling. At the time, it was denominated as "pounds", "shillings", and "pence" (£. s. d.). One pound was made up of 240 pence, with 12 pence to 1 shilling and 20 shillings to a pound. The change from imperial to metric arrived in Fiji on 13 January 1969. Gold sovereign issued as £1 coin in 1900s, would today be worth about £800.

Perspectives of British Colonial Rule in the Fiji Islands

middlemen and suited everyone. Bartering had helped Grandfather Algu to set up a business to support his family.

The community as a whole suffered the vagaries of sugar-cane production – the time lag between cane harvesting and payment – caused problems for the local shopkeepers and their customers.

Disappointingly, the future continued to present more problems than solutions. With no prospect of new industries or help from the government or the plantation owners.

Cane production ceased. The area was not commercially viable. The crushing at the Tamanua (Navua) Sugar Mill was wound down, and growing ceased in 1923. Families on whom the closure had an impact were cut adrift without compensation or help to relocate. Many left the township in search of opportunities elsewhere, and those with a suitable skill set established small enterprises to make ends meet. Most had small plots of land, which helped them survive.

Suva was the service-based capital of Fiji and was the seat of government offices. Most professionals and technicians practised there, and it was where a growing community of post-indenture labourers came to escape the cane fields.

The influx provided a ready customer base for most businesses. From clerks to artisans, all needed provisions and services of some sort – from barbers to carpenters – all were there, ready, willing, and able to satisfy every need of the growing population. The young and ambitious capitalists, with ready cash, looked for opportunities to set up enterprises at a moment's notice.

So, for Ram's family, Suva was perhaps the only choice. They relocated to Muanivatu, a quiet suburb, and rented a family home. Later, they found a shop with two rooms and storage facilities in downtown Suva, located on Marks Street, a busy commercial thoroughfare. They set up a general store selling homewares and tobacco.

I recall visiting the Marks Street shop as a child with my sister Manorama, towards the end of the war. The place was dim and sombre, with dark, heavy curtains still languid from its moorings high above the door and windows. The fear of a

Japanese invasion was still in the air, although the danger of a real invasion had passed; however, the mind remained conscious of the possibilities of a surprise attack.

From time to time, a strictly observed curfew was imposed: the covers and screens on the windows stayed in place until the war was over. The austerity experienced was reflected by the items on display in the shop. Imported tinned goods and loaves of bread stood in a small wooden and glass cabinet, placed next to a cash drawer built into the counter. The drawer contained the proceeds of the day's sales. In another area of the shop were odd tools, including tin openers, screwdrivers, assorted hammers, and other items.

Set in the centre of the shop, on top of a solid wooden block, was a large coil of the popular rolled-up tobacco. Its display attracted some older addicts of the stuff, which had a pronounced odour, not quite to our liking, that permeated the atmosphere. This tobacco was dispensed in pieces cut to size with a sharp knife, measured by a wooden dowel template and cut to that size on a hardwood block.

Impact of Sadhu Vashist Muni on Education

Vashist Muni was born in Benares (now Varanasi), India, in 1888; he arrived in Fiji in 1920. His meetings attracted farmers from far and wide. He set about easing their minds. He told them that the government had other things to deal with, and that, by working together, they could bring change and improvement themselves. He informed his attentive listeners that his purpose was to assess their needs and to help them where he could. His presence was reassuring to the farmers: at last, someone was there to listen to their grievances and concerns. The government's apathy and indifference were legendary; all it was concerned about was that sugar production should continue uninterrupted – nothing else mattered.

However, in 1921, Muni felt their frustrations; as a last resort, he advised them that there were no easy solutions to end their misery, and that the strike action they had proposed was justified. He counselled the leaders to keep the strike peaceful and focused, but not to expect a positive response. Muni's open support for the farmers was unpopular in government circles; he was suspected of being a spy sent by Gandhi. After less than a year in the colony, he was deported.

With inadequate resources – lacking capital, assets, and technical expertise – the farmers were embarking on a journey into an uncertain future. They were resolute and determined to avoid the pain of earlier years. They had seen and experienced hunger in India and hardships as labourers in Fiji's cane fields. However, they had been toughened by their continuing difficulties and were not waiting for or wanting handouts.

Vashist Muni's intervention was invaluable and timely. It gave the people hope and encouragement to build a future founded on self-help. Hindus, Muslims, and Christians alike hung on to every word of his advice and were motivated by it. He was non-political and non-sectarian: he was there for all and devoted to improving the lives of men and women. His realism encouraged the farmers when they felt overwhelmed by hopelessness and despair, and when they were being marginalised by the administration. People recalled his words, stood united, and put together the pieces to shape their future.

During his brief period in Fiji, Muni opened schools in the northwestern part of Viti Levu. He also established schools in Lautoka and the Navua district. Today, the institution he founded in Navua, about thirty-five miles from Suva, is the Vashist Muni College, which caters to students of all races up to secondary level.

In school, Ram showed promise, and the teachers often reported his keen ability to grasp key points and learning. His progress was steady enough to convince a businessperson and a family friend, Mr Apa Bhai Patel (of A. J. C. Patel Bros of Ba), to offer to pay for his education. Mr Patel planned to send Ram to New Zealand to qualify as a lawyer or accountant, once he had completed his schooling in Fiji.

Our grandparents had met Mr Patel on a trip to Ba, and they had become firm friends: as business folk, they had much in common. Whenever he travelled to Suva, Mr Patel stopped over in Navua to visit the family. Mr Patel had a son, Babubhai, who was about Ram's age. When they were older, Ram and Babubhai

Early Years

enjoyed an occasional tipple of Scotch together, when it was available.

Ram was the youngest of three children in the family, but, as the only son, having an older sibling pass away, he was expected to be the breadwinner for the family. Our grandmother declined Mr Patel's offer to pay for Ram's education; she preferred to educate him locally. Some had notions that a period spent in a foreign country changed habits, led to drinking alcohol, and resulted in marrying a foreign lady.

Ram was pragmatic and sensitive. He observed the challenges his parents endured: the 1918 pandemic, the mill closure, and the subsequent financial losses, which pushed many into desperate situations. Imagination, intuition, determination, and a large dose of fortitude that underpinned their survival drove them and others like them to emerge from desperation and near penury to see their offspring reach financial security and freedom from want. Job done.

Their eternal optimism kept the door open for fresh starts. Seeing all this made a deep impression on Ram as he grew up. From listening to the stories of family and friends about their living and working conditions, he decided that he wished to be neither a shopkeeper nor a farmer. The hardship experienced by his family was never to be repeated – not by him.

Education – that elusive universal aspiration of the poor – was a concern for most Indian parents. Schools in the areas they settled were few. Those that existed tended to provide a very basic curriculum in mostly poorly constructed timber and metal outbuildings in a compound, generously donated by a community member.

Schools with trained teachers and books were rare; in time other schools run by missionaries came along, but they cost money. With deliberation and careful evaluation of their resources, some farmers were able to send their offspring to these schools. Ram was one of them and he noted the details in his application to the civil service.

Until 1926, when the family went to Suva, Ram was sent to the Methodist Mission School, which was run by Miss C. J. Weston. In Suva, he attended the Seventh Day Adventist Mission

School, where Mr Burnes and Mr G. M. Masters taught him. In 1929, the family moved again. This time, he settled down at Samabula Government School. This school was headed by Mr Sewak Masih, under whom he obtained the School Leaving Certificate and a scholarship to the Teacher Training Institute in Davuilevu in 1931.

Mr Sewak Masih was Ram's most important mentor and made a lasting impression on the young, impressionable student. Ram often spoke positively about Mr Masih, especially when in the company of friends such as the Revd. Ramsay Deoki and Mr R. H. Ram Narayan. Mr Masih was a role model: he practised what he preached and encouraged his students to adopt sound, regular habits. It was a source of comfort to Ram that he could revert to his old teacher and mentor at a moment's notice. In personal development terms, this friendship was priceless.

Change of Direction

In 1933, Ram graduated from the Teacher Training Institute, but his stint in the teaching profession was brief, lasting only a year. He became disillusioned with the prospects it offered and decided to find an opportunity where he could express his talents and mounting ambitions. His friends could not convince him to view the teaching profession in a positive light. They reminded him of its status and security, as well as the joys and rewards that would come from imparting knowledge to the young and preparing them for a secure future. He believed his friends were dedicated individuals and respected their views, but he had to follow his intuitions and insights and make his own way. He was in his twenties and still had time to enter a more open and competitive environment.

He had no regrets about his training as a teacher: he used to say that it was a "noble profession". His former colleagues were now firm friends, and the associations lasted a lifetime. He admired those who continued in teaching and dedicated their lives to bringing out the best in young men and women.

Early Years

The Next Move: A Change for the Better?

While Ram worked out his notice, following his resignation as a teacher, he learned about a vacancy for an *interpreter* at a legal firm. He had a good command of Hindi and English, so he decided to apply. He reasoned that he had nothing to lose. If the worst came to the worst, he could return to teaching: teachers were always in demand at missionary schools, government schools, and private institutions.

Good character references and approval from the Education Department soon cleared the way. He was offered the position of interpreter, with additional duties as the law clerk's assistant to Mr Leleu, Mr J. M. S. Park, and Mr W. L. Donovan. He was now committed to an unfamiliar world, where he began working on January 1, 1935. He was not qualified in legal matters, nor did he have dealings with the law. He was excited to learn a new craft and do his best to prove himself capable and diligent. He borrowed law books and discussed technical matters with the chief law clerk.

These were relatively easy matters to deal with, but facing his mother was going to challenge his abilities to the limit. Explaining why he had gone from a respected teaching career to something unfamiliar with lesser prospects, as he was not a qualified lawyer.

Ram's new job required him to translate documents and letters, interpret for the firm during client interviews, and attend court as an interpreter and translator accompanying the legal team. He assisted the chief clerk in his work when he was not needed as an interpreter. He sat in on interviews with him, and sometimes with the solicitor. Soon he acquired a good knowledge of the legal system, procedures, legal jargon, and the law. He met a variety of people who had interesting views and stories. He also noted that, apart from a few Europeans, most clients he encountered were Indians: farmers, businessmen, and employees dealing with issues ranging from theft to unfair dismissal, as well as those with business partnership and family law problems. Providentially, this new position laid the foundation for his future. He saw opportunities and openings in unpredictable and also in unexpected areas.

Perspectives of British Colonial Rule in the Fiji Islands

Ram spent two years with Leleu, Park & Donovan, which were invaluable. They provided Ram with a steep learning curve. The experience and knowledge he gained were a game-changer. Mr Leleu was a good communicator and mentor: attributes Ram found valuable. Here, he found an interest in accountancy and taxation. He took it up seriously and enrolled in a bookkeeping course with a correspondence college in New Zealand. He was subsequently promoted and received a salary increase of £1 per month.

On 31 December 1936, Ram left Mr Leleu's firm. In April 1937, he joined the larger law firm of Ellis, Munro, Warren & Leys. There, he was appointed Senior Law Clerk, in addition to his other duties as an interpreter; he was paid a salary of £262 per annum. His duties included frequently attending court with the partners. While at this law practice, he borrowed law books from the firm's library and took an advanced course in accountancy.

After a full day at the office, Ram continued to work with local businesses, helping them with their tax returns and enquiries. Few understood the income tax regulations, and these startups benefited from the expertise of a local man. These were key, formative days for Ram. He got his act together early, was focused, and assessed his potential as both a legal operative and an accountant.

His private work added an extra £110 per annum to his income. He had now achieved the level of financial shelter he so much wanted, despite giving up a secure position in teaching. He built a cash reserve and increased his investment in a life policy with the Queensland Insurance Co.

At Ellis, Munro, Warren & Leys, Ram had access to Australian and local tax ordinances and tax manuals. He absorbed the technical data of this complicated topic. He put himself to the test by preparing and presenting income tax returns for his clients and was confident enough to appeal to the Commissioner of Inland Revenue on their behalf, as and when the occasion demanded.

In time, his work was noticed, and he was asked to prepare the legal firm's accounts and tax returns. He excelled in

Early Years

his new responsibilities, and his skills and capabilities were not lost on his employers. He became the Accountant and Senior Law Clerk at Ellis, Munro, Warren & Leys, within a couple of years of joining the firm and served until 1948.

At the end of the Second World War, Ram's clientele increased. His clients included Narain Construction Co. and S. P. Parekh Bros in Suva, as well as Nabi Buksh in Nausori township and other businesses in the locality. He soon received enquiries and clients from as far away as Ba and Lautoka in the northwest of the island, which was more than a day and a hundred miles away, reached only by a tortuous, gravel road.

18

Home Life

Ram had one sister, my aunt Bachhi or "Tabbu", as Ram preferred to call her. After Ram got married in December 1937, Aunt Tabbu continued to live with him and his new bride, Tapeshwari, in Amy Street. Before my grandparents settled in Suva, Tabbu had lived with them in Navua and helped in their shop in Naitonitoni. There, she had close friends and was happy in the quiet rural area, close to the sea.

Aunt found Suva too crowded and unfriendly and tended to stay at home to help with the chores and our growing family. In 1943, she married Basdeo Dhanna. The marriage was a grand affair conducted from our Amy Street home. A marquee was set up in the large rear garden, with a separate, secluded tent for a couple of busy cooks and assistants. The Dhannas raised four daughters – Nirmala, Urmila, Premila, and Prem Lata – who all now live in Sydney suburbs.

Uncle Basdeo Dhanna had a successful private hire and taxi business, which he initially operated from various locations in Cumming Street, Suva. A large section of Cumming Street was vacant land. It had become derelict after a fire gutted part of the street in 1923. The fire's point of origin had been opposite the greengrocers Leong, Lee, Parshottam & Co. The derelict area was cleared up and used as an open market, with taxi stands. The entire street was a hive of commercial activity. Uncle later relocated to Victoria Drive, next to the Cable & Wireless Co. building, opposite the Sabrina Buildings.

During the 1960s, Cumming Street continued to develop thanks to the enterprise culture of the immigrants; there were shops, such as Brijlal & Sons, in a mini shopping mall. The famous Musadilal & Sons sweet shop was also located here, as were Kwong Tiy, Wahley's Butchers, eateries, pharmacies, duty-free shops and of course barbers

Home Life

Toorak, Suva

It was in early 1937 that Ram acquired a large property on Amy Street, Toorak, an inner suburb of Suva. The family settled there after his marriage on 18 December 1937. We lived there until August 1955, when we moved to 11 Herbert Street, which was later renamed 73 Knolly Street. The house was sold to the Fiji Football Association when Mother resettled with family in Melbourne, shortly after Ram passed away.

A parade of shops near our Amy Street home included a *halwai* (Indian sweet) shop, an ice cream parlour, a K. W. March & Co. grocery shop, its bakery, and a Chinese general store at the corner of Toorak Road. Across from this business was the Methodist Church: a prominent landmark, connected with Dudley House School. The area was cosmopolitan and vibrant: people of different backgrounds – Fijians, Rotumans, Chinese, and Indians – lived and worked together, and the commercial services were facilitated by the Chinese and Indians.

On Amy Street, our next-door neighbours were the Columbus family on one side and the late Manu Tupou and his family on the other. Manu was a voracious reader; he and I would discuss new books as I came across them. I was able to afford books and shared them with him. He was particularly interested in those about Mahatma Gandhi and read all that I had on the man, including Gandhi's autobiography, *The Story of My Experiments with Truth*.

Tupou senior had seen service during the war in the Pacific; he survived, although he was injured when a Japanese bayonet glanced off his thumb. The Japanese did not survive, however. The last we saw of the Tupous was in 1955, when we moved to Herbert Street. Manu Tupou later pursued a Hollywood acting career, appearing in television shows and films, including *Hawaii* and *A Man Called Horse*.

The rear section of our Amy Street property had two large rooms and one smaller one. They were rented to Mr Hemraj Daya and his family. In one room, he crafted tortoiseshell jewellery, as well as other trinkets and functional items, including bangles, necklaces, brooches, and paper knives. He used a part of the large kitchen for storage, work, and cooking. Ram saw an enterprising young man in Mr Daya and so helped to set him up as a dealer, with a retail outlet in Suva town. He later acquired a taste for Scotch whiskey.

After the Daya family vacated the rooms, Mr Jagjivan, a young jeweller, moved in. He married soon after his arrival, and our family grew close to his. We have maintained that connection. Members of his family now live in Canada, England, and New Zealand.

Grandfather's Influence

During the 1940s, Ram's maternal grandfather, Haripal Thakur, visited our house on a weekly basis. He was an erudite man who could quote parts of the Vedas in Sanskrit, which fascinated Ram, who was glued to his every inflexion. Ram found peace and knowledge with his grandfather, who mentored him in the basics of the Sanskrit language and literature. They were both interested in the attention the Europeans, especially the Germans, were now giving to the language, which the latter were translating into German. Both Ram and his grandfather were concerned with the lack of interest in the language. An exception was the Swami Dayanand, whose initiatives included founding the Arya Samaj, the Hindu reform movement that leant heavily on religious texts, as propounded in the Vedas.

Haripal Thakur – Nana - was a slender person whose usual attire was a white shirt, a dhoti (the traditional Indian men's ankle-length loincloth, wrapped around the waist and the legs, resembling trousers), and a white turban, neatly bound on his head, which he never removed. Mother knew his usual arrival time and always had piping-hot, traditional Indian kedgeree ready. This was prepared and cooked according to his strict instructions. It was a simple dish, drenched in ghee, and it had a sweet aroma from kesar, an ingredient he particularly liked. It satisfied the hunger of both Nana and his great-granddaughter.

He was fond of all of us, but Lalli was his favourite great-grandchild. She was about three years old at the time. He would sit her cross-legged on the dining table before him. He fed her first; he would watch her, smile when she started to chew, and then load the next spoonful for himself. I would get a morsel or two – as an afterthought! I was not in the same league as my sister; I always stood by in anticipation.

The food was served on a deep, polished brass plate reserved for him. No one talked except when he said something. Lunch was a quiet affair when he was present.

His daughter, our grandmother, had no hand in preparing or serving the food. Father and daughter's disagreements apart, he was friendly, enjoyed his family's company, and told old stories of his early days in Fiji. He ended his visit with a quick chat with our mother about lunch. She would have her sari's veil drawn lightly over her head and her palms together, as if in prayer, while listening intently and silently, her head slightly bowed in respect. He was always complimentary and kind, and then left, with his palms joined.

In about 1950, we had not seen our great-grandfather for a few weeks. One evening, just as we had finished dinner, an unknown visitor called. As I opened the front door, he asked me to fetch *"Pita ji"* ("father"). When Ram came to the door, the stranger put his hands together in greeting and told Ram: *"Aap ke Nanaji ab nahe rahe,"* which means: "Your grandfather is no more." This news was not expected: there was no prior indication that our great-grandfather was in ill health, although we had not seen or heard from him for some weeks. The man informed Ram that "Thakurji" had died peacefully in his sleep in his room in a rented flat at the end of Toorak Road, not far from Kruppa's store and a short distance from where we lived on Amy Street.

The funeral took place from our house; the cremation itself was at the Vatuwaqa Cemetery and followed Hindu Vedic rites.

19

Vuci

Ram's work would take him to the opposite side of the island of Viti Levu, to Ba and Lautoka, where he would spend a few days to a week on business for private clients. During his absences, the family spent a lot of time in Vuci *(=Vu-thee)* – a suburb of Nausori – just twelve miles from our home in Suva, the capital city.

We travelled there with our mother on a bus owned and operated by a cousin, Ram Hit. Cousin Ram collected us and our baggage from Amy Street: yes, the bus drove up to our front door. The trip was fun for us children, but not for Mother, because she had to keep an eye on us and because the Queen's Road was bumpy. The government never maintained this vital trunk road, even for safety's sake. Accidents were common and many, but that didn't bother the colonial sahibs.

Soon, all discomfort was forgotten: the arrival at Nani's house more than compensated for the discomforts of the road. As the trimmed hibiscus arch and the hedge, running the entire width of the property in Vuci Road, came into view, we knew we had reached our destination and got ready to jump out.

Nausori was the birthplace of commercial sugar production in Fiji. From being an obscure mill village in the Rewa district, it was transformed into a bustling commercial centre within two decades of its opening in 1882, thanks to the activities established by indenture-free farmers. Many retail outlets and services grew, and by the 1950s, people had established deep roots, both personally and commercially. The living rooms of new timber-clad houses were adorned with simple furniture, produced by local carpenters. The kitchens had wood-fired stoves, and water was usually sourced from a nearby well. On the few roads, taxis appeared, which serviced the town and surrounding villages. This microcosm of the farming village model was replicated throughout the islands.

Vuci

The immigrants, now most quite *"Fijianised"*, began their journeys of life anew with a new language: the Fiji patois, with its attendant idioms, which condensed the differences of religion and culture into a single *Fiji baat* or Fiji Hindustani language. Once concerned about their survival in foreign and hostile conditions, these young men and women rose to meet the challenges and demands of a hostile employer and an equally demanding natural environment.

The growing purchasing power of the close family units helped the economy to grow. New ventures and centres of trade springing up in townships and villages provided work. Wages earned were no longer being squirrelled away and kept in tins under mattresses. Cash was king, which meant that there was growing encouragement among the populace to innovate and take small chances to increase capital. The community balance sheet was becoming robust, and with it, there was an increasing confidence in the outlook.

My maternal grandparents were assigned to various plantation locations before they were released from their indenture agreements. Once released, they settled on Vuci Road, where they immediately began to grow vegetables on small plots and sugar cane on a few acres of leased land. They were resourceful and took great pride in working on their own estate, propagating and sowing their cane seeds, and cutting and delivering harvested cane to the mills. They were proud of their achievements. Their success was evident in financial terms. Now, at the dawn of another decade – the 1920s - their prayers were about to be answered in the shape of a house – financed by saving pennies and shillings – which they planned and built with their own hands.

Nani's large family included five of her sisters' children and five of her own. She educated one child from her small sugarcane holding: her only son, Shiu Nath. She enrolled him at the Marist Brothers School in Suva. He later graduated as a teacher and joined the civil service, working in the government printer's department.

Across the road from Nani's house was a Fijian primary school. Indigenous Fijian teachers lived and worked in the small, local sugar-cane farming community. We had close relationships with the teachers and the community from that village and school. We often saw our elders in conversation or sharing food with the teachers or workers. When the ladies from the village felt like it, they popped around to Nani's place for a *talanoa* (chat), socialising with refreshments; they were always welcome visitors. Nani's house was open to many of the school's staff, who were friendly and protective towards us.

No government administrator or any chief had reached the village. The communities shared many local and social activities, interacted and reciprocated as equals and with respect, enjoyed one another's company, and shared joys and disappointments. This was not unique to my family or village, but rather typical of most sugarcane-growing areas, where the chiefs and government representatives had little connection.

New Era of Post-indenture Fiji

Fiji's growing consumerism, especially after World War II, established a need for goods and services that had seen little expansion during the preceding decade. New merchandise flowing through the economy and rapidly exchanging hands whetted the appetite for more and varied products. The preference for new fashions and styles, as well as modern features found in imported clothes and foodstuffs, prompted businesses to import goods in sufficient quantities to meet demand.

Small businesses expanded, and the demand for white-collar professionals such as bookkeepers and clerks increased. Ram saw his clients also expand. G. B. Hari & Co., along with other drapers and tailors, expanded their trade, while Whaley's Butchers, which had interests in an abattoir in Nasinu, saw a significant increase in their turnover. Mr Harm Nam of Whaley's and his sons were astute businessmen. On occasion, Ram would visit their residence in Suva Street for work and sometimes for a social drink or two; the Nams remained in contact with him until the mid-1960s.

Vuci

Property Developer

<u>An Ambitious Enterprise</u>
By the late forties, Ram was continuing to expand his private clientele. One such new client was Mr (later Sir) Sathi Narain. The association began with Ram advising Mr Narain on his accounting and taxation matters for his fledgling construction and furniture enterprise in Amy Street. With time, the professional relationship developed into a lasting friendship and business partnership. Mr Narain had an office with staff, including a draftsman. He also owned a workshop, located on Amy Street, that manufactured furniture for both private and commercial use.

Ram and Sathi acquired a prime location close to the workshop, at the corner of the High Street and Amy Street, where they planned to build a commercial complex, comprising shops and a cinema. The venture failed as the site was not ideal at the time for a large multipurpose mall in the centre of a large residential conurbation. Ironically, the area today is a highly commercialised part of Suva, owing to its expansion as a major port and business centre.

Investing in property was an early ambition for Ram. He struck a good deal when he purchased his home in Amy Street in 1937 and followed that with the acquisition of a plot of hilly land on Augustus Street, which at the time was a single-file dirt track that led up hilly terrain and ended in Brown Street, near the Colonial War Memorial CWM Hospital.

<u>Gordon Street</u>
The next project was a building on Gordon Street in the 1950s that contained four apartments. The plot was in a depression, about twenty feet back from Gordon Street, opposite the premises of a Chinese merchant family: the owners of K. W. March. It was just down the road from Knollys Street. Sathi Narain suggested that Mr Sami, a young architect Mr Venkataiya, who had recently graduated from an Indian university, draw up plans for four flats. The construction was undertaken and completed by Narain Construction Co. Ltd.

Perspectives of British Colonial Rule in the Fiji Islands

Augustus Street

The area was primarily desolate, with only a few houses visible. The land was reached by a short walk from the end of Toorak Road, which formed a "T" junction with Augustus Street, and then turning left to walk up the track for about two hundred yards to reach the property.

Ram sold the building for £2,575; the property had cost him £1,100. This whetted Ram's appetite for more real estate ventures. The profit later came in useful for something he planned on a larger scale. An opportunity arose to purchase a residential property in Carnarvon Street.

The Carnarvon Building

The next project was significantly more ambitious. A timber residential building stood on the spot. In 1951, Ram began the Carnarvon Building project by levelling the land to prepare the foundations. The new three-storey apartment block, with two street-front shops, cost £12,300 to erect. He began the project with a loan from the Bank of New Zealand. The building was centrally situated, next to Suva Motors Ltd's Spare Parts Division, and approximately fifty yards from the junction of Gordon Street and Carnarvon Street. It was an ideal location for busy professionals and government officials. It was within easy reach of the Government Printers, Carnegie Library, Suva Sea Baths, government buildings, and the Fiji Broadcasting Company. The project was a major undertaking and sought the services of an experienced architect. Mr Marlow of Fiji Builders Ltd was the person he chose to plan the redevelopment. The Suva City Council approved the plan, and the contract was awarded to Narain Construction Co. Ltd. With additional work, the total costs escalated to £16,000, and the building was completed in 1952.

During the year of construction, Suva suffered a severe earthquake, but to everyone's amazement, there was not a single crack in the unfinished building, even in the parts that had just been plastered. Once the building was completed, Ram leased it to Mr C. D. Narayan for a period of six years. All the apartments

Vuci

were rented out to Royal New Zealand Air Force (RNZAF) officers based at Laucala Bay, Suva.

However, the lessee gradually suffered from a decline in rental income. By 1959, the RNZAF and commercial seaplane operations at Laucala Bay had declined as Nadi International Airport was increasingly used by commercial flights from Fiji to New Zealand and Australia. The seaplanes were operationally untenable, primarily due to a lack of infrastructure and limited land available for the development of repair and other support facilities. A further obstacle to seaplanes was the development of aeroplanes that took off and landed on specially prepared landing strips. The valuable and pleasant real estate became redundant and later became the site of the new University of the South Pacific, the first university in the South Pacific.

From 1961, the Carnarvon Building underwent gradual transformation. After the lease reverted to Ram, he set about restructuring the apartments into offices, cafes, and restaurants. Burroughs Ltd, an office equipment company, and a driving school were the first businesses to occupy the repurposed site.

An increasing demand for offices led to the erection of a seven-storey building in the 1970s at the rear of the existing block; the front section comprised a nightclub and restaurants. This building project was Ram's last. When he retired on a civil service pension in 1961, the Carnarvon Building was the obvious location at which to set up his accountancy and taxation practice.

<u>11 Herbert Street</u> (later renamed <u>73 Knolly Street)</u>

In 1947, the father of Miss Lila Ramsamuj, a nurse with the Health Department and a colourful personality, purchased the freehold of 11 Herbert Street from Sir Howard Ellis (a solicitor and former civil servant) for £1,000. Miss Ramsamuj leased the property to Mr Tui Johnson (the father of Mr W. G. Johnson, the Managing Director of Carpenters Ltd). In August 1955, after eighteen years in Amy Street, we moved into 11 Herbert Street. We settled in at the end of 1955, after the completion of extensive renovations and extensions. These included a new, custom-built kitchen, a fully tiled bathroom, a dining room, a storeroom, and an extra bedroom at the rear. A new "Dux" hot water system supplied the residence with instant hot water in the kitchen and bathroom. The new, enlarged garage had, at its rear, a servant's quarters, a shower room, and a laundry. Some planning issues related to the length of the garage were objected to by the Suva City Council but resolved by appeal, with the assistance of Mr Andrew Deoki, a solicitor, politician and a personal friend of Ram.

After Ram passed away, the property was sold to the Fiji Football Association.

Matanitabua Street

A building from the Amy Street project was demolished, and the usable timber was retrieved and removed to a site in Matanitabua Street, off Rewa Street, where Ram had acquired another plot on a hillock to build two three-bedroom flats. This venture, completed in 1952, was also in partnership with Sathi Narain. Mr Ram Khelawan of Nausori was assigned the contract to build. He was a conscientious man, but his employees did not perform to the standards required by the construction specifications. The cost of the build was £2,300.

Moti Street

This project on Moti Street, off Rewa Street, was undertaken in late 1966 and was to be Ram's last project. I had significant input into the construction of this residential site, overseeing it from inception to completion. The total cost of labour and materials amounted to £2,000. It was sold within one week of construction for £4,000.

20

Colonial Civil Service

A Civil Servant is an officer – a servant of the Crown working in a civil capacity and who is not the holder of a political or judicial office. Also, the holder of certain other offices in respect of whose tenure of office special provision has been made; [or] a servant of the Crown in a personal capacity paid from the Civil List.[1]

The colonial civil service departments, under the direct administration and direction of the Secretariat, include the Defence Department, the Treasury, the Inland Revenue Department, the Foreign Affairs Department, and the Labour Department. The service does not include government ministers, who are political appointees, nor does it include members of the armed forces, the police, or local government officers.

The first British civil service was established in the eighteenth century to support the expanding administration of the increasingly influential and powerful British Empire. Parliament's role grew, as did its legislative powers, which were devolved to ministers and secretaries of state. Colonial governors' roles were more clearly defined, with anticipated outcomes in the colonies that laid the foundations or continued to address the particular demands of the land and its people. Each colony was unique, and the Colonial Office (CO) had its own expectations regarding the colony's financial stability, profitability, constitutional reforms, and peaceful transitions to eventual freedom.

Universal commercial expansion during the nineteenth century necessitated changes in the expertise required to collate,

---

[1] "Civil Service (United Kingdom)", Wikipedia (last edited 20 February 2025), https://en.wikipedia.org/wiki/Civil_Service_(United_Kingdom), accessed 20 February 2025.

analyse, and disseminate ministerial decisions. A civil service college was established in 1806 in Haileybury near London. This followed a visit to China by British officials who observed the workings of the Chinese imperial government departments. However, adherence to hierarchical traditions of patronage and bureaucracy limited the scope of competent officers from lower social classes to lesser posts.

Changes were later introduced to update the administrators on the ground to reflect the rapid growth of the colonies and their changing demographics. These brought new enthusiasm and a revival of the spirit to travel into the unknown. Recruits were selected on merit and trained before being let loose in departments across Britain and in overseas territories.

Following the Trevelyan–Northcote Report of 1854, the groundwork for a permanent and credible "Home Civil Service" was established. A system without patronage, purchase, or political bias formed the basis of the new civil service at home and in the colonies: neutral in its views on political matters and unbiased about the current government's social and economic policies. It became an institution that was admired as a model of effective administration and was replicated elsewhere.

From 1954, civil servants were appointed to the Colonial Service or its later incarnation, Her Majesty's Overseas Colonial Service. Local administrations in the respective colonies were now responsible for the retirement pension arrangements of civil servants. The pensionable age was sixty-five years. Expatriate officers in Fiji were also entitled to take a six-month "long leave" every three years, which effectively reduced their three-year terms of active service to two and a half years. The colonial treasuries, of course, bore all the costs.

Transfers of governors and district commissioners from one colony to another had little effect on substantive matters. Neither did they make much difference in practical terms, but their experiences were meaningful when it came to major decision-making. For example, Governor Gordon's assessments and his decision to import Asian immigrant labourers into Mauritius and elsewhere were replicated in Fiji.

Colonial Civil Service

The Colonial Office did not coordinate policies and executive decisions among departments; it dispensed regulations across all the colonies, with oversight of compliance, and served as an intermediary with the governors. Anthony Kirk-Greene recounts how Mr Amery, the Secretary of State for the Colonies, highlighted this dilemma in 1927 during a Colonial Office conference. He discussed the fact that he did not deal with a single Colonial Service, but with three dozen self-contained administrations: "Each Colonial Government and each Colonial Service has grown up on the spot by a continuous process of local evolution." He went on to describe how each governor and each service was autochthonous.[2]

Governors had absolute discretion and independence. In Fiji, this dispensation ranged from decisions based on flawed reasoning, such as the perception that indigenous Fijians were incapable of higher learning, which had consequences for their prospects and relationships with other communities.

Selected Fijians were in the civil service, but none were in demanding decision-making posts – even those who had the good fortune to be educated in the world's top universities, funded by the Crown. Upon their return, they were mostly appointed to nominal positions in departments or interfaced with villagers, serving the establishment as loyal and dedicated servants wherever they were posted in the colony. Were the chiefs better servants of the people or better servants of the Crown?

In the absence of a programme to train local civil servants in the colony, the future development, integrity, and consistency of the administrative services were a concern that only time could decide the outcome.

On balance, no imperial power had anticipated relinquishing control of the real estate it had acquired. Consequently, educational programmes were measured and delivered as and if demanded by vocal and foresighted local leaders. Alternatively, it was left to the educational policies of

---

[2] Anthony Kirk-Greene, *On Crown Service: A History of HM Colonial and Overseas Civil Service, 1837–1997* (Bloomsbury, 1999), p. 31-33.

respective colonies to address their immediate and pressing needs.

At independence, the transfer of power in Fiji seemed seamless. Many expatriate officers continued their services under their new masters.

21

Invited to Join the Civil Service

> I think there is only one ideal that the British Empire can set before itself in this regard, and that there should be no barriers of race, colour, or creed which should prevent any man by merit from reaching any station if he is fitted for it . . . But such a principle has to be very carefully and gradually applied because intense local feelings are excited.[1]

The end of the war had repercussions on other aspects of the colony's growth and its future prospects. Demand for technicians, clerical staff and others increased as the need arose for improved telecommunications, modern amenities and infrastructure. Most government departments were impacted by the shortage of experts or trained staff.

The rising number of company registrations and individual start-up enterprises foreshadowed the future direction of Fiji's growing commercial development and the government's response to its immediate needs to regulate and control, benefiting the colony's financial state.

The government was now under pressure to find qualified and experienced staff for many departments. The Inland Revenue, which had to meet the increased turnover of enquiries, revenue collection, and tax assessment, lacked suitable officers.

The need for financial and other services to meet the consumer demands for the growing immigrant communities set the government to seek entrepreneurs in other colony's. Soon word was put out among the business communities of Gujrat and Punjab in British India and Chinese from Hong Kong of

---

[1] Declared by Winston Churchill at the 1921 Imperial Conference; quoted in Avery Forman, "Racism, Colonialism, and Britain's Legacy of Violence", Working Knowledge (12 April 2022), https://hbswk.hbs.edu/item/racism-colonialism-and-britains-legacy-of-violence, accessed 11 February 2025.

opportunities in the islands. The second wave of smaller scale immigrants arrived on Fiji's shores to stage the second phase of economic expansion.

Small stores appeared in the communities. – exchanging goods for cash was now underway. Lending and borrowing and hiring - indeed the full enterprise culture that was unimaginable just a couple of decades before was now accepted as normal part of everyday activity.

By 1940s the farmers had settled as fully fledged residents of the colony. They were dedicated to the land of their birth as any Fijian or other race. They were optimistic about the future and looked for new opportunities to grow their income and wealth.

Ram noticed the changes. Demands for his services increased, and his family saw less of him as he worked late into the night to meet the demands of the Inland Revenue. All this was in addition to his responsibilities at the law office, where he presented himself on time at 8 a.m. every day.

The civil service was also hard at work to bridge the gap in its services. The shortage of experienced staff was felt, and the Secretariat permitted the Commissioner of Inland Revenue to seek out and appoint a suitable local accountant as an Inspector of Taxes, which was its immediate need.

Ram's work and presentations were closely observed by the department for some years, as revealed during his interviews with Mr Watson of that department. So, it was no surprise that he was shortlisted as a potential candidate for a key post.

The Commissioner of Inland Revenue, in consultation with the Secretariat (a branch of the Executive Council), made a decision. He authorised Mr Watson to interview Ram, with a view to recruiting him for the civil service, specifically as an Inspector of Taxes in the Department of Inland Revenue.

Sir Howard Ellis was a leading solicitor and a former civil servant in Fiji. He was also a senior partner at Ellis, Munro, Warren & Leys and Ram's employer. Mr Watson arrived at Sir Howard's office and declared his purpose for the visit: he wanted to recruit one of Sir Howard's employees.

Invited to Join the Civil Service

The shortage of officers following the events of the preceding few years had taken its toll. Many former professionals in the dominions never returned from the European and the Western Pacific battlefields. Their loss resulted in severe shortages of essential bureaucrats in both the nearby dominions and the outlying dependencies for which the Colonial Office in London was responsible.

Sir Howard called in Ram and introduced Mr Watson. When he saw the Assistant Commissioner with Sir Howard, he felt uneasy. His mind raced to the last set of the firm's accounts he had submitted. His fears were soon put to rest when his boss revealed that Mr Watson had come to invite Ram to work for the Inland Revenue Department. Ram objected: "But, Sir, I am not looking for another job!" He was happy at the firm and had no complaints.

Mr Watson explained that the position offered was that of an inspector of taxes, and he would be pleased to have Ram on the team. An inspector of taxes! That position would be a massive deal for a simple accountant/law clerk in a solicitor's office: one who had no experience as an inspector of taxes, nor of any type of work in any government department. He had not dreamed of becoming a civil servant – least of all, an inspector of taxes!

He was direct and clear in his mission and seemed determined to get his man. He was even prepared to agree to Ram's terms. He had secure employment and had not intended to move, but if the commissioner agreed to *his* terms, he would consider it in consultation with the firm's partners. He later intimated that he did not expect the Secretariat to accept his terms, in which case he would have been happy to continue at the firm.

Mr Watson spoke enthusiastically with Sir Howard about Ram's record as monitored in the department. Ram stood in astonished silence as his work was discussed and what he, a talented young man, might achieve was open to him – there were no limits, Mr Watson opined.

When Ram had worked as an intermediary between his clients and the Inland Revenue, he'd had interactions with the officers of Mr Watson's department. He was familiar with their names and positions. At that time, all the senior officers were expatriates. The final decision for the appointment for such a post was subject to approval by the Secretary of State for the Colonies in London. So, Ram was uncertain about the eventual decision, and he waited patiently.

Things were moving rapidly, but he needed time to mull over this momentous decision. A lot was at stake. He had personal clientele in his accounting portfolio, which he was keen to retain – if possible, under civil service rules. He looked ahead and considered his options and chances. As a professional, he was aware that nothing is risk-free, but he must make his decisions based on the current situation and possible future trends.

His decision to accept the invitation would rest on *his* terms. He was aware of certain aspects of government service: one had to accept the government's terms as laid down in the Colonial Rulebooks and the General Orders. He was a reluctant applicant, but pressures were present: there were advantages to status, promotions to higher grades, and a pension. He was encouraged by his colleagues to accept this "a once-in-a-lifetime chance to join an elite group".

He hedged his bets: he was going to apply, but on his terms. If rejected, he had his future in his hands; if accepted on his terms, he had nothing to lose.

He was concerned about his clients, whom he had known for some years and with whom he was on good terms. It crossed his mind that they might feel betrayed in some way. Additionally, he maintained an excellent relationship with the staff and partners at the law firm. Lastly, he had established his private property portfolio, which generated a good return and covered his loans. He was financially secure and needed nothing more.

Later, he discussed this invitation with Sir Howard, who concurred with Mr Watson's view of Ram's work and potential as a tax expert: he was a worthy candidate. Sir Howard urged him to take this "once-in-a-lifetime" job. He said he would lose an able and conscientious employee, but that he was proud of Ram's achievements, as this approach from the government implied. He looked forward to Ram's progress as a civil servant.

Questions for Mr Watson

Government officers can be transferred at will to any location where their services may be required. Ram decided to address this and other conditions with the Secretariat. If Mr Watson and the department needed him, they would have to agree to his conditions; after all, he was not desperate to join the Inland Revenue, and they needed him more than he needed them.

Ram prepared his questions, including his reservations, for Mr Watson for their next follow-up meeting. The typical queries about promotions, salary grades, and the probation period were ironed out during their conversations, but he needed reassurances about his written submissions [2]. He was also concerned about the possibility of expatriates returning to the civil service. If conditions in the dominions and Great Britain improved, would the department recruit an expat and release him from its employment?

Ram reached an understanding with Mr Leys, a partner at the law firm, that if his terms were not acceptable to the Commissioner and the Secretariat, he would not pursue the matter and would continue with his duties at the office.

He had an enormous respect for Sir Howard and loyalty towards him and his partners. He had gained much from the association with the firm, including the time to study and pursue his interests and businesses during his spare time. Given the freedom and opportunities during this period, it was challenging for him to leave his colleagues and many of the firm's clients that he had worked with since joining the firm in 1937. He had Sir Howard's blessing, and he would leave on good terms.

The Secretariat agreed to Ram's terms and acknowledged his concerns, dispatching the appropriate forms for Ram's attention and completion.

---

[2] Please see Ram's terms and conditions in Chapter 22, below.

Perspectives of British Colonial Rule in the Fiji Islands

Ram, now in his mid-thirties, had arrived at an important fork in the road. He was sure of his prospects at the law firm. Although the next steps might be fraught with unknowns, there were great possibilities and opportunities. He had established himself in a commanding position to develop further as an expert in taxation, which was his particular interest and forte. Unofficially, he was the firm's taxation expert and consultant, as well as a law clerk and accountant. He was now on a new track, from his perspective and insights, embarking on a gold-standard career where he could indulge in his expertise and excel.

His property portfolio was a sensitive issue. He could not, as a civil servant, continue to run his own business. His properties required continuous attention: rent collections, property maintenance, and addressing tenants' complaints and issues between them all had to be attended to. Ram discussed these matters with Mr Leys, who agreed that the firm would continue to represent Ram's business interests as agents and legal counsel. Mr Leys was given general power of attorney to execute what was necessary.

At his next meeting with Mr Watson, Ram discussed his terms and concerns. He put forward his terms and would resign from his firm *"only if the appointment was arranged on [his] specific terms and conditions".*

For the record and as a statement of fact at the inception of his application, he prepared a detailed statement of disclosure of his financial affairs and who would manage his portfolio in the future. He said that as a public servant, he had no direct interest or control in any part of his business. If there were potential concerns about conflicts of interest, all these would be resolved before Mr Watson left the colony for an appointment as Commissioner of Inland Revenue in Hong Kong.

22

Ram Sets His Terms

Ram was setting off on a new journey. From his humble beginnings on the Navua plains, to Chief Law clerk, Accountant and property developer, and now his prospects and fortunes would be measured and tempered by rules and regulations.

All the doubts and hesitations helped to consider both sides of the argument. It was time now to decide.

Ram wrote the following letter, detailing his situation and leaving no doubts about his concerns and future intentions. If his application was accepted on *his* terms, he would resign from the law firm; otherwise, he was happy with his current arrangements.

A draft of Ram's conditions was discussed with Mr Leys, Ram's mentor, legal adviser and confidant. The final terms, dated 27 September 1947, were presented to Mr Watson, who conveyed them to the Secretariat, which, in turn, responded with a formal application form.

> Central Building,
> Suva.
> 27th September 1947
>
> Mr W. F. Watson
> Suva
>
> Dear Mr Watson,
>
> During the past few weeks, I was considering my position as regards my joining the Government Service as an Inspector of Taxes. Now I have come to a conclusion in the matter, and I think it would be better to place my views before you while you are here.
>
> 2. You are no doubt aware of my total income

each year from the various sources and is continuously increasing year by year. Sources of my income, as you know, are:

	1946	1947 Estimated	1948 Estimated
Accountancy etc.	£827	£1100	£1200
Ellis & Munro Salary	£262	£272	£285
Interest from Investments	£203	£250	£275
Rents collection	£58	£92	£140
	£1350	£1714	£1900

My income, even in the prior years, from the bookkeeping alone, as I have returned for income tax purposes, was £840 for 1944 and £637 for 1945, and in addition to this, as you know, I had other sources of income.

3. In view of the privilege of the Government Service for overseas and other leave facilities and to secure peace, rest, and tranquillity, I have decided to take up an appointment (permanent) as a senior inspector of taxes at a salary of £600 to £720 per annum BUT in case a vacancy for a senior inspector of taxes at a salary of £600 to £720 is not at present readily available THEN I am willing to take up an appointment on a permanent basis, of an inspector of taxes on an initial salary of £600 p.a. on the following terms and conditions:-

(a) That my post be a permanent and pensionable one, and

(b) That my commencing salary be at the rate of £600 per annum, and

(c) That my salary be increased at least at the basis of £600 to £720 per annum after the expiration of the first two years of my service or earlier upon creation of a post for the senior inspector of taxes or any other post or posts created in lieu thereof bearing salary at the rate of £600 to £720 per annum or above.

Ram Sets His Terms

(d) That I should be the first man after Mr Wheatley for promotion to the post of Surveyor of Taxes or any other post or posts created in lieu thereof if I prove useful and competent for that post.

(e) That I should not be required to be transferred to any other place in the colony or to any other department where work other than accounting is required, and

(f) That I should not be required to appear for any examination, either it be examination "H" Language or any other departmental examinations, and

(g) That my appointment should not be subject to any probation at all. It should be made on a permanent basis straight out as I understand from you can be done, and

(h) That I should not be required to commence work before the 1st March 1948.

4. As you are now permanently leaving the colony on transfer, I would be glad if you would kindly take this matter up either with Mr Thompson or Mr Donovan and if they approve of my appointment on these lines, please let me know, and I will then tender my resignation to Ellis, Munro, Warren & Leys. If my appointment cannot be accepted on these lines, then I am not prepared to resign from Ellis, Munro, Warren & Leys and join the Civil Service.

I will very much appreciate your early attention.
Thanking you.
> Yours sincerely,
> (*sgd*) Ram Charitra

The next few weeks were a tense period of uncertainty about whether Ram's terms would find favour with the government. The terms (a) to (h) above were clarified verbally with Mr Watson before he officially committed them to him.

Ram's terms were unambiguous and direct. He would resign from his present position only if the government accepted him on the terms he had outlined: *"if they approve of my appointment on these lines, please let me know, and I will then tender my resignation to Ellis, Munro, Warren & Leys"*. Mr Watson was non-committal about Ram's personal terms and promised to do his best to get the Secretariat's approval.

The Revenue needed his services, and he was well positioned to set out the conditions on which he would be happy to apply.

There was no question of joining the civil service at any cost.

Civil Service Application

Ram handed the completed application forms to Mr Watson on 6 October 1947 and accompanied him to Mr Thompson's office at the Secretariat, where he waited outside. Mr Watson returned and said that it was *"all fixed up, except there might be some delay [in getting a reply] because the 1948 estimates have [yet to be] approved by the Secretary of State for the Colonies"*.

The clearance and acceptance of the application arrived from London in time for him to start his duties as a civil servant, as agreed, on 1 March 1948. Mr Watson's recommendation to the Secretariat that Ram Charitra be accepted *without further requirement to appear for any other examination* was accepted. The terms and conditions put forward by both parties were agreed by the Secretariat, including the amendments suggested by Ram.

In his application, he noted, among other things, the following information about his education:

> Methodist Mission – Miss C. J. Weston, 1925–1926.
> SDA (Seventh Day Adventists) Mission – Mr Burns and Mr G. M. Masters, 1927–1928.
> Samabula Indian Government School – Mr Sewak Masih.
> Passed School Leaving Certificate and obtained Scholarship, 1929–1930.
> Teachers Training Institution, Davuilevu. Mr Adamson and Mr Mowson.
> Passed Teachers Grade 4th Examination - 1/1/1931–30/6/1933.

Ram Sets His Terms

References from Mr W. F. Watson and Mr A. D. Leys, and an education reference from Mr Sewak Masih, accompanied the application form.

The Outcome

Before his departure to his next assignment in Hong Kong, Mr Watson wrote to Ram on 20 October 1947:

> Before leaving the Colony on transfer, I wish to express my appreciation for your excellent work as a tax agent. It has been a pleasure to receive your well-prepared returns, and in this regard, I consider your work would compare most favourably with registered Australian tax agents.
>
> 2. I understand you have applied for the position of Inspector of Taxes, and it is my opinion that you would make a very good Inspector. With your experience as a tax agent and your local knowledge of taxpayers, I consider your prospects would indeed be bright in the Inland Revenue Office.
>
> 3. Should you be appointed an Inspector of Taxes; I wish you every success as an Inspector. In case you continue as a tax agent, I am sure you will give my successors the same excellent returns as you have lodged during my nine-year stay in Fiji.
>
> Yours sincerely,
> (*sgd*) W. F. Watson

The following letter, dated 27 February 1948, was sent by the law firm of Messrs. Ellis, Munro, Warren & Leys. It notes Ram's qualities and abilities as an employee during the eleven years he worked with them.

<u>To WHOM IT MAY CONCERN</u>

Mr Ram Charitra has been in our employ since June 1937, when he joined our staff as a clerk and interpreter. Since June 1944, he has been the senior clerk and interpreter in the office. He has handled our Indian clients very efficiently and appeared to have their confidence and has shown considerable ability in assembling and sorting out information in complicated transactions.

In 1942, when we were working with a reduced staff in our accountancy department, we found that he was able to do bookkeeping, and for the rest of the war, he took over the keeping of books for various estates and companies for whom we acted.

He is obviously very interested in accountancy, and the work which he did for us in this department was very capably carried out. Ram Charitra has also shown a keen interest in Income Tax problems, and we consider that he has good appreciation of that side of accountancy work and also of the Income Tax Ordinance. He has also gained experience by keeping books in his own time for a very large number of Indian businessmen.

Ram Charitra is a very hard worker and capable of using his initiative and has carried out his duties for us very satisfactorily. We have found him to be very reliable and of good character and we believe that he bears a good reputation in his community. He now leaves us to join the Government Service, and we are sorry to lose him.

Ellis, Munro, Warren & Leys,
(*sgd*) A. D. Leys

Terms and Post of Inspector of Taxes Offered

The application was successful. Mr A. J. Thompson of the Secretariat offered Ram the terms, detailed in a letter dated 24 December 1947.

Colony of Fiji

The Secretariat,
Suva.
24th December 1947

Sir,

I am directed to refer to your application for appointment to the Civil Service of this Colony dated 6 October 1947 and to offer you appointment as an Inspector of Taxes in the Accountant-General's Department with salary at the rate of £600 per annum in the scale £400 x 25 - £600 and with effect from the 1st March 1948. Your appointment will of necessity be temporary in the first instance, but as soon as the 1948 Estimates are approved by the Secretary of State for the Colonies and an additional post of Inspector of Taxes is created, steps will be taken to make your appointment permanent. You would be required to produce a satisfactory medical certificate.

>   I am,
>   Sir,
>   Your Obedient Servant,
>
>
>   *(sgd)* A. J. Thompson
>   For The Colonial Secretary

Mr Ram Charitra,
Box No. 149,
Suva.

January 1948: the Offer and Terms Are Accepted.

Ram was delighted with the terms offered by the Colonial Secretary. He joined the department on 1 March 1948. He formally accepted the offer as follows:

> C.F. 29/37
> c/o Post Office Box No. 149,
> Suva
> 12th January 1948
>
> The Honourable,
> The Colonial Secretary,
> The Secretariat,
> Suva.
>
> Dear Sir,

> I Thank you for your letter of the 24th of December 1947, offering me an appointment as an Inspector of Taxes in the Accountant-General's Department, with a salary at the rate of £600 per annum. I also wish to thank you for the extension of time to the 1st March 1948 you have so kindly granted to me in order to enable me to take up my duties as from that date.
> I hereby accept the appointment offered to me and I would assure you that I will always endeavour to discharge my duties entrusted to me to the satisfaction of the Head of Department concerned. I herewith forward to you the medical certificate of my health.
>
> > Thanking you.
>
> > Yours faithfully,
> > (*sgd*) R. Charitra

In short, the position offered would become permanent when the following conditions were met:

1. if the estimates were approved by the Secretary of State for the Colonies.
2. an additional post of Inspector of Taxes was created.
3. a satisfactory medical certificate was provided.

Ram's terms and conditions that preceded his application to the civil service were not rejected, modified, or commented upon, and included no contrary terms or reasons that Ram might find unsuitable, causing him to withdraw his application.

The Secretariat's offer constituted a binding legal arrangement, which Ram accepted and subsequently resigned from Ellis, Munro, Warren & Leys.

He wrote to Mr A. D. Leys:

> My untold loyalty to you requires me to inform you that I am applying for an appointment of an Inspector of Taxes on the permanent establishment with the commencing salary of £600.00 per annum. You know that I have always endeavoured to the best of my ability to be loyal and faithful to you in

discharging my duties during the past ten or eleven years of my service and that there has been constant harmony and goodwill and continued friendship between us. I have no complaint or dissatisfaction of any kind with which I ever can say that I have the slightest desire to leave any one of you. I have always appreciated your goodwill and friendship in the past, and I desire to reciprocate the same in a similar spirit in future…

23

First Day at the Office

What lies behind us and what lies before us are tiny matters compared to what lies within us.[1]

In terms of financial institutions, Ram trod the ground that no local-born person of colour had done; he now sat with some authority, in a senior position, among officers considered his superiors. The post seemed ready-made for him. His years of problem-solving for his tax clients had prepared him well, and the Inland Revenue officers were fully aware of his penetrative insights and abilities as they had observed and monitored his correspondence for nine years.

On the first day, 1 March 1948, when he walked in, accompanied by the Commissioner, a respectful atmosphere prevailed during his introductions to the staff. His new colleagues – with the two exceptions of Mr David Rahiman and Mr Basavanand, both junior officers – were expatriates from Britain, Australia, and New Zealand.

Indications of Tensions Ahead

The presence of a non-European in a department that had never appointed an "outsider" naturally sparked curiosity, but this was a significant departure from the department's normal practice, and in some quarters, it was not as welcome a change as one might have expected in the post-war world. For Ram, it was natural, and he expected the net to cast wider, tempting more local expertise to enter the service. He had worked with people from all races, primarily Europeans, throughout his eleven years at the law firm. His educational records from an early age also

---

[1] Ralph Waldo Emerson

First Day at the Office

showed that most of his tutors were Europeans, so working with expatriates came naturally to him. From his perspective, he was among fellow professionals, and that was all that mattered to him.

Increasing numbers of Indians were becoming taxpayers, so it seemed apposite that someone from that community was among the higher-ranking tax officers. It also aligned with the government's declared objectives to train local talent for work in the colonial administration. There was, however, not much evidence of progress at that level. This change was forced upon the government by the crises caused by the war. The government's attitude was one of lethargic disinterest in change. The dichotomy between the expected localisation and the temperament of the ruling elite seemed a bridge too far. The dominant class's impulses towards self-preservation triggered resistance and reluctance to relate to "others".

Ram settled down to a routine as an inspector of taxes. He enjoyed his job and found his colleagues to be amicable. They ensured that he was familiar with office practices and procedures and that he knew where the various forms, stationery, and references were stored. He found he shared much familiar ground with them: families, relationships, and hobbies. Politics apart, there was much they had in common, but they were unwilling to admit it. Some had been in Fiji for many years and were familiar, not least, with the wet tropical conditions in Suva, its local politics, social issues, and the expanding commerce in the city.

Questions from his colleagues about his application and education soon dominated conversations. He did not possess accounting qualifications from an institute they recognised. How could he then be expected to deal with complex or unusual cases from taxpayers and corporations? Was he up to handling corporate tax matters? They were aware and familiar with his expertise, so some questions he faced were blatantly racist in origin. He kept his cool. "Sometimes I thought they were insane, not idiots or racist!" he told me once.

The questions were limited only by the questioners' imaginations and the depth of their preconceived notions and prejudices. Why had he left teaching? Surely, he would be more useful to his community as a teacher. Wasn't there a shortage of teachers? All true and relevant. But why had "they", the expatriate officers, left their own countries to seek employment in the colony?

The "wind of change" was still some distance off, over the horizon. However, the belief among the settlers and the administration that the colony had a credible programme of localisation was one reflected by the overconfident chiefs. Some no doubt saw the steady economic development of the islands and conflated it with political and administrative progress.

At the time of Ram's induction as a civil servant, he had a good reputation among the growing Indian business fraternity and projected fair financial growth year after year. As a civil servant, he was earning less pay than before his move to the department, especially when considering his investments and fees. However, he had no regrets as this move had its advantages: on retirement, he would have a government pension, not to mention the status that usually accompanied work at high levels in government. The expertise and experience gained from his position at the Inland Revenue Department would be an invaluable asset in private practice – if he had the opportunity to practice again or if he needed to. In addition, his business affairs were in the capable hands of his solicitors, who executed deals under the power of attorney he had given to one of the partners, Mr A. D. Leys.

24

Terms of Employment Changed Without Notice

Britain is obliged to set up a new and more positive standard of our duty and obligation towards the peoples to whom this House is in a position of a trustee.[1]

Whatever transpired in the department, Ram's natural stoicism carried him through some unwelcome innuendos, but he continued nonetheless. However, little did he realise at the time that he was surrounded by officers who were determined from the outset to remove him from their midst. Localisation was not a serious government objective.

Two were particularly active and "hands-on" about trying to remove Ram, and no obstacle was too small or too big to put in his way. The rest were not able to help him: they had their own future security and promotions to consider. Their positions weren't permanent; they hoped to renew their contracts, and they wanted nothing to jeopardise that. There were, however, a few who sympathised but were powerless against the powerful departmental heads.

Perhaps the ire of his adversaries should have been directed at the Commissioner and the Assistant Commissioner, who had initiated Ram's move to the Department. "*Sacre bleu!* - They had even accepted *Ram's* terms to get him into the Revenue." Ram's hope of seeing this posting through to this retirement soon took a downturn. His future seemed insecure – if not at its end.

---

[1] Leopold Amery, Hansard, HC, vol. 118, col. 2174 (30 July 1919), quoted in John T. Ducker, *Beyond Empire: The End of Britain's Colonial Encounter* (Bloomsbury, 2020), p. 13.

Perspectives of British Colonial Rule in the Fiji Islands

Ram had barely settled down to his new routine before an unexpected communication landed on his desk.

One month and seventeen days after his employment had started, the Secretariat varied the original contract. His mind went back a generation when the plantation managers disregarded the indenture contracts with the labourers. *That* document was not worth the paper it was written on. The similarities are uncanny except for the time and situation.

This revised arrangement would not have been accepted, and Ram would not have resigned from his previous employment. The deceit practised by the administration's Secretariat was unprofessional and indeed, beyond reprehensible.

No consultations, no reasons, no prior notice or intention of changes, and no complaints filed against him to justify a variation of the original arrangement of employment were advanced.

The General Orders authorised no such unilateral action to break an existing arrangement. This action was a clear breach of contract initiated from within the department. It was executed by the Secretariat against an employee whom it had preferred, accepted, and employed.

Ram was now in a vacuum. He had resigned from his former firm, and he was thrust into an unknown and unpredictable situation.

The new terms imposed additional conditions not previously discussed during the negotiation period, and especially between 27 September 1947, when Ram's terms were put forward, and their acceptance by the department on 24 December 1947. This new dimension left Ram in a tricky position. Should he continue according to the new terms (although not previously agreed), take the department to court, or resign from the service he had joined only six weeks before? He discussed the matter with friendly colleagues and decided to stay at his post, following the arrangement agreed upon with Mr Watson in 1947, and dealing with the consequences as they arose.

The two contracts were different: this latter version asserted terms he had explicitly ruled out.

Terms of Employment Changed Without Notice

The Seal of the Secretariat

The Secretariat,
Suva,
Fiji.
17th April 1948

Sir,

Subject to your acceptance of the terms of this letter and to the production of a satisfactory medical certificate you are hereby appointed to be an Inspector of Taxes, Accountant-General's Department, in the Civil Service of this Colony, with effect from the 1st of March 1948.

2. You will receive a salary at the rate of £600 per annum in the scale £500 x 25 - £600. Your incremental date is the 1st March.

3. You will be required to contribute to the Government Employees' Provident Fund at the prescribed rate in accordance with the Government Employees' Provident Fund Ordinance (Cap. 45) and to the Widows' & Orphans' Pension Scheme at the prescribed rate in accordance with the Widows' & Orphans' Pension Ordinance (Cap. 46). Copies of these Ordinances may be seen in your department.

4. Your appointment will be on a probationary basis for a period of not less than three years with effect from 1st March 1948. While probationary it may be terminated by one month's notice on either side or by payment of one month's salary in lieu of notice; but you will be liable to instant dismissal in the event of incompetence, misconduct, or insubordination.

5. You will be subject to all regulations governing the Civil Service of this Colony which are now in force, or which may be promulgated from time to time by the Governor.

6. You will be liable to be transferred at any time to another branch or department of the Colony's Service.

Perspectives of British Colonial Rule in the Fiji Islands

I am,
Sir,
Your Obedient Servant,
(sgd) A. J. Thompson
For The Colonial Secretary

Mr Ram Charitra,
u.f.s The Accountant-General,
Suva.

Significance of Changes

This was the first sign that Ram had been ensnared into working for the government under false pretences. His only wish was to indulge his favourite occupation of working out complex interpretations of taxation regulations with like-minded colleagues in challenging cases.

He also wanted to demonstrate that not only could he have a career as a civil servant, but also that anyone could, provided they applied themselves diligently, and that the government was open-minded and fair in its terms of service, available to all deserving candidates. He believed that there should be no preconceptions, misgivings, or hesitation about working at a senior level with European expatriate officers – most were fair and open-minded - after all, the customary decency and integrity of the British were legendary.

Naturally, Ram wished to learn the cause or causes of this unusual turn of events from the Secretariat.

To preserve the integrity of this change, a senior officer removed Ram's original letter of appointment, dated 24th December 1947, from the department's secure filing cabinet. The original copy, also signed by Mr A.J. Thompson, was now lost forever.

The "lost" letter was the legal letter of appointment, based on the terms negotiated before Ram's application. No one witnessed its removal, nor did anyone admit to its whereabouts. The missing letter was replaced by a copy of the above letter dated 17 April 1948 – falsely implying that no other prior contract existed – except, of course, one that Ram had in his possession.

Terms of Employment Changed Without Notice

A nameless senior staff member had fired the first salvo at a non-European senior officer. Was this a warning to others, also perhaps to warn him that his future in the department had limits to his expectations?

This episode at the beginning of his civil service career was disturbing and nerve-wracking. The position at his former firm was now filled. His future seemed uncertain, and he felt insecure about what was to come next. It was possible to interpret the abrupt and unexpected change as a challenge to his character and temperament. His time at the law offices had been happy, and he had built up good relationships with all people, colleagues and clients; he saw no reason for this abrupt change in the brief period he was in the department. There were no complaints from colleagues or the taxpayers.

The relationship of his previous incarnation as an accountant was that of a "master" and "servant". Both parties knew their places, and there was little to no likelihood of coming into proximity to form friendships. Dealings were strictly professional and at an arm's length,

He had expected that he and his new colleagues would establish a closer working relationship. Ram was sociable and always approachable. He was a good listener and always patient. His success during his periods as a legal clerk, accountant, and tax agent can be attributed not just to his expertise but also to his temperament and personality.

Now, as colleagues, there were bound to be challenges, and he was determined to do his best, being open and professional. Ram would have continued happily at the legal firm had the Secretariat not been so dishonest. He was accepted as a civil servant under false pretences, and this corrupt and unethical approach disturbed him, coming as it did from the highest officials in the land.

They had misled him into accepting his terms, then refuted them without explanation. What could be read into this? Distrust of some of the most senior officers? Confidence is built on mutual respect, predictability, and consistency. He was losing confidence but had to remain constant and focused. He had his future ahead of him, but now the greatest Empire was showing signs of cracks, having to resort to deception.

Now that the Secretariat could not be trusted, could he survive in this toxic environment? The experience revealed a side not visible from a distance: there could be no immediate resolution, but perhaps not jumping to conclusions might be the preferred option.

His entry into the Inland Revenue would lead him into the hidden world of expatriate civil servants, whose erratic tendencies often led them to ignore rules and regulations. It gave him insight into the inconsistencies that perhaps pervaded the entire colonial administration. He saw evidence of their condescending and demeaning conduct throughout his period as an officer of the Crown. The expatriates appeared to rule the colony with a degree of disingenuousness and hypocrisy. Yet, somehow, the outside world perceived them to be dedicated, honourable men, providing selfless public service.

Ram's tenure in the department was marked by primaeval sentiments unsuited to the developing post-war, impressionable colony, such as these islands. He reported and complained about all that transpired and affected his position in his detailed petitions to the Governor.

25

Recommended for Professional Status

The changes to the contract do not appear to have had any visible impact on or altered Ram's responsibilities or duties. He continued with his routine and decided that he would not give anyone a reason to complain or object to his presence under any circumstances. Those early days of uncertainty seemed long ago. Not much had changed since then, and it was work as usual. Were his concerns unjustified? Was there anything to be worried about? So far, so good... and it appeared that things were better than he had anticipated.

In the early days when Ram was at the Inland Revenue, unknown to him, his work was monitored. Mr Watson, the Assistant Commissioner, added weight and some cheer when he suggested that Ram may apply to a professional body to be recognised as an accountant by the broader community. Qualifying staff members in his department were registered as associates or fellows of these institutes, and Ram was free to make an application.

The Secretariat maintained a comprehensive list of recognised, relevant institutes and organisations in Australia and Britain that were recognised by the civil service departments. Consultations with colleagues followed, and Ram decided to apply to the Society of Commercial Accountants of England and Wales, registered in Bristol, England, the patron of which was the Duke of Edinburgh.

The significance and relevance of these institutions were discussed with Mr Watson before a formal letter of application was drafted. All officially recognised designations were published in the Civil List when such announcements were made.

Perspectives of British Colonial Rule in the Fiji Islands

On official Inland Revenue notepaper, Mr Watson wrote in support of Ram's application to the society:

<u>TO WHOM IT MAY CONCERN</u>

22nd May 1948

THIS IS TO CERTIFY that Mr Ram Charitra was appointed an Inspector of Taxes in this Department on 1st March 1948. Mr Charitra has had long experience in the preparation of accounts and returns of income; he is a conscientious and industrious officer and shows promise of becoming an expert Inspector of Taxes.

2. I consider Mr Ram Charitra a suitable candidate for admission to the Society of Commercial Accountants.

(sgd) W. F. Watson,
ASSISTANT COMMISSIONER OF INLAND REVENUE

Ram was admitted as a Fellow of the Society of Commercial Accountants by letter, dated 29 July 1948, and entitled to use the designation F.Comm.A. He was confident of the future and that the success or failure of his tenure would be determined purely through his work, and there were eagle-eyed scrutineers looking out for slipups.

The Commissioner of Inland Revenue, Mr R. B. Ackland, wrote in his report of 9 September 1948:

This is to certify that Mr Ram Charitra has been an Inspector of Taxes in this department for the last six months. Prior to joining this office, Mr Charitra had long experience in the preparation of accounts and returns of income and the knowledge so acquired has fitted him for his present post. Mr Charitra is an able and industrious officer and shows promise of becoming a very efficient Inspector of Taxes.

On 10 January 1950, he applied, through the Commissioner of Inland Revenue, to include the designatory letters after his name on official documents. The Secretariat

Recommended for Professional Status

approved the request, and his name was subsequently inserted in the following year's Civil List, with the appropriate letters. This practice continued for *six years* without interruption

Recommended for the Post of Assessor

During Mr Ackland's management and supervision, and three years after the terms were altered, any concerns that Ram had seemed to be a distant memory. He had settled in and developed good working relations with his colleagues and the taxpayers, and his progress reports were complimentary.

In May 1951, Mr Drysdale, the Deputy Commissioner, prepared a report on the general work activities and efficiencies of all the officers of the Inland Revenue Department for the Secretariat. This report followed a departmental exercise to revise salaries.

> To: Mr Ram Charitra,
> u.f.s Commissioner of Inland Revenue
> Ref. FEO 29/801
>
> 23.7.51
> PROMOTION
> Dear Sir,
>
> I am directed to inform you that you have been selected for promotion to the post of Assessor in the Inland Revenue Department. Your promotion will be subject to confirmation by the Secretary of State for the Colonies.
>
> 2. You will be eligible to receive a salary at the rate of £750 a year on the scale of £750 x 30 – (840) x 40 - £1,000 and will retain your incremental date. Your promotion will take effect from the 24th of April 1951.
>
> 3. In other respects, you will remain on your existing conditions of service.
> *(sgd)* A. L. Baker

Perspectives of British Colonial Rule in the Fiji Islands

For The Colonial Secretary[1]

Ram was promoted to Assessor, effective 24 April 1951. Mr Drysdale expected this promotion would be subject to Ram's taking certain examinations. However, the Secretary of State for the Colonies followed the Colonial Secretary's recommendations and the advice from his Permanent Secretary, and confirmed Ram's promotion, without need for an examination. This was accepted by the department.

The appointment was subsequently published in the *Fiji Royal Gazette*, no. 45, dated 28 November 1951.

Revised Terms Exploited

However, double standards were at play. The first major shots to destabilise Ram, a properly installed civil servant, began with Mr Drysdale's first steps to remove him. The Commissioner planned either to remove this local officer from the department or to make his situation untenable by impeding his progress through the department.

Following the unannounced change of Ram's civil service contract on 17 April 1948, Mr Drysdale and Mr Philbrick, his deputy, took the position that Ram was incompetent and unqualified for the responsibilities entrusted to him, despite his promotion and the confidence reposed in him by Drysdale's predecessors and indeed, himself in his report.

Both senior officers, archetypal professional opponents, were now setting up to assert their influence and achieve their goal, now that Mr Ackland and Mr Watson were gone.

The reasons for their actions were not clear; they did not reveal any problem they encountered with his work, if any, or that he was an unsuitable person to occupy a position of some importance in the civil service.

Even though Ram's appointment was made at the highest level, Mr Drysdale insisted that the post should be

---

[1] Petition to the Colonial Secretary, 14 May 1956, p. 2.

confirmed only after the relevant examination. He wished to have the last say in Ram's promotion, and if he could stop it by saying that an examination was needed, even though (officially) it was not, he would be adamant that it was.

Ram resisted and challenged this decision, arguing that Mr Mayze – a junior officer – *was confirmed without an examination by the Commissioner.* He discussed this with Mr Drysdale and returned disappointed. Ram reminded Mr Drysdale that he had entered the civil service based on the offer made by the Secretariat on 24 December 1947, which did not include examinations as prerequisites for confirmation of an appointment. But this was of no interest to Mr Drysdale. As far as the Commissioner was concerned, that was his ruling, and he would adhere to it regardless of any inconsistencies observed.

Mr Drysdale further contended that Ram's appointment was invalid without the relevant examination and that there were no legal grounds for the appointment to be confirmed. The Secretariat, however, thought otherwise and held that the confirmation would stand.

The manner of Mr Mayze's appointment created a precedent that Mr Drysdale would find difficult to reverse. His defence was that it was "an *error*" but that the position would stand! The Commissioner of Inland Revenue was in breach of the General Orders, which were known to the Secretariat, but the culture of the establishment obstructed justice and fair resolutions.

Mr Drysdale's actions exposed the cronyism and corruption at the heart of the colonial civil service. Rules that set a stable and predictable environment were not enforced. Established procedures were discarded at will.

Senior Positions Out of Reach

Given fair play, Ram could or should have been the next Senior Assessor. The position would have indicated a significant and momentous breakthrough: an achievement for the colony, as indeed, it would have been for this locally recruited civil servant. It would have been a recognition of the British colonial policy of localisation, and lent credibility to the oft-mentioned intentions of Fiji's colonial administration to localise. Such an agenda, however, was not of concern to the Commissioner of Inland Revenue. He was on a mission.

The Inland Revenue's senior managers neither expected nor thought it possible that a local person would be able to achieve the proficiencies needed to be accorded such a senior post as to be within spitting distance of becoming the head of the department.

Under the present incumbent, promotions were to be predetermined by prevailing ideology, rather than merit. However, Ram believed in British justice and fair play. He thought that he would achieve promotion on merit when the time and opportunity were ripe. Much was at stake during this colonial period, when public policies were not subject to scrutiny and debate, and public servants were not accountable.

1951: Appointed *Acting* Senior Assessor

The position of Senior Assessor in Ram's department became vacant. He applied to the Colonial Secretary for the post on 15 September 1951. On 13 December 1951, the Colonial Secretary replied: *"The question of your further promotion does not at present arise as there is no vacancy in the Senior Grade."*[2] A clear and unequivocal official statement.

The denial of a vacancy puzzled Ram. On 9 January 1952, he followed up with a request to be appointed as an *acting* senior assessor. He was duly appointed to the position; his appointment was backdated to 22 December 1951, the date he assumed responsibility. The post had been vacant for five months, and Ram hoped that he would be the next occupant as of right. He was experienced, capable and entitled to it. With a couple of notable exceptions, his colleagues indeed had expected him to be the next Senior Assessor. However, a *temporary*, acting post was available, and Ram was eligible and accepted it. This arrangement ended on 2 July 1952. He was then reappointed again as Acting Senior Assessor by Mr R. B. Ackland, the Commissioner, from 1

---

[2] Petition to the Governor, Sir Ronald Garvey, 25 January 1955.

June 1953 to 8 March 1954. Mr Ackland retired on 1 June 1953, and Mr Drysdale assumed the position of Commissioner.

Appointment Not Published

As was customary, all departmental appointments and promotions were reported in the *Fiji Royal Gazette*, but Ram's appointment was notable by its absence from 20 April 1951, No.18, which did not carry the official announcement. However, all the other temporary appointments were published. When Ram investigated the matter, no explanation or reason for this omission was given. Silence. Was it an oversight or a deliberate act? These apparently minor actions were irritating and unnecessary, but they had consequences and were deliberately omitted from the official announcements.

Corruption in the Colony

Corruptions take many forms, from perverse decisions and irregular actions, which may or may not include sleaze and foul play. The outcome must benefit the perpetrator at the expense of another. During Ram's period of service, the practitioners of this dark art emerged from the closet were the Assistant Commissioner of Inland Revenue, who later became the Commissioner, and his deputy, Mr Philbrick. These two were officers with great responsibility, tasked with collecting national dues. A significant part of their time, however, was spent on trivial pursuits, including trying to remove an officer they feared threatened their positions. Their attempts took many forms, ranging from serious to puerile.

The blatant lies – practised at the highest level – directly implicated the Colonial Secretary and others and exposed their clumsy attempts to deny Ram's legitimate claims. The organisation was a "closed shop", tightly controlled with the blessings of the highest authority in the land. They were protecting the colony and were responsible for the White Man's Burden.

When Ram was told that "there [was] no vacancy in the Senior Grade", the Commissioner was secretly searching for a senior assessor in *Australia*. News reached Fiji that Mr Drysdale had advertised the vacancy in the *Sydney Morning Herald* as late as April 1952, while denying that a vacancy existed! Here, a senior officer in the civil service was free to lie to his officers and, possibly, to an executive officer of the government. This serious misjudgment was one that the Secretariat tolerated, with *no* consequences for the perpetrator.

Mr Drysdale had misrepresented the facts to Ram and possibly to the Secretariat. He drew the Colonial Secretary's attention to the irregular practices, including making false statements in the department. [3]

A further twist in this wretched saga came to light. If Mr Drysdale had not succeeded in procuring an Australian officer as a result of the position advertised, he would have considered appointing a *friend* of an expatriate senior officer in his department. This unknown prospective Senior Assessor was then employed by W. R. Carpenters & Co. (Fiji) Ltd as an accountant. However, Drysdale could not do so when it became an open secret that the vacancy was advertised in the Sydney newspaper.

The Colonial Regulations were clear about promotions. They were based on merit and seniority. Ram qualified on both counts. The Secretariat undoubtedly colluded or turned a blind eye, enabling a capricious senior officer to disrupt the work and progress of a colleague. The principle governing promotions as incorporated in the 'Terms of Service and Salaries Revision Committee', headed by Mr Snell, a retired judge, published as Legislative Council Paper No. 25 of 1946, stated:

> "(a) Paragraph 41: *Promotion by Seniority*. Colonial Regulation 32 reads: 'Claims of officers for promotion will be considered on the basis of official qualification, experience, and merit.'" The *New Zealand Official Yearbook, 1939*, p. 872, says "that the determining factors as regards the promotion of officers are efficiency and suitability. Only when it is not possible to

---

[3] Petition to the Administering Officer, dated 29 June 1952. Ram recalled that he had no objections to the advertisement in the Sydney Newspaper, but a similar announcement in the Fijian press would have been welcome and would have absolved him of any misunderstanding.

Recommended for Professional Status

separate officers on these grounds is recourse made to seniority."

The 'Fiji Secretariat Circular', no. 53, of 10 December 1943 sought to expand the Colonial Regulation. Its essential remark was that in considering promotion, the Civil Service Board had regards to the character and qualifications of the candidates... personal merit, experience and suitability as well as seniority... other things being equal the senior candidates will normally be selected.

(b) Statements have been made from time to time that it is the Government's policy to fit in local youths in the higher post of the service if they possess experience and are suited for it."

As it then stood, the Colonial Regulations and General Orders were options available to the Commissioners, but these did not seem to impress them. Neither Mr Drysdale nor Mr Philbrick, the Assistant Commissioner, had any intention of following regulations.

The cause of some of Mr Drysdale's irrational acts seemed to lie elsewhere. According to a petition Ram had presented to the Governor,[4] Mr Drysdale's irritation stemmed from an incident that occurred in September 1951. Mr Drysdale, then the Assistant Commissioner, had asked Ram for a half-share in his freehold real estate in the Carnarvon Street building project, which, at the time, was in its planning stages.

To Mr Drysdale's dismay, Ram declined the proposition. Ram thought of the dangers that were there: signs pointed to insinuations of corruption in an important government department. It would have taken little encouragement for an outsider to cause public disquiet at the business transactions between government officers in the department.

Even if the two, as "partners", had been completely "on the level" possible discussions and disagreements over

---

[4] Petition dated 29 June 1952 handed to the Commissioner Mr R.B. Ackland in which Ram complained about the reasons for Mr Drysdale's state of mind and his lack of co-operation sympathies for Ram's legitimate demands.

contentious arrangements would have been detrimental to the department's continued professionalism. The property in question was in a prime location in the city; Ram was not going to take chances by sharing in the business venture, even with a personage as august as the Assistant Commissioner of Inland Revenue. He had never gambled, and he was not going to start now. The reason for declining the request seemed obvious, but this refusal, along with its proper disclosure to the higher authorities, according to the rules, was not appreciated by Mr Drysdale.

Mr Ackland, the Commissioner, was on holiday in England during the Carnarvon Street episode, and Mr Drysdale was the Acting Commissioner. On his return to Fiji in January 1952, Mr Ackland was informed by Ram, quite correctly, of the half-share request by his fellow officer, Mr Drysdale. A copy of the letter to the governor was on Mr Ackland's desk. Following a discussion with Drysdale, the Commissioner took no further action: Mr Drysdale said that he had only made an enquiry about the property. Mr Drysdale never forgot nor forgave Ram for this incident.

Appointment Ignored

A vacancy arose for the post of senior assessor when Mr Wheatley was promoted to the post of Assistant Commissioner. Ram was posted to act as Senior Assessor, effective from 24 April 1952 (page 2 of the Petition dated 25 January 1955).

Before Mr Drysdale departed for Australia on holiday on 22 December 1951, he arranged all the temporary appointments of officers in the department. As was the practice, he ensured that the office continued to function efficiently during his absence. He fulfilled and recorded all the posts except one: he took no notice of Ram's promotion and did not publish it in the *Fiji Royal Gazette* as was required. All the other appointments appeared in issue no. 18 on 20 April 1951.

Recommended for Professional Status

Thus, officially, Ram's appointment was not recognised and therefore not remunerated. [5] Ram again considered his options. How much longer could he tolerate deliberate actions such as this? The "higher authorities" – the Colonial Secretary and the governor - were no doubt aware of Mr Drysdale's malicious designs aimed at one individual in his department, through Ram's many petitions and pleas for justice. Would they heed another one? Ram did the needful and sent off his petition – even if no action was taken, it would act as a record of a Commissioner's personal crusades directly impacting on his promotions and future security.

When Mr Ackland – the Commissioner – appointed Ram for his *second* period [6] as *Acting* Senior Assessor, effective 22 December 1951, it was recorded on 8 February 1952 in issue no. 9 of the *Fiji Royal Gazette*, on p. 33.

Change at the Top: A Series of Irregularities

There was restraint during Mr Ackland's period in charge of the department, thanks, it would appear, to his confidence in this local officer. Mr Drysdale bided his time until he took over from Mr Ackland on 1 June 1953 as Commissioner.

His first act was to shorten the duration of Ram's post as Acting Senior Assessor, which had been scheduled to last from 1 June, 1953, until 18 August, 1954. Drysdale brought forward the end of the term to 8 March 1954, and recorded the change in the *Fiji Royal Gazette*, no. 34, 12 June 1953.

In September of that year, he *confirmed* Mr Mayze in the post of Senior Assessor, *without* reference to any examination (*Fiji Royal Gazette*, no. 47, 4 September 1953). Both Mr Drysdale and his deputy Mr Philbrick consistently held that passing the prescribed examinations was the sole criterion for confirmation, and that the rules *must* be followed. Neither the General Orders

---

[5] Petition, 29 June 1952, p. 2.
[6] Ram's stints acting as Senior Assessor: 1. From 22.12.1951 to 2. 7.1952; 2. From 1. 6.1953 to 8. 3.1954; 3. From 3. 7. 1955 to not known.

nor the Colonial Regulations granted discretionary powers to Commissioners to waive rules; however, when an exception was made, it created a precedent that had to be followed in similar circumstances. However, questions about the lack of exams arose only when Ram's promotion was in question. The rest of the expatriate staff were waved through to their new posts without exams.

On 19 August 1954, the position again became vacant, remaining so until 3 July 1955. For *eleven* months, no person was responsible for this crucial post. Ram's experience and merit carried weight and credibility; they fitted him for the senior position and "in the same precedence as he already acted on two previous occasions".[7] Although he was the man best placed for promotion according to seniority and entitlement, Mr Drysdale again refused to accede to that request.

The administration continued to shelter behind the pretext that there were no vacancies. His misfortune was that he was up against a hostile individual, aided and abetted by an unfettered colonial administration.

Governors, all with many years of cumulative experience from different parts of the empire, mostly from colonies similar to Fiji, were the ideal administrators to oversee and promote good management in all departments. During Ram's tenure in the department, governors, from Sir Brian Freeston to Sir Ronald Garvey and Sir Kenneth Maddocks, adopted the age-old practice of seeing only what they were advised to see by their officers, which was a compelling practice but one that effectively condoned potential misconduct by officers.

Ram's petitions for justice were all futile, time-consuming exertions. Allowing officers to submit petitions served only to mollify them, assuring them that their complaints were being heard. Ram's pleas for promotion to the post of Senior Assessor were all ignored and, at times, even unacknowledged; thus, his grievances were not resolved. The governors' implied support of the miscreants was a restraining

---

[7] Petition, 25 January 1955, p. 2.

feature that was embedded in the colonial management of administrative affairs. The governors' inaction or inability to scrutinise and test the veracity of complaints was a dereliction of duty and a perversion of justice.

No colonial governor gave serious consideration to Ram's petitions. Many quotations are reproduced in this biography, making it easy to deduce the autocratic nature of colonial justice, which was shaped by its own unique twist on classic British "justice" and the "rule of law."

Even breaches of the General Orders were overlooked; it seems that they were no more than an opaque government instrument that served only to display some sort of order-based administrative system.

Ram was repeatedly given the acting senior assessor position but never confirmed as the senior assessor. No one questioned his abilities as a technician during his tenure in the department or elsewhere. There was never an adverse reaction to his periods as Acting Senior Assessor, from 22 December 1951 to 2 July 1952 and from 1 June 1953 to 8 March 1954. As a matter of course, this state of affairs was a great injustice to Ram; it also had negative implications for the colony's prospects and those hoping to develop and acquire expertise in complex administrative matters.

Mr Drysdale's Unpredictable Actions

As a colonial principal and head of an important department with rights, privileges, and power, Mr Drysdale essentially directed the fate of his subordinate officers. He was not justified in terminating Ram's acting senior assessor appointment only to appoint a junior officer, Mr Mayze, in his place. This was contrary to General Orders, but he was not concerned with such minutiae. Reasons were not proffered, nor was any complaint recorded or lodged by any colleague about Ram's work, integrity, or relationship with his colleagues or taxpayers.

Another side of Mr Drysdale comes to light. As a Commissioner of the Inland Revenue Department, he had to be an archetypal representative of an efficient administrative system that would, perhaps, continue to run the affairs of a prosperous nation in the future.

The precursor to this abrupt decision appears to be that Ram had submitted a report against Mr Drysdale's financial tendencies to make some money on the side as these were proscribed under the General Orders s.44(b). He had lent £500 to a businessman, Mr Fong Lee, registered under Mortgage Reference No. 53057 and as *required by regulations*, he had failed to report the transaction to the Colonial Secretary.

The reported breaches, with evidence, reached the Governor. Mr Drysdale was not admonished or cautioned - another example of government corruption in the colony. The governor's see-nothing and do-nothing attitude towards his senior officers only encouraged erratic officers to get away with actions bordering on criminality.

To add to his woes, Ram was not paid for the period from 24 April 1951 to 22 December 1951, despite his repeated requests. He was aware that this was an effort to provoke a reaction from him. He reported the "oversight" and brought the omission to the attention of the Administering Officer, through the Colonial Secretary and reported that he was owed -

> an Acting Allowance of the post of Senior Assessor be paid to him in respect of the period 24th April 1951 and 22nd December 1951 being the period during which he has also discharged the like and the same duties as he has performed and discharged since the 22nd of December 1951.[8]

The Administering Officer and the Commissioner remained silent, and the debt was written off.

Mr Wheatley, who held the post of Assessor, was appointed, on 11 April 1951, to act as *Deputy Commissioner*. Again, on 24 April 1951, he was promoted to Senior Assessor during his acting tenure as Assistant Commissioner. Mr Wheatley had

---

[8] Petition, 29 June 1952, p. 2, paragraph 1.

leapfrogged from *Assessor* to Deputy Commissioner, a position usually reached after a stint as a Senior Assessor, not before.

Secretariat Declines Mr Drysdale's Nominees

The General Orders guide civil servants in the proper conduct of their business. The officers, without exception, are required to familiarise themselves with all government notifications and executive orders that affect appointments, promotions, dismissals, and even breaches of government rules. These important rules were quite often flouted, as already seen above, without consequences for the offending officer, as the following instance also illustrates. Ignoring all the rules, Mr Drysdale appointed Mr W. A. Lewis, an officer junior to Ram, to be the *Senior Assessor*.

To their credit, the Secretariat declined to confirm Mr Lewis, as it refused to condone breaches of regulations. Determined to have his way, Mr Drysdale tried to employ an alternative candidate again in contemptuous defiance of the Secretariat. On 8 September 1954, he appointed Mr J. C. Davis in place of the now-rejected Mr Lewis.

Now, an exasperated Secretariat demanded an explanation of why precedence had not been followed, and why Ram, the only officer eligible, had not been appointed to that vacant post.

Undaunted, unimpressed and unyielding, Mr Drysdale refused to appoint Ram. He again petitioned the Governor with no positive result; the latter referred the matter back to the *Commissioner* for advice instead of to the Secretariat for an appraisal. Submissions to the Governor – the font of British justice in Fiji – were futile.

Even the Secretariat's request for an explanation about why Ram was not selected for the post was not answered by the Commissioner. Frustrating and demeaning, working for the British colonial civil service represented values not worthy of the traditional trust and expectations reposed in the Crown.

To avoid the issue, Mr Drysdale left the position *vacant* rather than be forced to appoint someone he had set his mind against. The Secretariat took no further action, and the fox was free to roam.

The Commissioner's influence over the Executive Council of the government was inappropriate and unacceptable. Whether the influence played a role or whether the Council lacked the powers to deal with errant heads of departments.

26

Further Attempts to Expel

Mr Watson never questioned or doubted his belief in Ram's abilities: Ram had a promising future in the Inland Revenue Department. However, due to his experiences during Mr Drysdale's tenure as Commissioner, Ram came to doubt Drysdale's suitability to head an important department. From Ram's documents, there was fair evidence of Drysdale's instability and unsuitability: his attempts to buy shares in a fellow officer's real estate project, lending money to a taxpayer, Mr Fong, and having his nominees rejected by the Secretariat were serious issues.

Examination Anomaly

The ideals of democracy and the rule of law held little value for the autocratic colonial institutions. The oversight and regulations had been practically undermined to serve their narrow purposes of convenience and inconsequential objectives.

Rules and regulations had serious purposes, including the orderly prosecution of official business and the seamless execution of mandates, which was the public perception. The reality was anything but that. For example, the question of examinations had now become a discretionary issue: the Commissioner excused some officers who were promoted without insisting on examinations; these individuals were all advanced to higher grades *without* following the General Orders. For example, one such appointment was that of Mr Mayze, Ram's junior, confirmed without exams and officially listed on page 263 of the *Fiji Royal Gazette*, no. 47, dated 4 September 1953.

Ram was also aware of the work of the Committee on Promotions, who were widely expected to widen the scope of exemptions. He expected perhaps that the Commissioners would examine the findings before finalising and determining the charges now against him for disobeying orders to appear for exams. When Ram objected to exams as a precondition for promotion, he was accused of insubordination and threatened with dismissal by Mr Philbrick, the Assistant Commissioner. He argued that he was within his moral and legal rights not to comply, citing precedents. With reference to the General Orders, the penalty prescribed for non-appearance at an examination was an "incremental penalty". Threats of dismissal were not among them or in the Colonial Regulations, but that did not matter to Mr Philbrick – he continued to intimidate.

It was general knowledge in official circles that the committee would remove exams as a promotion requirement. In his petition to the Governor, Ram wrote:

> That the question of examination was to be left over in abeyance until after the Report of the Promotions Committee was out. Mr Drysdale further stated that he anticipated that the Committee may do away with the question of examination altogether. He [the Commissioner] asked your humble petitioner not to do anything in the matter until the report of such Committee was published, and if then, the examinations were still applicable, he suggested applying for exemption on the grounds that no examinations were required in view of the Secretariat's letter of 24th December 1947. It is most regrettable that Mr Drysdale, on the one hand, assured your humble petitioner that no action would be taken in the matter of examinations, pending the result of the Promotions Committee, and on the other hand, whilst he was away on leave and the Report of such Committee was still being considered, Mr A. S. Philbrick, the Acting Commissioner of Inland Revenue, took advantage of his official position, power and authority and wilfully forced the issue. This was an act designed to misleading one for the purposes of trapping him.[1]

---

[1] Petition to the Governor, Sir Ronald Garvey, 11 May 1956, p. 7.

Further Attempts to Expel

Mr Drysdale had given assurances after the Secretariat unilaterally changed Ram's contract of employment without giving reasons.

> "Mr Drysdale...suggested to apply for exemption on the grounds that no examinations were required in view of the Secretariat's letter dated 24 December 1947."[2]

Mr Philbrick, also an expatriate and in a position of power, whose power and authority went unchallenged by the executive, forced the issue and attempted to bring it to a defining moment that would mean Ram had to accept the illegal order, resign, or be dismissed.

Ram decided to call Mr Philbrick's bluff; he declined the invitation to sit for the examination and waited. The anticipated threat of dismissal did not materialise, but the failure was not a victory for Ram. It was just another aspect of the department's culture. Additionally, Mr Philbrick could not ignore Ram's professional capabilities and his official duties as a competent officer.

Judging from the glowing reports of all the Commissioners, past and present, his work was exemplary. It was a moot point why only Ram, a non-white officer, should be tested to assess his capability and competence for the work. Mr Philbrick had to accept Ram's performance at his desk; he had no adverse comments in that regard. Neither did Ram's other colleagues ever have cause to complain about how he discharged his duties.

"Efficiently Discharged His duties"

Ram's concerns about his colleagues' continuing harassment and their preoccupation with exams were beginning to weigh on him, and he had considered leaving the service. However, as an eternal optimist, he always looked to the future; he hoped for better days, when his colleagues would reflect on their actions and activities, considering their possible causes and

---

[2] Petition, 11 May 1956. p. 7

consequences, and come to a just accommodation with their consciences.

He had no doubts about his abilities, only about his colleagues' temperament and mindset.

On good days, and there were many of them, the department performed as a single friendly unit with little evidence of the undercurrent that may have flowed through its veins and sinews. He could not square the circle because he found that promotions came, despite all the futile exercises of his superiors to undermine him. He was promoted *despite* his continued refusal to comply and their persistence in ordering him to comply.

The undeniable facts were there. Frustratingly for Drysdale and Philbrick, he was not a candidate they could dismiss without some very serious blunders.

The following Certificate of Increment was prepared by Mr Philbrick himself on behalf of the Commissioner of Inland Revenue. It certified that –

> Ram Charitra, holding the post of Assessor, has discharged his duties with efficiency, diligence, and fidelity. *There have been no* adverse entries in the Efficiency Record Book against this Officer.
>
> Mr Ram Charitra, whose salary is at the rate of £750 by £30 to £840 x 4 – £4000 at present, draws £810 a year and is due for an increment of £30 with effect from 24.4.1954.
>
> Dated: 12 April 1954 [3]

Unwarranted Removal of Designatory Letters

The contrast between the Assistant Commissioner Philbrick's complimentary words and his actions were stark. One might be forgiven for thinking that Mr Philbrick had important matters to attend to. Inventive and not short of original

---

[3] Emphasis added.

Further Attempts to Expel

stratagems, Mr Philbrick's behaviour continued undeterred and unhindered as before.

His next project: Ram's designatory letters. He next questioned whether the designatory letters awarded to Ram were from a recognised institution. It would have been more appropriate to direct that question to the former Assistant Commissioner and the Secretariat, which stocked and supplied forms to its appointees from institutions recognised by the department and senior officers. Others who were holders of similar designations were not in Mr Philbrick's sights.

Mr Philbrick's line of enquiry begged this question: what prompted him to re-examine an issue without cause, many years after the designation was awarded with the blessings of the senior officers? This new investigation was as unnecessary as it was pointless. It was nothing more than a display of power by a shallow-minded officer.

Ram records in a letter dated 10 January 1950, that Mr Philbrick asked whether the Society of Commercial Accountants was a recognised body. Ram replied in the affirmative and reminded him that his predecessor, Mr Watson, had initiated the process of application to that particular institute.[4]

Information on professional bodies was available from the Secretariat. The organisation of particular interest was based in Britain, and after a discussion with Mr R. B. Ackland, the previous Commissioner, Ram began the registration process. The questions now being asked by Mr Philbrick, eight years after the event, seemed irrelevant and unwarranted. In effect, was he questioning the probity of his predecessors and the Secretariat?

Upon enquiry, none of Ram's fellow officers who possessed the diploma were approached by the Acting Commissioner with similar demands. Ram was not in breach of the institute's regulations, nor did he breach departmental rules for such registrations. The request to view the syllabus was impulsive, vindictive, and mischievous.

---

[4] Petition to the Governor, Sir Ronald Garvey, 14 May 1956, p. 15.

Ram suggested that the Assistant Commissioner's request would be valid and relevant only if Ram were a senior assessor and/or on a salary of £1,450, in which case answering such a request would be mandatory. He had reached neither milestone.

What transpired between Mr Philbrick and the Colonial Secretary will remain a mystery, but he seemed to have induced the Secretariat to withdraw Ram's designatory letters from all official publications without further discussions or reference to Ram. Once again, this was reminiscent of the earlier unilateral withdrawal of the original contract. Colonial administration at work in the Fiji Islands.

By its Circular (No. 40 of 1955), dated 12 October 1955, the Secretariat initiated the move that executed Mr Philbrick's orders and omitted the designatory letters, F.Comm.A., after Ram's name from the *Fiji Royal Gazette*.

With no recourse to an impartial adjudicator, Ram sought legal advice and instructed Messrs A. D. Patel & Co. to object to the unwarranted removal of these letters to which he was legally entitled. The Assistant Commissioner produced no evidence to justify the withdrawal of recognition. No breach of the institute's rules was reported, nor were there any infringements of the General Orders or of Colonial Regulations in connection with his responsibilities.

Ram's lawyers wrote to the Colonial Secretary:

[It] appears that on or about 19th August 1955, the Acting Commissioner of Inland Revenue, Mr Philbrick, suggested and recommended to you that the designation of F.Comm.A. be removed from our client's name in the Civil List to be published for 1956.

Following the suggestion and recommendation of Mr Philbrick, you have taken out the designation after our client's name in the Civil List of 1956, in spite of the protest made by our client in writing and addressed to the Acting Commissioner of Inland Revenue dated 18th October 1955,

Further Attempts to Expel

and the contents whereof must have been passed on to you by the Acting Commissioner in the execution of his duties.

It is further significant that while our client's designation of F.Comm.A. is removed from the Civil List of 1956, the same designation of another Civil Servant has been retained in the same list. This savours not only of discrimination but also amounts to defamation of our client, as it gives a strong impression to those who read the list that our client must have been removed from the Roll of the Society of Commercial Accountants of England due to some professional misconduct on his part.

No doubt that by now, the Government have sufficient reason to realise that Mr Philbrick right throughout acted maliciously against our client to do him every possible harm and went to the length of making a false accusation against our client, which led to the appointment of Commission of Inquiry and the subsequent withdrawal of proceedings by the learned Attorney-General against our client. Our client also feels aggrieved that Mr Drysdale did not acquaint you of the true position before the Commission of Inquiry was appointed as was his duty and delayed the matter until he was actually called to give evidence before the Commission, and thereby putting our client to considerable worry, expense, humiliation, and degradation from his post.

It appears to us that Mr Philbrick's action in the matter amounts to a criminal act as well as a civil wrong, and Mr Drysdale's conduct in the matter at least amounts to a tort.
Before taking any further action in the matter, we would be grateful to know what amounts, if any, the Government is prepared to make to our client and what steps, if any, they propose to take against the officers concerned.

> We have the honour to be,
> Sir,
> Your Obedient Servants,
> A. D. Patel & Co.

Perspectives of British Colonial Rule in the Fiji Islands

The Commissioner was unmoved. His membership of the institute was not affected. Aided and abetted by others and flushed with success, Mr Philbrick continued to plague Ram.

The removal of designatory letters was an unjustified and gratuitous action that only massaged the ego of one spiteful officer. That Mr Philbrick could take such action without the intervention of an adjudication committee pleased him, as it was one rare success he could claim. The Governor also remained silent, thus condoning the action.

Probationary Period.

We have seen the machinations of senior officers. The extent to which they interfered in the promotion process meant that Ram was never confirmed as a permanent member of the civil service. He was on probation throughout his tenure and remained on probation until he retired.

It is not easy to comprehend the contradictions. Whereas, on the one hand, he received glowing reports and was promoted, on the other, he was deliberately and continually hindered from advancing to achieve permanent status as a civil servant.

He petitioned the Governor, Sir Ronald Garvey, to set aside the probationary period and to confirm his appointment as a civil servant in terms of the Secretariat's letter of 24 December 1947. He further requested that the unilaterally changed terms be set aside [5]

He goes on to say that -

---

[5] Petition, 14 May 1956. p. 1: (b) the Secretariat's letter of 17th April 1948 [containing the unilateral change of his employment terms] be set aside as null and void and of no effect on the grounds that terms thereof were not consistent with those contained in the offer made for appointment in the first instance as otherwise one's career can very seriously be jeopardised, if a change in an offer, can subsequently be permissible in law.

Further Attempts to Expel

it appears that for some reason no consideration has so far been given to the facts and substance contained in the said petition dated 14th December 1955 nor any steps taken for setting up an investigating commission as was requested in the said petition.[6]

Ram retraced the communications from the Secretariat and reiterated in his submission of 14 May 1956 that the employment was to be purely temporary in the first instance, until such time as the 1948 estimates were to be approved by the Secretary of State for the Colonies. In the submission, he states:[7]

Upon approval of the 1948 Estimates by the Secretary of State for the Colonies, your humble petitioner's appointment was to be made permanent unconditionally and without the addition subsequently of further terms or conditions of whatsoever nature or kind.

He reminded the Governor, in paragraph (f) of the petition, that

... everything hinges on the validity of the letter dated the 24th of December 1947 ... At this stage, the following issues arise for consideration: what was the Secretariat's real object in writing this letter? If the object was to offer an appointment, then what were the terms and conditions and whether any of the terms so offered require specifically your humble petitioner to sit for an examination? Whether this letter is valid and, after its acceptance by your humble petitioner, binds the Government as to its contents and whether its breach is permissible by law, whether this letter stipulates the sitting for any examination, if not, how can one or, for that matter, the Acting Commissioner of Inland Revenue read into it a "requirement" that is not there?
What is the legal presumption in law in the absence of a specific provision in a written contract? Certainly, what is not

---

[6] Petition, 14 May 1956. p. 1. Para 3.

[7] Petition, 14 May 1956. pp. 3 & 4 paragraph(d) (iii)

Perspectives of British Colonial Rule in the Fiji Islands

> provided for in writing in the offer and acceptance thereof, nothing further can be subsequently incorporated therein.
> In view of the foregoing submission, there is no question of any examination, and consequently no question of insubordination arises, and there the charges brought by the Acting Commissioner of Inland Revenue should be set aside and regarded as groundless, and if there is any doubt in the matter, it should be in favour of your humble petitioner . . .
>
> This is the legal presumption on which legal authorities can be produced . . . There is no room for any intendment, and if there were any, it would have been incorporated in the said letter precisely on the same lines as other terms and conditions inserted therein.
>
> (g) Notwithstanding anything to the contrary, your humble petitioner accepted the Government's appointment by letter dated the 12th January 1948 relying in good faith on terms and conditions offered to him by the Secretariat's letter dated 24th December 1947, not knowing whether any further conditions were to follow.[8]

The points raised were valid. It was also stated by the Secretary of State for the Colonies in London that Ram's appointment was to be made permanent *unconditionally... on approval of the 1948 Estimates;* that was eight years ago.

The Governor, again, took no notice of the Secretary of State's direction, nor did he intervene to rectify the situation. That "justice" is blind took on a whole new meaning in colonial Fiji.

The British Governor did not inconvenience himself or interrupt his routine by replying to a series of apparent wrongs imposed on his civil servant. The many petitions to the font of justice and fair play received no response, and the bullying continued unabated.

According to the General Orders, the initial probationary period was set at *three* years, which, in Ram's case, expired on 28 February 1951, when his position was to be made permanent.

---

[8] Petition, 14 May 1956. p. 4.

Further Attempts to Expel

However, the continued obstruction to regularising his position as a civil servant can justifiably be laid at the feet of the Governors. The proverbial buck did not stop with them. The Secretary of State and the Colonial Office were out of sight and regarded as irrelevant and extraneous to Fiji's administrative needs. Having considered all aspects of this local civil servant's expertise, abilities, and experience, if his racial orientation were not black, the post of Senior Assessor and indeed that of the Commissioner would have been his for the asking.

Courtesy Title "Mr" Removed

So far, we have seen that Ram was not promoted despite recommendations from the Secretariat; his salary was not paid for work done during his period as an acting senior assessor; designatory letters were removed from official publications; and his probationary period was not applied according to stated rules. Now, let us see how low the expatriate civil servants could reach.

It has to be said that while the governors never responded adequately, if at all, the government machinery, such as the disciplinary committees and the commissions of enquiry to which Ram was subjected, always found in his favour. Allegations brought against him, time and again, proved fruitless, as they appeared to be a concoction conceived out of prejudice or caprice, or both. It was becoming increasingly challenging to expel him because there were no grounds on which the spurious allegations were based. The alternative was to frustrate and *provoke* him into making a self-destructive error.

Ram's steadfast, unfaltering, and unflappable disposition frustrated his antagonists, who could not engineer his dismissal from the department, however hard they tried. Consequently, Mr Philbrick became preoccupied with irrelevance, triviality, and spitefulness. He appeared to have had a free pass to misuse his publicly funded time and position.

The extent of the pettiness cannot be imagined or exaggerated until one learns that, on 7 September 1955, Ram wrote a letter to the Acting Commissioner of Inland Revenue to protest about a small matter that had irritated him, which he later included in his petition to the Governor:

Perspectives of British Colonial Rule in the Fiji Islands

Sir,
I feel you will appreciate my bringing the following small matter to your official notice. You will note on the attached Circular that whilst each and every other officer whose name was shown on the list for distribution of the monthly statistics for August has a prefix of "Mr". I am referred to as "Ram Charitra". I would appreciate it if, in future, "Mr" could be placed before my name on a similar list. Of course, if you desire to drop the use of "Mr", would you please do so in all cases as these savours of discrimination.[9]

Income Tax Assessed incorrectly... by the Commissioner!

As required, Ram completed his tax return, disclosed his personal and rental income as a taxpayer, and handed the documents to the *Assistant Commissioner*, Mr Philbrick, for assessment.

Mr Philbrick was in a good mood, gloating because of his rare "victory" with regard to the courtesy title. Nevertheless, he was still on his warpath; he now decided to concoct a plan that might hurt Ram's pocket. He saw an opportunity to take liberties with Ram's income tax return.

Mr Philbrick assessed the tax return in a way that reduced Ram's allowances because, as he remarked to Ram, "You can afford to pay it!" He was not joking. At last, for Ram, Philbrick lost all credibility as an objective and neutral civil servant, whose purpose is to assess tax liability regardless of the financial or social status of taxpayers.

Ram's reaction was typical. In his petition, he records his conversation with the Deputy Commissioner:

> (c) In April 1955 you [Mr Philbrick] pointed out to me to a return of income and remarked what a mighty income that taxpayer had derived. After a discussion, you stated I was

---

[9] Petition, 14 May 1956, p. 11.

Further Attempts to Expel

wasting my time in this department. You suggested that I leave Government employment as I would earn much more. Again, in June 1955, when we were working in the Residential Tax Building, you passed similar remarks on two occasions, hinting to me to leave the service as I was well off and able to earn much more outside.

(d) In July 1955, soon after Mr Drysdale left the Colony on leave to the UK, you raised the tax assessment on my 1954 income without reference to me, and when doing so, you made no approach on me for any discussion whatever as you had previously suggested. You assessed my 1954 income without allowing any initial depreciation on the Carnarvon Building. Later, when I took recourse to law and made an objection against the assessment on legal grounds, you issued an amended assessment but still maintained the disallowance of the initial depreciation to a greater degree in respect of which the matter is now being taken to Court of Review.[10]

Ram stated on 5 September 1955 that his taxes (Ref. 31845B/C301), dated 8 July 1955, were incorrectly assessed. He presented his version and explained his objections in an appeal through his solicitors, Messrs Ellis, Munro, Warren & Leys. The tax assessment on his income from the Carnarvon Building, which was completed at a cost of £12,636.10.1, was incorrect -

> "I claim that the said Carnarvon Building was a building used for commercial purposes and that I am therefore entitled to a deduction of an initial allowance of 10% for depreciation in addition to annual depreciation aforesaid and that my total 1954 income for purposes of assessment of tax should accordingly be reduced to the sum of £1185.5.8".[11]

---

[10]Petition, 14 May 1956. p. 13

[11]Ram's objections to the Assessment dated 8.7.1955. No. 31845B/C301 in his submission dated 5.9.1955. Assessment issued by Mr Philbrick, the Acting Commissioner of Inland Revenue.

Mr Philbrick responded on 8 October 1955 and accepted, in part, Ram's submission. He issued an amended assessment but rejected the more significant issue of the ten per cent initial depreciation.

Ram claimed that the depreciation applied to the entire building, not just to a part of it. Mr Philbrick's assessment applied depreciation only to that part of the "building, which was used for Commercial purposes, i.e., the two shops".[12]

According to Ram, there were precedents where depreciation was allowed on the building as a single unit, rather than splitting it into parts to designate some for commercial use and others for private use.

The Assistant Commissioner and Ram were familiar with the issues; both knew the correct position, but Mr Philbrick insisted that any adjudicator would accept his version because he was the senior officer. He continued -

> (e) On 9.7.55, I received from you the tax assessment on 1954 income. A few days later, when I requested an extension of time until 30.9.55, you appeared, in some degree, to be unwilling to grant such an extension of time, although you granted similar or greater facilities to outside taxpayers. When I told you that Mr Drysdale (*the Commissioner*) had already kindly consented to the due date for payment of tax being September and pointed out to his note made in his handwriting on my 1954 tax return, you ultimately granted me the required extension accordingly. Thereupon when I asked you whether you were prepared to reconsider the question of disallowance of initial depreciation claimed on Carnarvon Building, you said the assessment was rightly issued "*and I could well afford to pay it without recourse to any hardship*".[13]

---

[12] Mr Philbrick's contention that the 10% depreciation should be allowed on account of just the two shops fronting the street, not to the entire building which was Ram's contention. Ref. 301. Office of the Commissioner, 8.10.1955.

[13] Petition, 14 May 1956, p. 13. emphasis added.

Further Attempts to Expel

The duty of an income tax officer is to calculate taxes based on the information lodged in the tax returns, without concerning himself with their affordability: strict objectivity is the order of the day. However, in a colonial environment, the rule of law was often an option, and it was applied as the expatriate officer deemed appropriate; in the case of a non-European taxpayer, this consideration did not arise.

On 4 November 1955, Ram's solicitors submitted that the appellant claimed that the Carnarvon Building was one used for commercial purposes, and that he was therefore entitled to a deduction of an initial allowance of ten per cent for depreciation on the cost of the whole building, as well as to the annual depreciation aforesaid. In addition, the tax on his 1954 income should have been assessed on the following basis:

Chargeable income as assessed under Awarded Assessment	£1514. 2.4
Deduct difference between	£1369.10.1
Depreciation claimed as above and	£ 286. 0.1
(£158 + £128) allowed under Assessment.	
Assessment and Amended Assessment	£1110.10.1
Chargeable income	£ 403.12.3

The Appeal

The appeal was heard on 26 April 1956 by Magistrate Mr E. Light at the Court of Review. Ram's appeal was successful. The magistrate concurred with Ram's conclusions based on precedents that the "building" was one whole unit and not split into "commercial" and "private" structures -

> In the present case, there are no words of doubtful construction, nor can it be said that there is anything in the Ordinance indicating the apportionment in such a case was complicated by the legislature. There is nothing to harmonise. In my opinion, until such time as there is a special provision for apportionment in such a case, the Commissioner has no power to apportion ... On the fact there can be no doubt that the Carnarvon Building is a building used for commercial purposes, although it is not "wholly" or "solely" used for such

> purposes. In my opinion, neither the Commissioner nor this Court can add these words. That would be in perversion and straining of the language.
>
> Accordingly, the appeal is allowed[14].

Ram noted in his petition to Sir Ronald that

> It obviously follows that Mr Philbrick was prejudiced towards your humble petitioner in discharging his official duties in that he took a mean advantage in issuing the tax assessment in direct conflict with the ruling policy of the department by not treating your humble petitioner on the same lines as other taxpayers and thus your humble petitioner was indirectly persecuted.[15]

According to Ram, Mr Philbrick was familiar with the cases quoted. He had hoped that by discussing the matter with him frankly and discussing the precedents, without prejudice to the case, they could avoid a judicial review. But Mr Philbrick was adamant and would not budge, apart from the minor concession he had made earlier. The Assistant Commissioner did not accept defeat gracefully; the verdict only intensified Mr Philbrick's dislike for Ram because he had lost against a "local chap". Ram did not gloat but considered it a sad indictment of a system that permitted such persons the freedom to range free in an important environment with gross racist tendencies.

Philbrick served no useful purpose in the colony other than to indulge in personality clashes and his unconstrained hatred of a colleague.

---

[14] The Appeal: The question is whether the appellant is entitled to the full initial allowance of 10% depreciation on a building used for commercial purposes. Appeal Allowed. Magistrate, Mr E. Light. 22. 2.1956.

[15] Petition, 14 May 1956. p. 14

27

Disciplinary Action and Commission of Inquiry

The Commission of Inquiry eventually got under way on 10 a.m. on 12 May 1956. The governor approved the following officers to serve on the Committee: Mr G.P. Sunders, Senior Magistrate (Chairman), Mr W.P. Ragg, Deputy Accountant-General, Mr N.G. Price, Personnel Officer, Public Works Department. The committee met in Puisne Judge's Chambers.[1]

The following letter from Ram's solicitors, Messrs A.D. Patel & Co., to the Commissioner, Mr Drysdale, throws some light on the case -

> Dear Sir,
>
> While we appreciate the evidence you gave before the Commission of Enquiry, our client Mr Ram Charitra feels aggrieved that had you informed the Honourable the Colonial Secretary of the true position in time, instead of keeping it to yourself until you were called as witness before the Commission of Enquiry by the learned Attorney General, out client would not have been put to all the expense, worry, humiliation and degradation of having to face a commission of enquiry.
>
> No doubt you will agree that as a head of a department, it was your duty to inform the Hon. The Colonial Secretary and His Excellency the Governor of the true position in time to save all subsequent trouble.

---

[1] Letter from the Secretariat. Ref. XP.2706 of 28. 6.1956.

Our client wishes to take proceedings against you, but we are of the opinion that if this matter could be amicably settled out of Court in view of the past good relations between you and our client, it would be in the best interest of both parties concerned.

We shall be glad to know which course you would prefer.

Yours faithfully. [2]
A.D. Patel & Co.

There is no record of the outcome.

Mr Philbrick's Final Mission

Ram was well aware of Mr Philbrick's keen eye on every assessment and deliberation he made regarding taxpayers' concerns.

Philbrick set out to achieve his final objective of removing Ram from his department altogether in one fell swoop. Dealing with Ram had become his mission; if it were to be left to him to remove a person of colour from the department, so be it. To Philbrick, this was a project worth the time and energy expended: it was something purposeful in his life! He still had arrows left in his armoury and did not hesitate to reach for the next one.

Mr Philbrick again brought up the old chestnut of examination. Ram again refused to sit the exam; he was threatened with disciplinary action for *insubordination*. Ram insisted, as he had done during Mr Drysdale's attempts to make him take the examination, that he was not contractually obliged to sit for it or any other. He quoted the original agreement issued by the Secretariat, dated 24 December 1947, in which no such obligation was imposed in terms of employment; he was able to begin his employment on 1 March 1948.

Disciplinary action against an officer can never be taken lightly. The parties concerned saw this as a grave turn of events

---

[2] Letter dated 4 December 1956 from A.D. Patel & Co.

because insubordination cases were rare in the colonial civil service. Ram's friends had heard of his problems and visited to offer support: they understood the bigotry and underhanded devices to which he'd been subjected. They also knew of another man in their community, Mr Ram Dhani, who was similarly persecuted. Mr Dhani was a headteacher; he was discriminated against just for being a good teacher and an efficient administrator. His students went on to secondary schools, and some progressed to tertiary institutions. Other talented people throughout the empire had experiences very like Ram's and Mr Dhani's.

Causes of the Threats

Following Ram's refusal, on 10 November 1955, to sit an exam, the Secretariat, on the advice of Mr Drysdale and Mr Philbrick, set in motion procedures, on 3 December 1955, to take disciplinary action against him.

Philbrick and Drysdale would have preferred to find an obvious way to dismiss Ram instantly. But immediate dismissal, though ideal, required evidence of serious misconduct and incompetence. They had nothing in their armoury to justify such an action. They had already lost the depreciation case in the magistrate's court and could not risk another loss. But the pressure had to be maintained because perhaps, just perhaps, Ram might unwittingly fall into a trap. So, they sought to keep Ram perpetually distracted with exams. They had to milk it for all it was worth. It was their only possible solution to a problem that had festered in their irrational minds; as a result, Ram would also have to contend with severe threats to his pension benefits.

He had successfully appealed to the Magistrates and won. But he had nothing else to fall back on to get relief from his detractors, who seemed to be pursuing a vendetta against him. He begged for justice in his appeals to the Governor for a "determination of the facts and substance", but no one was listening. Despite the continuing shenanigans in the department and the administration, he never lost faith in the ideal of fair play he believed to be at the heart of the British justice system.

Perspectives of British Colonial Rule in the Fiji Islands

Whether he was justified in disputing the request to fulfil something not in the agreement he had originally signed was a legal question. The second contract, issued by the Secretariat at the advice of an unidentified officer, contravened the original agreement. Drysdale and Philbrick knew that the later version, which contained unilaterally altered terms, would be of no use in a court of law, but Ram's resignation would, de facto, achieve their purposes.

If it were only a question of appearing for an examination, set and marked by independent professional tax experts, Ram would have had no reservations or hesitations in accepting the challenge. But Messrs Drysdale's and Philbrick's tendency to meddle and prevent a fair outcome did not imbue Ram with confidence. He confessed his fears to Mr Richardson, a colleague and confidante, that he was uneasy at the prospect of his papers being marked by the antagonists who had been consistent in their efforts to harm his prospects. Mr Richardson suggested he give it a go to see what happened. So, Ram voluntarily appeared for the initial exam and passed. His fears and doubts about it all began to fade, and he agreed to appear at the next, confident that he could pass anything they threw at him. However, the outcome of that trial was disappointing.

During the postmortem after the exam, he sat with his office colleagues, including Mr Richardson, and discussed the questions and the answers. All agreed, without exception, that Ram had answered correctly, and they conservatively calculated that he would pass with a *minimum* of seventy per cent; the pass mark was sixty per cent.

Ram's examination results were declared at 47%. The other two candidates gained 91% and 87%. Not only Ram, but also the entire department, was shocked and disappointed by the deliberate manipulation of results. Could this really happen in a British colonial administration? Some of Ram's colleagues had claimed that one officer, in particular, had "little hope of getting 31%" after they had conducted a postmortem together, similar to Ram's, but he was awarded 87%! Despite the visible surprise among Ram's colleagues, Drysdale and Philbrick offered Ram

Disciplinary Action and Commission of Inquiry

their commiserations and said, "Better luck next time," their tongues lodged firmly in their cheeks.

Everyone understood that the Commissioner and his assistant had perpetrated an injustice. Ram asked for a review, which was immediately and emphatically denied as if they had expected he would make such a request.

Ram had given it a go, following encouragement from his colleagues, but his fears had been justified. He noted in his petition to the governor that his expatriate colleagues were not required to take exams but were promoted. For example, both Mr Wheatley and Mr Mayze were promoted without the word "examination" crossing the lips of the Commissioner or the Assistant Commissioner.

In his petition to the Governor, he expressed his doubts about the integrity of the examination "O" results held on 3 June 1955. He directly accused the Acting Commissioner, saying that he had been "purposely failed by the markers, one of whom was the Acting Commissioner of Inland Revenue [Mr Philbrick]".[3]

Ram implored the Governor to have the papers checked and verified by an

> (h) outside independent and qualified persons duly conversant with the Income Tax Law and practice . . . Soon after the examination was over, on the same day, your petitioner discussed the questions and answers with two other colleagues, who also sat for the same examination on the same day, and the answers they said they had put in the papers, in respect of two or three questions, were quite incorrect, as they were instantly verified with Mr D. J. Barnes when the subject matter of those questions and answers were referred to him for decision. The next day when your humble petitioner had an interview with Mr Drysdale, your humble petitioner purposely asked him whether those particular questions were correctly answered by the others. Mr Drysdale's answer was in the affirmative. Mr Drysdale had not realised at that time that

---

[3] Petition to the Governor, Sir Ronald Garvey, 14 May 1956, p. 5.

those questions and answers were already referred to Mr Barnes by all the parties for his decision. For this reason, the papers of examination "O" held on 3rd June 1955 of all candidates should be rechecked.[4]

According to General Orders 437, on the failure of an examination, the Acting Commissioner should impose an "incremental penalty", which the Commissioner, inexplicably, did not do. Instead, he pressured Ram to sit further tests, which he would no doubt again manipulate.

Regulations did not specify the need for a resit. It was not in the Commissioner's or anyone else's gift to institute any other "penalty" or give other instructions.

> (j) The aim and object he was attempting to achieve was apparently something else . . . It was for the Acting Commissioner to take action for my failing to pass an examination. It is therefore submitted that the charges laid down against you humble petitioner for misconduct and insubordination are unjustified and incorrect.[5]

Exams had their ramifications. Promotions required examinations; Ram had to comply with the Commissioner's orders to sit and pass the required exam to confirm his permanent employment.

It was not the *examination* that concerned Ram but the dishonesty and treachery. Ram's experiences in his appeals to the colony's governor confirmed this state of affairs. What was exposed to the light of day, during this period, was the fact that a non-European had no place in the upper levels of the department's hierarchy.

The numerous petty attempts to denigrate his status, by removing his courtesy title and the designatory letters after his name, meant that there was little value in the relationship and that they could devise or invent little else to achieve their objective. The impact of the obstructions for the last several years had its

---

[4] Petition, 14 May 1956. p. 5
[5] Petition, 14 May 1956. p. 6

Disciplinary Action and Commission of Inquiry

corollaries. Clutching at straws, Mr Drysdale and Mr Philbrick were now on a psychological war path to force him into submitting to their demands:

> (k) On the 10th November 1955, the Acting Commissioner of Inland Revenue wrote a threatening letter to your humble petitioner, intimidating him with the various intended actions – paragraph 4 states: *"You are to be informed that you are still on probation after 7½ years' service and that action to regularise your position must be taken forthwith. You are to be informed that if you do not qualify yourself for confirmation in your appointment by passing the requisite examinations at the next opportunity, consideration will have to be given to the termination of your probationary period."* [emphasis added] It is respectfully submitted that usually, one is not expected to be intimidated by the written threat of dismissal or termination of appointment should one fail to pass an examination. In view of the threat in this letter and as your humble petitioner had already once sat, without prejudice to his rights under a letter dated the 24th December 1947 and, as in case of failure, ordered to sit again, was an incorrect procedure on the part of the Acting Commissioner, your humble petitioner never had any further faith in the integrity of the Acting Commissioner.[6]

Ram was as adamant as his adversaries were to insist that he follow their terms. In addition, precedent *was* established in the appointment of Mr Mayze. The Secretariat's approval confirmed and legitimised the arrangement. That this was inconsistent with current rules mattered little.

In his petition to the Governor, Ram pleaded

(a) that his probationary period be set aside and that his appointment be confirmed on a permanent basis in terms of the Secretariat's letter dated 24 December 1947, *without recourse to any other terms and conditions not being already specified therein*, [emphasis added] and

---

[6] Petition, 14 May 1956, p. 6

(b) [that the] Secretariat's letter dated 17th April 1948 be set aside as null and void and of no effect on the grounds that the terms thereof were not consistent with those contained in the offer made for appointment in the first instance as, otherwise, one's career could very seriously be jeopardised, if the change in an offer were subsequently permissible in law.[7]

The governor remained stubbornly mute despite the overwhelming evidence of injustice. No governor to date had shown any cause for concern or made enquiries into the repeated cases of harassment, even out of curiosity as to what his civil servants were up to – if anything.

Insubordination charge

Ram was now formally accused of gross insubordination. In his petition, Ram wrote that the reason for this accusation was that having been ordered on the 10th of November 1955 and again on the 3rd of December 1955 by the Acting Commissioner of Inland Revenue to sit for examination "O" . . . he refused to sit and did not in fact sit for that examination.

> "That on 2nd December 1955, your humble petitioner committed an act of gross misconduct in that he alleged to the Acting Commissioner, as justification for his refusal to sit examination "O" that by virtue of a document in his possession, he was not required to sit for civil service examination which claim was not genuine and not made in good faith.[8]

The document in Ram's possession was the letter containing the original terms and offer of Inspector of Taxes position with effect from 1st March 1948.

As with his previous petitions to the Governor, dated 25 January 1955 and 11 May 1956, his current efforts had no effect,

---

[7] Petition, 14 May 1956, p. 1.
[8] Petition, 14 May 1956, p. 2.

Disciplinary Action and Commission of Inquiry

and he was charged with gross insubordination. He had clearly stated his reasons for disobeying, but that did not impress the Commissioner, who was determined to have another go at dismissing him from the civil service.

The Disciplinary Committee was established and chaired by Mr W. P. Ragg. Both sides were legally represented. However, the Attorney-General responsible for pursuing the action was unable to produce evidence to justify the action. He withdrew the dismissal action, along with the accusation of insubordination against Ram.

Again, there was no victory for Mr Drysdale and Mr Philbrick, but the exercise wasted much of the government's time and resources. Their motives were never revealed, as much of their effort was simply wasted in their unachievable attempts to destroy an officer whom they had selected for a vacancy they were unable to fill with a suitable candidate from abroad.

28

The Accountant-General's Department

The late Mr Ram "Monkey" Narayan, formerly of the Treasury Department, retired and lived in London. When he visited me at my residence in Mill Hill, London, in the 1990s, he spoke of Ram Charitra's principled stand against his wayward colleagues. These are my recollections as noted at the time -

"…your dad had an analytical approach to his work and his technical skills were unmatched in the department. They feared his rise to important post that could reveal their past failures. That's my view, who knows what motivated their hostilities towards him. They would have expelled him in an instant if they found fault. He served at a high level – Senior Assessor! so they were confident in his abilities – they had to keep him out, somehow, but under tight control…"

The respect that Ram's expatriate colleagues (excluding his superiors) had for him was muted. It was not the done thing in mixed societies to be in awe of a person of colour. Mr Narayan cited one exception: Mr Richardson, who spoke up during their general conversations, said, "They just want him out of the way."

The culture of departmental malpractice and corruption had to change. The Governor and the Secretariat were complicit and continued to let the departmental heads rule the roost. Nonetheless, the Secretariat did exercise its powers on occasion, such as in the cases of Mr Lewis and Mr Davis, when it stopped the Commissioner from appointing these two officers to positions for which they were inadequately qualified.

During his three-year secondment, beginning on 27 August 1956, to the Treasury department, Ram established a reputation as an accountant who was fearless and no respecter of shoddy work.

The Accountant-General's Department

Mr Griffiths was the Accountant-General at the time. As was usually the case with other colonial civil service heads of departments, he was surrounded by people of similar sentiments, character, and skills. His ability to oversee his department lacked depth and commitment, and he never brooked any criticism of his junior officers when they were found to be deficient. Hence, the numerous cases of misinterpretations of ordinances led to miscalculations of the pensions of former officers.

While working on the pension files of retired officers or those transferred to other postings in the South Pacific, Ram found errors that he brought to Mr Griffiths' attention. He was surprised that Mr Griffiths was none too happy to be faced with his officers' discrepancies. He had signed them off, not giving a second thought to casting an eye over them before approving them. Ram was told that those files were none of his business, which was untrue; they were, in fact, his responsibility. In addition, the Accountant-General, detached from reality as he was, accused Ram of substandard work!

In April 1958, Ram was assigned to work on the Provident Fund. He and his colleagues encountered a problem involving the clarification of a particular interpretation of an ordinance (Section 11 of Cap. 53). This interpretation of the ordinance had been followed since 1938, when it was passed. The Accountant-General had not troubled to satisfy himself that the calculations matched the will of the legislators. No one possessed the depth of knowledge and understanding to apply the figures as originally intended, resulting in apparent consequences for the retirees, those who contributed to the fund, and, indeed, for the government.

Ram referred the query to the senior accountants, Mr S. M. Waddingham and Mr W. P. Ragg, but both stood by the old decisions and accepted Mr Griffiths' explanations. Ram found their attitude odd; he was confident of *his* version and decided that the only remedy was to refer the matter to the Attorney-General.

The Attorney-General's decision was eventually published, but Ram was not informed. He made several attempts to obtain the report, but Mr Griffiths insisted that the decision had not yet been communicated to him. Ram took him at his word, bided his time, and waited. Due to the nature of its activities, the Attorney-General's department did not usually take that long to deliver a verdict, but Ram was confident about the outcome, so he decided to wait a bit longer.

Eventually, in September 1958, as Ram was reviewing some live files concerning the Widows' and Orphans' Pension Scheme, he came across a file that seemed out of place. It had been hurriedly inserted: it was upside down. Upon examination, Ram discovered that it was the long-awaited reply (No. 95) from the Attorney-General, dated 23 April 1958. Mr Griffiths had been a bit economical with the truth when he told Ram that the file had not come through. The Attorney-General had, in fact, conveyed his decision on interpreting Section 11 of Cap. 53 *five* months before!

When Ram read the file, he discovered that the Accountant-General and his senior colleagues had stubbornly proclaimed that their interpretations were correct. Ram's request for an explanation of how he had arrived at this conclusion was not adequately answered. As the head of an important department, the Accountant-General was incomparably incompetent and clumsy, not to mention devious.

In a petition to the Colonial Secretary for transmission to the Governor, in March 1960, Ram did not mince his words. He stated that the Attorney-General had concurred with his interpretation contained in a submission dated 19 April 1958. The decision was concealed and not communicated to colleagues interested and involved in the matter.

The moral responsibility lay with Mr Griffiths to amend the errors in the files, thereby preventing possible losses to the pension fund's contributors. Ram felt that it was unlikely to happen because Mr Griffiths had disagreed with the AG's conclusions.

> I said that I felt very sad to see that the Attorney-General's decision was not conveyed to me in respect of which I had gone to the extent of preparing a legal submission in my own time. I asked him what the idea was of concealing that decision

from me. Thereupon, Mr Griffiths appeared extremely indignant and said I was wasting his time. I said I was not wasting his time but was instrumental in saving his prestige from future criticism, which might have arisen from a wrong interpretation of Section 11 of Cap. 53. He said he did not entirely agree with the legal interpretation he had received from the Attorney-General and that the matter was still receiving his personal consideration.[1]

It was time for Mr Griffiths to take action to defend his position, and he began with a vicious attack on Ram's work!

Initially, he warned Ram to stay within his remit. Second, he contended that Ram's work did not meet the standards expected of an assistant accountant in his department. Third, the Accountant-General's interpretation of the ordinance in question would stand.

Ram explained in his petition to the Colonial Secretary that his reasons for disagreeing with the Accountant-General's and other accountants' versions were as follows:

> In April 1958, when I was handling some of the Provident Fund duties, my colleagues encountered a problem that required clarification on the interpretation of Section 11 of the Cap. 53. This matter was discussed between me, Accountant "E", and other officers of that section. Although
>
> Accountant "E" and other officers, as aforesaid, agreed with my interpretation of that section of the Ordinance, however, they pointed out that the practice in the Treasury and the ruling given in past by Senior Accountant "B", as well as the Accountant-General himself, was quite different on Section 11 of Cap. 53. On that occasion, I was also informed that the Treasury [had been] pursuing that particular policy ever since the Provident Fund Ordinance was first introduced in 1938. As I was fully confident that the Treasury's existing policy was quite wrong on the point of law, I requested Accountant "E" to discuss this matter with Mr S. M. Waddingham, Senior Accountant "B", as well as with Mr W. P. Ragg, who then, as

---

[1] Petition to the Governor, 21 March 1960, p. 4.

far as I can remember, was acting as Accountant-General, in order to confirm their definite ruling once again on that Section of the Ordinance. After this was done by Accountant "E", he came and informed me that he had discussed the matter with Mr Waddingham and Mr Ragg, and that they both were still of the same opinion and confirmed the exiting policy as being correct. I was then very much surprised and asked Accountant "E" whether he was prepared to forward my legal submission to the legal department and obtain the Attorney-General's ruling in that matter to see who was right and who was wrong. Accountant "E", after discussing the matter with somebody, informed me that my proposed legal submission could be forwarded to the Legal Department provided it went through the proper channel, that is, through the Accountant-General. I agreed to that, and, in a couple of days, I handed in my legal submission which reads as follows:

"Sir,

"A case has been brought to my notice wherein a contributor, upon resignation, requested that the Accountant-General, by a letter authorising him [to do so], pay the refund of his contribution into the bank account of another person (hereinafter called 'B'). For some reason, the contributor was unable to call at this office himself personally to collect the refund of the contributions which is due and payable to him. For some unknown reason, the contributor also desired and directed the Accountant-General to pay such a refund of the contribution into the bank account of another person. 'B' took no part either directly or indirectly in the matter. Section 11 of Cap. 53 imposes certain restrictions on assignments and attachments of accumulated contributions whilst in the hands of the Accountant-General. The questions which give rise to consideration are whether the provisions of Section 11 of Cap. 53 have (a) any bearing on a case such as this, (b) whether such provisions could impose any lawful restriction on the part of the contributor from getting his refund paid into 'B's' account, and (c) whether the Accountant-General could lawfully turn down contributor's application by virtue of the power conferred on him by Section 11, Cap. 53, which reads:

The Accountant-General's Department

'Subject to the provisions of this Ordinance, no deposit, bonus or interest on any such deposit shall be assignable or transferrable or liable to be attached, sequestered or levied upon for or in respect of any debt or claim whatsoever.'

"2. In view of the facts that:

(a) 'B' is not a party to a contract nor took part in the transaction,
(b) The transaction is a voluntary one on the part of the contributor, without being subject to confirmation by 'B',
(c) There is no 'offer' and 'acceptance' on the parts of the contributor and 'B' to constitute an assignment or transfer,
(d) There is no valuable consideration for the purposes of either an assignment or transfer to make the same valid in law, and
(e) As the contributor's request to the Accountant-General for payment of the refund of his contributions to 'B's' Bank Account does not in any way constitute either 'assignment', transfer, or attachment.

"It is my opinion that the contributor's request does not fall within the ambit of Section 11 of Cap. 53. It is submitted that 'B's' position is that of only an 'agent', through whose medium or agency, the refund of the contributor's providient fund contributions is to be received. Therefore, it is submitted that the action taken by the Department would appear to be incorrect. I would be grateful if the matter were referred to the Legal Department for a decision in case you disagree with my views expressed herein.

"3. It is also my opinion that assuming there was a debt due by the contributor to 'B', even then, the contributor's application to the Accountant-General requesting and authorising him to pay the refund of his contributions into 'B's bank account does not come within the intendment of the legislature. The intendment of the legislature is clear. It places restrictions on assignments, transfers, and attachments, etc. Nothing could be read into the Section, nor anything could be subtracted from it. The Ordinance must be read as it stands, giving an ordinary meaning to the legal phraseology and its application.

Perspectives of British Colonial Rule in the Fiji Islands

Assignment and transfer, referred to in Section 11 of Cap. 52, refers to documentary assignments and transfers with valid consideration whereby a contributor sets unto the assignee a specified sum of money. Such an assignment or transfer must be signed by both the assignor and assignee, and they must be absolute unless otherwise specified therein to the contrary. As regards attachment, sequestration and levy in respect of a debt referred to in Section 22 of Cap. 53, they refer to only judgment debt in which case the process prescribed by the Courts must be followed in respect of which Section 11 of Cap. 53 imposes restrictions.

(sgd) "R. Charitra,
19.4.58"

Then –

"A few days later, I was informed by Accountant 'E' that the Acting Accountant-General had written to the Attorney-General for his legal opinion on the issue involved and that I would be informed of the decision in due course. After waiting for some time, I inquired whether a reply from the Attorney-General was received but the answer I got indicated that the matter was still under consideration, although in fact it had already been received. By this time, Mr Griffiths had returned from overseas leave and had resumed duty as Accountant-General. On one or two occasions, I again enquired about the reply, but no definite answer was given to me. When I called for my TPF 2365, I saw my submission, as aforesaid, was there, but not the reply from the Attorney-General.

"During the month of September 1958 or thereabout, I was going through some of the dead files in connection with the Widows' and Orphans' Pensions. During this period, I sighted Mr Ram Swamy Naidu's file – TPF No. 4376, and, ongoing through it, I remembered the incident of his Provident Fund case, in respect of which I had made a legal submission and received no reply. Consequently, I came across the Attorney-General's reply – No.95, dated the 23rd April 1958, conveying to the Accountant-General the legal decision on the interpretation of Section 11 of Cap. 53. It is respectfully submitted, Sir, that the Attorney-General's decision was on the

The Accountant-General's Department

same lines as that contained in my legal submission of the 19th April 1958. Consequently, I took the TPF 4376 and saw Mr Griffiths on the subject. I said that I felt very sad to see that the Attorney-General's decision was not conveyed to me, in respect of which I had gone to the extent of preparing a legal submission in my own time. I asked him what the idea was of concealing that decision from me. Thereupon, Mr Griffiths appeared extremely indignant and said I was wasting his time. I said I was not wasting his time but was an instrument in saving his prestige from future criticism, which might have arisen from a wrong interpretation of Section 11 of Cap. 53. He said he did not entirely agree with the legal interpretation he had received from the Attorney-General, and that the matter was still receiving his personal consideration. I thanked him for the reception he had given me and moved out of his office in view of the resentment he had shown. It is humbly submitted that, Sir, from my legal submission dated the 19th of April 1958 on the interpretation of Section 11 of Cap. 53, and the Attorney-General's decision thereof, as conveyed to the Accountant-General under reply to No. 95, dated 23rd April 1958, the following points give rise to consideration:

"That the interpretation that was from time to time given on Section 11 of Cap 53 by Senior Accountant 'B' and the Deputy Accountant-General, as well as the Accountant-General himself, was absolutely wrong in point of law,

"That from the date when the Provident Fund Ordinance was first introduced in 1938 to the time, I took up the matter in April 1958, how many cases of an unlawful act, arising from the wrongful interpretation of Section 11 of Cap 53 by the Treasury's Senior Officers as well as the Accountant-General himself, were committed and cases of injustice perpetrated,
"That the incorrect interpretation of Section 11 of Cap. 53, as aforesaid, indicates nothing but an inefficiency,

"That, in the light of the Attorney-General's decision under his letter No. 95, dated 23rd April 1958, in TPF No. 4376/11, my legal submission, dated the 19th April 1958, on Section 11 of Cap. 53 was testified to be correct. Sir, does not this in itself go to show that the standard of my work in the Accountant's-

General's Department was better not only than the Assistant Accountant's but also than that of other senior officers, including the Deputy Accountant-General?

"That the concealment and suppression by the Accountant-General of the Attorney-General's said reply, as aforesaid, could convey a wrong and false impression to the members of the public. In the circumstances, one might, upon hearing the incident, feel that it is the Government that advocates such a sharp policy to be practised by heads of Departments, notwithstanding the factual reality that it was, in this case, the Accountant-General who perpetrated a clever and cunning move himself in the arena of discrimination. Sir, this also goes to show how the Government, at times, is criticised for something for which it is not responsible.

"4. In January 1959, while I was working on computations of registered pensions of the various officers, I came across a case where the arrears of contributions to Widow's & Orphan's Pensions amounting to £108.6.8 were still outstanding and had been overlooked since January 1957. I picked up this in the course of my duties and brought the same to the notice of the Department by the following communication:

"Accountant Section 'E'

"Re: J. E. Perry-Johnson – TPF 213

"This officer resigned w.e.f. 14.8.54 and selected to continue to contribute to Widows' & Orphans' Scheme – vide (61) in TPF 213. The rate of his contribution was £52 p.a. or £4.6.8 per month. His contributions have not been received despite our letters of (63) and (67), nor has he advised us of his intention to cease. The officer better be asked to make up his mind one way or the other. If he wants to continue to contribute further, he has to pay up the arrears amounting to £108.6.8, made up as follows:

1957 Contributions at £52 p.a.　£52. 0. 0
1958　"　　　"　　"　　　 52. 0. 0
Contributions for the month of

The Accountant-General's Department

January 1959 at £4.6.8 p.m.   4. 6. 8
                                £108. 6. 8

of
if
"His future contributions w.e.f. 1/2/59 will accrue at the rate of £4.6.8 per mensem, ceasing on 7/1/1967. On the other hand, if he does not wish to pay up his arrears, as aforesaid, we will then have to work out the reduced registered pension w.e.f. 1/1/57. His registered pension is £326.10.9 w.e.f. 1/1/54, and this will apply to him if he continues to contribute throughout the period of contribution as he elected to do so in terms of (61). I have picked up this from the big Ledger and later called for the TPF, etc.

(sgd) "R. Charitra,
13/1/59." [2]

Ram exposed the arrears amounting to £108.6.8 that, without his intervention, might not have been discovered. The senior officers had overlooked it for at least two years. He questioned Mr Griffiths' judgement and expertise as a senior officer. The Accountant General had behaved like a spoilt child; his hiding the Attorney-General's decision was a gross act of deception practised on his officers, whose pension funds were adversely affected by his decision, and those subordinates who had to follow incorrect instructions. His work as the head of the department fell short of the high standard expected, and he was too proud to seek the Attorney-General's views to ensure that no contributor to the fund suffered.

Mr Griffiths was hostile and refused to accept any corrections, which showed him and his senior officers – all expatriates – to be inept and professionally unfit for purpose. The discovery of outstanding arrears was not an exception; rather, a culture of sloppiness, combined with a lack of care and oversight, created a dangerous precedent.

Other cases, recorded in the Petition to the Governor, dated 21 March 1960, on pages 7 and 8, also concerned the

---

[2] Petition, 21 March 1960. p. 5

Widows' and Orphans' Pension Scheme, which Ram recalculated and found to contain errors.

These included the case of Mr D. C. C. Trench (no TPF ref. no. "Refer to Big Ledger" is noted). The discrepancies lay undetected from 1946, when the first error occurred. Again, in Ram's view, this resulted from a misinterpretation of the relevant ordinance, i.e. Section 5 (7) of Cap. 54.

In the case of Mr M. L. Bernacchi (TPF 241), an incorrect annual contribution rate was quoted, and consequently, the Treasury collected the incorrect contribution, effective from 5 August 1952. In 1952, Mr Griffiths' department fixed and subsequently collected Mr Bernacchi's annual contribution at the rate of £90 per annum, instead of £84, £126, or £60 per annum. Mr Bernacchi, however, had elected to contribute at the higher rate. Ram calculated that, in this circumstance, the correct rate of annual contribution was £126 per annum, effective from 5/8/52, instead of £90. The arrears of unpaid contributions amounted to £229.3.3. Ram addressed the issue as follows on page 9 of his petition at paragraph 3 as follows:

> (a) this officer elected to contribute at a higher rate of time and a half w.e.f. 1/12/43 which has not been as yet revoked or altered even until today.
> (b) Since at the time of transfer from Fiji to Malaya w.e.f. 22/8/44 he again elected to continue to contribute at the same higher rate, and –
> (c) Since he was transferred to G.&E.I.C.[3] on a salary of £2100 p.a.

It is submitted that in the circumstances the appropriate and correct rate of annual contribution was £126 w.e.f. 5/8/52 and the arrears of unpaid contributions resulting from a wrongful calculation of rate amount to £229.3.3 and made up as follows:

1/1/52 to 4/ 8/52 at £ 36 p.a.	£21. 7. 9
5/8/52 to 31/12/52 at £126 p.a.	51 2.11

---

[3] Gilbert & Ellis Island Colony.

The Accountant-General's Department

	72.10. 8
LESS:	
Total amount paid in 1952	<u>59. 7. 5</u>
	13. 3. 3
1953: 6% on £2100 = £126 less paid £90 =	£36. 0. 0
1954: 6% on £2100 = £126 less paid £90 =	£36. 0. 0
1955: 6% on £2100 = £126 less paid £90 =	£36. 0. 0
1956: 6% on £2100 = £126 less paid £90 =	£36. 0. 0
1957: 6% on £2100 = £126 less paid £90 =	£36. 0. 0
1958: 6% on £2100 = £126 less paid £90 =	<u>£36. 0. 0</u>
	<u>£229. 3. 3.</u>

He continued on point of law:

> "...it is submitted that whether we can legally enforce the collection of arrears resulting from short payment of contributions amounting to £229. 3. 3 due to the fault attributable to this Department in advising the officer as to the incorrect rate of contribution. The officer has a strong case. As his defence he could reasonably submit that had he known before that the higher rate of annual contribution would go up as high as £126 p.a., he would have then elected to pay either the compulsory amount of £60 or normal contribution of £84 on full salary. On these grounds the officer has every justification to call for a refund of contributions collected in excess of either £60 or £84 p.a., as the case may be. I fail to find any authority in the Ordinance whereunder we are empowered to refund any contribution illegally or wrongfully collected. There is also considerable doubt whether the provisions of Section 32 could be invoked in case such as this."

In October 1958, Ram chanced upon the case of Mr B. A. Doyle (TPF 2371), the former Attorney-General, whose pension contribution rate was similarly incorrectly assessed; the wrong amounts were being collected for his contributions. This resulted in arrears of £68. Ram drew the Accountant-General's attention by memorandum, dated 21 October 1958. Characteristically, the Accountant-General responded with indifference.

Perspectives of British Colonial Rule in the Fiji Islands

Then there was the case of Mr J. J. C. Suckling (TPF 232). Similar errors were found. No one, not even the Accountant-General, had concerned themselves with any care and attention to detail with regard to the regulations. The contributors had departed, retired, or transferred to posts in other colonies and lived in blissful ignorance of shortfalls or overpayments in their pension funds for the rest of their lives. I would hazard a guess, and I wouldn't be too far out if I speculated that once Ram had exposed the misinterpreted calculations, each one of them, Mr Griffiths included, dashed in to examine their own files.

However, the Accountant-General, still with blinkers on, would have none of it and told Ram that interpreting the law was not his business. Ram's responsibility, according to Mr Griffiths, was "to calculate registered pensions" and that he was not to interpret the ordinance that prescribed the actual manner of calculation. It was absolutely absurd, thought Ram, for anyone to say that any calculation of registered pensions under Cap. 54 could be done without reference to the interpretation of various sections of the ordinance.

For the purposes of calculating the registered pensions, the first and foremost duty of an officer is to comply and observe the proper interpretation of the whole ordinance; otherwise, the calculations will be inaccurate, "as I myself discovered was the case in the Treasury to which references are herein made. Can anyone or, for that matter, Mr Griffiths himself, calculate a single registered pension of a contributor without first obtaining a proper interpretation of the various sections of the ordinance? If not, on what grounds was Griffiths justified in saying, 'It is not one of Mr Charitra's duties to interpret the Widows' & Orphans' Pension Scheme ordinance but to calculate registered pensions.'" registered pension that his wife was entitled to in case of his death.

On 6 October 1958, Mr A. A. Wright (TPF 756) wrote to enquire about the amount of his pension his wife would receive on his death. It was up to Ram to respond. He discovered that the rate of contribution was incorrectly assessed in March 1932 and brought the matter to Mr Griffiths' attention before his reply to Mr Wright. "…It is necessary to recover the arrears of W & O

The Accountant-General's Department

contributions in the sum of £123. 9. 8 outstanding since 1932…An error occurred at the time he was promoted to the post of Secretary for Native Affairs, effective from 17/3/42, when his annual salary was increased to £1000. It appears from salary records that, although his salary was increased, no step was taken to collect the increased rate. This discrepancy, however, was audited year after year and passed as correct between the years 1932 and 1942.

Mr Griffiths did not reply to the memorandum and continued to remain silent. His silence, however, meant that either he accepted Ram's interpretation, as supported by the Attorney-General, or he completely rejected the legal position.

Instead of welcoming such a work and expressing his appreciation in the matter, he gave a clear sign of personal dislike towards the submission because it involved some of the senior officers of his Department.[4]

Ram continued to infer

"That in view of the standard of my submission, as herein before appearing, can one still reasonably place any reliance on Mr Griffiths' reports in which he said that "my work was not of the standard that was expected of an Assistant Accountant"? How would the standard of work of the Auditors, who audited the accounts from 1932 to date, and the senior officer, who was in charge of the Pensions Section in the Treasury, be classified in comparison with my work in view of the discovery of this error? [5]

Treasury officers were beyond criticism. None dared to contradict the Accountant-General until Ram appeared and took the bull by the horns. Everything revolved around the interpretation of regulations as one would expect, and one might

---

[4] Petition to Sir Ronald Garvey. 21 March 1960. p. 22.
[5] Ibid.

also be expected to accept the opinions of the government's team of legal advisors.

Mr Griffiths, if he had been a reasonable person, he might have accepted the official legal opinion. However, under the circumstances, he found himself in a delicate position. Having to agree with Ram's interpretations would call into question the preceding twenty years of errors endorsed by him, his predecessors, and the accountants in the department, all of whom had followed the previously misunderstood interpretations. It was therefore imperative that this local accountant be put in his place. Ram highlighted the superior quality of his work:

> In the light of Attorney-General's decision, under his letter No. 95, dated 23rd April 1958, on TPF 4376/11, my legal submission, dated the 19th April 1958 . . . was testified to be correct . . . does not this, in itself, go to show that the standard of my work in the Accountant-General's Department was better not only than the Assistant Accountant's but that of other senior officers, including the Deputy Accountant-General" [6] ?

Despite being vindicated by legal opinion, Ram was threatened with dire consequences for daring to challenge the Accountant-General's opinions. As an officer dedicated to his duties, Ram had responsibilities and was accountable for the assignments on his desk.

The Fijian colonial superstructure was organised to give the heads of departments plenary powers with impunity. However, without any system of accountability, certain members of the administration could range free and loose. Mr Griffiths was one such example. He could not bring himself to accept his own legal expert's opinion.

Senior officers, such as Mr Garnett and Mr Waddingham, were like peas in a pod; they supported the

---

[6] Letter addressed to the Colonial Secretary for transmission to the Governor dated 21 March 1960. p. 4 paragraph (d)

The Accountant-General's Department

Accountant-General. All of them had a hand in maintaining the false narrative that *they* were always correct, even when the evidence clearly showed that something was amiss.

In another case, Ram discovered the contributions to the pension of Mr Bevington [7] who was the government's Financial Secretary, were incorrect. The error had not been noticed by Mr Griffiths. Ram continued to ferret out old files he suspected contained irregularities. He recalled in paragraph 12, page 23 [8] of his petition to the Colonial Secretary:

> By March 1959, in the course of my official duties, quite a number of cases of wrongful and erroneous calculations of Widows' and Orphans' Pensions, as mentioned in this submission, were brought to the notice of the Accountant-General for necessary action but he, unfortunately, gave no decision thereon. It would appear that the reasons for his being so silent in the matters I brought to his notice were:
>
> (a) THAT the errors to which I had referred were committed by *senior officers* [emphasis added] of his Department to which he had, in some cases, himself inadvertently given previous sanction. Giving a definite decision thereon, one way or the other, meant creating an embarrassing situation for himself and,
>
> (b) THAT my submission on the interpretation of the provisions of the Widows' and Orphans' Pension Ordinance, Cap. 54, which pointed to various errors, was a correct one.[9]

Mr Griffiths' brashness and conduct made Ram decide to test the water personally. He sought Mr Griffiths' authorisation to increase his own pension contribution. Would the Accountant-General stick with his own interpretation or the revised and correct version? Ram wrote:

---

[7] Petition 21 March 1960. Paragraph 11. p. 22.
[8] Petition to the Governor. 21 March 1960. Paragraphs 11-12. p. 23
[9] Petition, 21 March 1960. p. 23.

Perspectives of British Colonial Rule in the Fiji Islands

Re Widows' & Orphans' Contribution: TPF 2356:

Sir,

As advised, I respectfully submit my application herein in writing. As a contributor to the Widows' & Orphans' Pension Scheme, on the present salary of £1250 per annum, the current rate of my normal contribution is £52 per annum. It is my intention to contribute to the Widows' & Orphans' Pension Scheme at a higher rate, and I will therefore be obliged if you would kindly let me know whether you will, under the Widows' & Orphans' Pension Ordinance Cap. 54, be so good as to allow me to contribute an additional contribution, increasing the current rate of my annual contribution from £52 p.a. in future and exempt me from the requirements, if any, of Section 5 (3) of Cap. 54, assuming that your answer is in the affirmative.

(sgd) R. Charitra,
31st March 1959

The Accountant-General replied:

Section 5 (3) of Cap. 54 states, *inter alia*, that "May be permitted so to elect at any time during his contribution term subject to the approval of the Governor after the examination of the contributor by a Medical Board."

(2) As I cannot authorise the additional contribution nor exempt you from being examined by the Government Medical Board, it will be necessary, before submitting your application to the Governor, for you to appear before the Government Medical Board.

(3) Do you, therefore, wish me to arrange a Government Medical Board for you?

(sgd) J. F. Griffiths,
2.4.59

In paragraph 3, note the tongue-in-cheek comment. But Ram countered and submitted to the Colonial Secretary as follows:

The Accountant-General's Department

> Even if I was declared medically fit by the Government Medical Board or, for that matter, if my application for an additional contribution was approved by His Excellency the Governor under Section 5 (3), I could not possibly, under any circumstances, be permitted by the provisions of Subsections (1) and (2) of Section (5) and Section 6 of Cap. 54 to contribute at the annual rate of £60 a year. Under the provisions of Subsection (1) and (2) of Section 6, only one of the two alternatives was open to me, viz: Either to contribute at the normal rate, that is 4% of my salary – £1250 = £52 p.a. or at an additional rate equivalent to time and a half of the normal rate, that is £52 plus £26 = £78 p.a.[10]

Ram had doubts and, once again, to ensure that his interpretation was correct, he sought independent legal advice. He consulted the Suva solicitors Messrs Hasan & Hasan to ensure that he had applied the correct legal interpretation.

The Crown had the perpetual right to nullify *illegal* contributions. At the same time, it also had the right to rectify positions upon the death of the pensioner and pay surviving beneficiaries the pension at a reduced rate, notwithstanding whether any additional contributions had been made. This would result in the beneficiaries receiving no benefit at all from the pensioner's higher rate of contributions.

Ram was advised to seek confirmation *in writing* from the Accountant-General that, after the Medical Board had declared him fit, the Accountant-General would allow Ram to increase his annual contribution from £52 per annum to £60. Further, he was advised that, after being declared medically fit.

> "It would appear that the Accountant-General had at once realised that the consequences which were to follow if he were to give a correct answer ... of my said letter. While the Accountant-General saw fit to give almost an appropriate reply to my inquiry ... he apparently evaded the points I had raised.

---

[10] Petition, 21 March 1960, p. 25.

He made no comment as to whether or not I could increase the rate of my annual contribution from £52 p.a. to £60 p.a. Sir, Mr Griffiths made no comment on that point because, on the one hand, Section 5 (2) and Section 6 of Cap. 54 could not authorize me to do so, and, on the other hand, he had done so in a number of instances, in respect of which I had drawn his attention. As a public officer, particularly in view of the fact that he is administering the Widows' and Orphans' Pensions Ordinance, it was Mr Griffiths' first and foremost duty to say to me, as soon as I submitted my first application to him, that even I was declared medically fit by the Government Medical Board, or for that matter, even my application for an additional contribution was approved by His Excellency the Governor, under Section 5 (3), I could not possibly, under any circumstances, be permitted by the provisions of Sub-sections (1) and (2) of Section 5 and Section 6 of Cap. 54 to contribute at the annual rate of £60 a year. Under the provisions of Sub-section (1) and (2) of S. 5 and S. 6, only one of the two alternatives was open to me, viz:

(a) Either to contribute at the normal rate, that is 4% of my salary - £1250 = £52 p.a. or,
(b) At an additional rate equivalent to time and a half of the normal rate, that is £52 plus £26 = £78 p.a.

Therefore, it was clear that my proposed additional contribution at the rate of £60 p.a. was not applicable in my case; even though Subsection ((7) of S.5 cannot compel a contributor to contribute more than £60 a year. To support this, I hereunder quote a part of the Colonial Secretary's letter to me of the 10.4.59; the sentence in the third line if the said letter commences:

"... in the first place I should explain that your "request to increase you contributions from £52 a "year to £60 cannot be considered under the "provisions of the Ordinance. Your rate of "contribution can only be increased by one half in "accordance with the provisions of S. 5 (2) or "(3)

The Accountant-General's Department

"of the Ordinance. Sub-section (7) of S. 5 of Cap. "54 has no application to a voluntary increase of "contributions, "which must conform to S. 5 (2). [11]

Mr Griffiths' response suggested that it was for the Governor to approve the increments. Again, he was incorrect. Only the contributions made under Section 5(3) of Cap. 54 required the Governor's approval. The ordinance *expressly* authorised the Accountant-General to approve other contributions if he thought that the conditions justified it, which they did in Ram's case.

Mr Griffiths was not up to it. The ordinance – indeed, the subject of pension contributions and the many computations required – were quite beyond him. He had all the resources from the executive branch and the legislators available, but his pride and ego prevented him from achieving the correct outcome, and he was too proud to accept Ram's calculations as correct. He was in charge and in control, having given his verdict. He enjoyed the blessing of the administration; therefore, barring any action taken in a court of law to review the ordinance, the matter was a dead issue. Ram was a civil service officer and therefore had to live with the department's decisions.

Accused of Substandard Work

Mr Griffiths may not have been directly involved in making the errors, but as the head of the department, he was ultimately accountable for all the errors and oversights, not least when the mishaps were brought to his attention. He responded to Ram's diligence by accusing him of substandard work.

Mr Griffiths met with the Colonial Secretary, and both discussed the implications of the unexpected discovery of the errors in the Treasury. Their reaction was to defend the long-standing but incorrect interpretations. Just in case Ram decided to go public, the Accountant-General pre-empted the possibility with an all-out attack on Ram's professionalism and integrity.

---

[11] Letter to Accountant-General. 31 March 1959. pp. 24-25

Although the Attorney-General had upheld Ram's interpretation of the ordinance, on 25 August 1959, the Colonial Secretary wrote to Ram, on Mr Griffiths' advice: "The Accountant-General has reported that your work is not of the standard which is expected of an Assistant Accountant." [12]

The case against Ram was spurious and vindictive. In his defence, Ram submitted to the Colonial Secretary his findings, during his secondment, of the miscalculations made over the years by the officers of the Accountant-General's Department.

Attack as a Mode of Defence

Ram defended his position and pointed out the errors he had discovered in the files he worked on. Before this intervention, no one was the wiser of the anomalies that lurked in those files. The colonial constitution limited the scope and intent of oversight; without recourse to independent arbitration, justice was subjective and coloured by personal motives or the administration's objectives.

No one in the hierarchy admitted there was a problem, and no officer, including the Accountant-General, provided explanations or reasons to support their contentions or suggest *where*, in their opinion, Ram had misinterpreted the legislation. Ram had no recourse to review: under the colonial constitution, the heads of department had the last say. If problems were referred to the Governor, he would bounce them back to the head of the department for advice. Expressions of the gravity of the situation fell only on deaf ears; the officers responsible were concerned primarily with protecting their reputations and prospects. Therefore, despite the Attorney-General's decision in Ram's favour, no corrective action followed.

---

[12] Petition to the Colonial Secretary. 21 March 1960. Ram was seconded to the Accountant-General's department. Accusations made were not substantiated by evidence of any errors of professional misjudgements. Ram disputed the interpretation of an Ordinance, and this was referred to the Attorney General to resolve. The AG found in favour of Ram. But the Accountant-General concealed the written legal decision.

The Accountant-General's Department

Whether in the public or private sectors, errors of a financial nature, however minor, cannot be overlooked. The public must maintain implicit trust in its Treasury Department; the utmost care and diligence of its staff are the order of the day.

The consequences of the administration's inaction deprived pensioners of the funds they anticipated for their retirement. For now, these were put under wraps, and the Governor's decision made no difference to the time spent on seeking to correct the errors. There would be no recompense for the affected pensioners or the colony's taxpayers, whose tax contributions to the Treasury were whittled away on wasteful pursuits. For Ram, his findings caused distress and disappointment within the hierarchy, resulting in stressful conditions that ultimately damaged *his* prospects as a civil servant in the department.

Causes of Discord

The regulations in question, the Widows' & Orphans' Pension Ordinance, were first introduced in 1938. The interpretation adopted by Treasury Department officers since then has never been questioned or reviewed in light of their clients' circumstances and status. Over the years, many departmental accountants followed like sheep and repeated the errors of their predecessors. Ram liked a challenge; he was not going to be held back by a bunch of intellectually idle officers. A great deal was at risk for the stakeholders who depended on the expertise and integrity of these officers for their retirement benefits.

What Ram found was just the tip of the iceberg. As we have seen, while working on computations for the registered pensions, he encountered irregularities in contributions to the Widows' and Orphans' Pension Scheme, which resulted in underpayments or overpayments. The files concerned were

J. E. Perry-Jones	File Ref: TPF213.13. 1. 1959
D. C. C. Trench	File Ref: Big Ledger. 25.11.1958
M. L. Bernacchi	File Ref: TPF241.22.12.1958

B. A. Doyle -
  The Attorney-General   File Ref: TPF 2371. 9.4.1959
Rattanji, Master Tailor   File Ref: TPF:7596. 9.4.1959
Late Mr J. J. C. Suckling   File Ref: TPF:232. 25.1.1959

Mystified, he wondered how the departmental audit system worked; the auditors did not appear to have matched the regulations to the calculations. How were the funds released? How did they reconcile and balance the superannuation and Provident Fund accounts, assuming that they followed the relevant ordinance?

Happy that the *Attorney-General* concurred with his interpretation, Ram felt exonerated by the government's top legal team. This mattered to him, but he was disappointed that the outcome did not impress the Accountant-General and some of his senior colleagues. The Attorney-General had no power to enforce his interpretation of the law enacted by Fiji's legislators. Nevertheless, Ram, the officer who discovered those delinquent documents, was within his rights to expose the errors and, with it, the true face of inefficiency, recklessness, and racism in the civil service.

29

Return to the Inland Revenue Department

Ram returned to the Inland Revenue Department after his eventful three-year stint at the Treasury. His nemesis, Mr Philbrick, now the Acting Commissioner, hoped to keep a tight rein on him following his return. Within days, Ram faced scrutiny for the amount of time he spent on the phone in the department. One day, Philbrick was unable to make outside calls because Ram was on the phone for a while. He wondered whether the calls were social or business ones. Philbrick needed an explanation, and quite rightly, too. He wrote to Ram[1] :

> From Acting Commissioner of Inland Revenue
> 14.10.1955
> To Mr Ram Charitra
>
> Re Telephone Calls
>
> On 10.8.55, mention was made in a staff circular that telephone calls were to be kept to a minimum.
>
> 2. Since you were brought back to this office, it has been noticed that you have had frequent inward calls, none of which appear to have been in *connection* with official matters. At least on two occasions today, when I have attempted to make calls, the phone was being used by you.
>
> 3. Please explain the nature of the reasons for these calls.
> *(sgd)* A. S. Philbrick,

---

[1] Ram's response: letter dated 16 October 1955.

Perspectives of British Colonial Rule in the Fiji Islands

Acting Commissioner of Inland Revenue

Mr Philbrick's memo was blunt and direct; it had all the hallmarks of his old proclivities. Ram's response was unequivocal and meticulous.

> 16th October 1955
> Acting Commissioner of Inland Revenue,
> Government Buildings,
> Suva.
>
> Sir,
>
> I thank you for your letter dated 14.10.55 asking me to explain the nature and reasons for receiving 2 telephone calls on Friday, 14th instant and other telephone calls in the course of 4 days – Monday to Thursday. You state in your letter under reference:
>
> "At least on two occasions today (that is 14th October) when I have attempted to make outward calls, the phone was being used by you."
>
> Apparently, you are more concerned about calls received on Friday the 14th of October, and I hereunder submit a summary of phone calls received during the period Monday to Friday.
>
> 1. TELEPHONE CALLS MONDAY TO THURSDAY:
> In the course of these 4 full working days, 6 phone calls were received. They were:
>
> (a) A phone call was received from Mr Albert Lee – an employee of Suva Motors Ltd, informing me that he had some mangoes for me and asked me to pick them up. He had received these mangoes from Lautoka for making pickles. I told him that I would either pick them up at 1 or after 4 p.m.
>
> (b) Another call was received from our Mr Basavanand wanting to know whether I would have room in my car at lunchtime for his daughter and himself. He said his car was under repair. At lunchtime, a lift was given to Mr Basavanand

Return to the Inland Revenue Department

and his daughter accordingly, and at the same time, lifts were also given to our Mr Lewis and Mr Giltrap.

(c) Another call was received from one Mr Ram Narain – an employee of MH Ltd – wanting to know the requirements and procedure for obtaining Clearance. He said he was given 3 months' leave and wished to go to N.Z. for a short trip. I informed him of the procedure to follow.

(d) Another call was received from my wife telling me that she was so sick that morning that she was unable to cook anything for lunch that day. She said the house servant had not come to work that day either. She said that she had nothing for lunch other than bread and tea. She said that if that would not do, then bring some roti and curry from town whilst coming home for lunch.

(e) A fortnight ago, I had made an arrangement for Swami Devendra Vijay to come home to recite and impart spiritual preaching at night between 10 to 12. As Swamiji's time is fully occupied from 6 a.m. to midnight each day, with heavy bookings in advance, the date given to me was Thursday the 13th instant, commencing at 10 p.m. As my wife suddenly became unwell, I sent a message cancelling the arrangement for Thursday night. On Wednesday the 12th instant, a committee member in charge of the functions rang me up at the office, asking me to confirm the cancellation – hence the wretched phone call.

(f) Another phone call was received from my wife telling and reminding me to make an appointment with Dr Oldmeadow to see her that afternoon. Appointments made with Dr Oldmeadow in the morning before 1 are attended to in the afternoon of the same day, and those made in the afternoon are attended to the following day. This call to me was just before 1. This was in connection with a painful lump that had developed in her abdomen as a result of a major local injection given to her about a fortnight ago.

Perspectives of British Colonial Rule in the Fiji Islands

2. TELEPHONE CALLS ON FRIDAY – 14.10.55.

(a) On Thursday night, I took my family down to listen to Swamiji's preaching in Suva Street. After parking my car in the street, I went up to Bhindi's yard or, rather, the arena where preaching and recital of hymns from Hindu scriptures are conducted each day and night. During the heavy shower, I came down to the car and smelt something was burning like rubber. I took no notice of the smell amidst heavy rain. I started the car, and as I reversed it a few yards up the hill, the engine stopped, and a heavy stream of smoke began to come out from the bonnet. It looked like the car might catch fire at any moment. In the meantime, a large crowd gathered, waiting to see the car ablaze any moment. Fortunately, a gentleman came and opened the bonnet and immediately took off a cord or wire from the battery and by doing so, the smoke gradually subsided. Upon further examination, it was discovered that some wicked person had made the wrong connection of some of the wirings whilst others were disconnected. Temporary adjustments were made in the night, and this enabled me to come home.

The next morning was Friday the 14th, when the car was given for repairs, etc., and it was in this connection that I received two phone calls. On Friday morning, I narrated this story to Mr Barnes, who said it would have been better if the car had burnt down; I would have had a new car from the insurance company. I told Mr Barnes that I agreed with him. At lunchtime, when I gave a lift to Mr Lewis and Mr Giltrap, I also mentioned to them the preceding incident.

(b) Another phone call I received on Friday was from the Hon. Vishnu Deo. He said he was raising funds on behalf of Swami Devendra Vijay to erect a very large temple in Bombay. Mr Vishnu Deo said that he wanted to come down to see me at home, and he asked me what time would suit me that afternoon. I told him 4.30 p.m. would suit me better. Hon. Vishnu Deo, no doubt, you are aware that he is a great talker, and he outlined a few of the objectives over the phone. I could not very well tell him to get off the line, although I suggested to him to have a full discussion when he came home that afternoon. At 4.30 p.m. the same afternoon, Mr Vishnu Deo

Return to the Inland Revenue Department

and 4 others came home, and after discussion, I promised them a donation of £10.10.0, for which they issued a receipt, which I enclose herewith for your perusal and return. I told them to collect this sum on Monday the 17th instant from Mr A. D. Leys.

3. As regards phone calls made to me, I must say that for days I received no calls at all. In any one week, the average number of phone calls received would not exceed 10. Would you call these "enormous calls" in comparison with others? Will you please come out with the truth and say what you have at the back of your mind and what you are aiming to achieve? It is not the phone calls irritating you; it is something else. Sir, if you do not wish to come out with these yourself, please do not hesitate to request me in writing, and I will myself disclose to you, as well as to the others above you, the aims and objectives you are attempting to achieve.

4. It appears to me from your general activities in this Department that you are not only taking undue advantage of your administrative powers, authority and position you are holding, but also ceaselessly attempting to exploit me on behalf of your friend Mr Drysdale on account of the two petitions I made on him which have not been, until now, presented to His Excellency the Governor. Your attitude in your official and personal capacity bears fruit to the statement made to me by Mr Drysdale on the 27th of January 1955 at the time when the petition was submitted on him for the second time. He had said:

"When Mr Philbrick or anyone else takes my chair, he would still be harder on you than I am – by seeing this Petition you made on me."

As a certain understanding was reached between Mr Drysdale and myself, that Petition was withheld [2] for the time being.

---

[2] Ram alludes to an understanding. I found these paragraphs on page 2 of Petition dated 25 January 1955 as appended within Petition of 14 May 1956, which might go some way to explaining why the petition was withheld. "AND WHEREAS the

Perspectives of British Colonial Rule in the Fiji Islands

It now appears to me that you are egging me on to proceed with the Petition in question. Will you please advise me whether or not you want me to proceed with that Petition?

Yours truly,
(sgd) R. Charitra

Mr Philbrick's reaction to Ram's strong response is not recorded. However, he calmed down and took no further action.

When it became known in the office what had transpired, friendly officers from the department visited Ram at home to encourage him not to be intimidated. In this circumstance, due to the sensitivity of the issue, it was the only way his expatriate colleagues could offer him moral support.

Finally, as if Mr Drysdale had nothing better to spend his time on, he took it upon himself to resurrect an old file. There was no rhyme or reason for this revisit, but with the thoroughness of a neurotic fanatic fixated on an ephemeral silhouette, he proceeded to dissect the agreement.

Ram responded to the Commissioner was as follows:

Inland Revenue Department,
Government Buildings,
Suva.

Petition dated 29 June 1952 was handed to Mr R.B. Ackland on 30 June 1952 for presentation to Your Excellency's government in relation to Mr Drysdale's unjustified activities in this office; a copy whereof is annexed hereunto.

AND WHEREAS in pursuance of the submission of the Petition above referred to, Mr Drysdale, on Friday the 11th July 1952, had personal discussion with your humble petitioner in the matter and requested for the withdrawal of such Petition stating that if Petition was presented to Your Excellency's Government he would not only have a "black spot" against his character but his chances for the post of Commissioner, upon the retirement of Mr R.B. Ackland, would be endangered. In view of: (a) Mr Drysdale's wife and child having died in a motor accident in Australia approximately three weeks prior to submission of the above petition, which had in itself brought considerable misfortune upon himself and required human sympathy."

Return to the Inland Revenue Department

14th February 1956

Sir,

This is to place on record that yesterday, you stated that, as a result of my submission to you of the letter dated the 1st, you required me to furnish you with a statement showing details of all properties:

- (a) Held in March 1949
- (b) Bought and sold since 1948, and
- (c) Erected during the period 1948 to date.

In compliance with your request, I furnished you, yesterday, the required information duly prepared from memory, without reference to book records and although I had no time at my disposal, nor was I asked to give reasons for the sale of some of the properties forced by circumstances beyond my control. The Assistant Commissioner is fully aware of the circumstances leading to such a sale in two instances, and the documentary evidence is available in respect thereof.

Be it remembered that when the first building was erected in 1949, and at the time when the Gordon Street land was purchased in August 1949, the matter of erection of buildings and flats was fully discussed with Mr R. B. Ackland when I was informed that there was no restriction on investments in properties. I had then informed him that all my property investments were managed and controlled by my solicitors, Messrs Ellis, Munro, Warren & Leys, and that I had no direct control over any of my investments.

At the time when I first joined the Civil Service in March 1948, I appointed Messrs Ellis, Munro, Warren & Leys of Suva, Solicitors, as my lawful and properly constituted attorneys to transact all business and things on my behalf and that such Power of Attorney is still not revoked.

This is also to be placed on record that you have also told me on several occasions that you yourself have already consulted the Honourable, the Colonial Secretary, on the matter of investment in properties and that you were duly informed that there was no restriction in respect thereof.

Be it known that there are other senior civil servants who are also carrying on a business, that of poultry, dairy, sub-division of lands and land deals as well as money lending on interest. You, too, Sir, lent £500 at 6% interest to one of the wealthiest and most prosperous Chinese merchants, Mr Fong Lee of Ba, under mortgage no. 53057.

This is also to be placed on record that in the past, I have already submitted my Balance Sheets and accounts from time to time, showing movements in the property investments and that these investments have always been carried out within your knowledge and that, until today, on no occasion you made any comment thereon.

In view of the fact that you have called for a statement in respect of my investments at a time when my Petition is still under consideration by His Excellency the Governor, I consider it most appropriate that a copy of this letter be sent to His Excellency for information, particularly those contained in paragraphs 5, 6, and 7 herein.

Yours truly,
(sgd) Ram Charitra

The Secretariat responded that as he, Ram, had previously disclosed the transactions in question, no disciplinary action was contemplated.

Memorandum

From the Colonial Secretary
Ref: CPF. 2706. 10.4.1956

Engagement in Commercial Properties.

CONFIDENTIAL.

Return to the Inland Revenue Department

I am directed to refer to your letter of the 14th of February 1956, addressed to the Commissioner of Inland Revenue, setting out business dealings in which you have engaged since 1947, and to inform you that it is considered that these transactions are such as to show that you are engaging in commercial undertaking, namely speculative building, contrary to the provisions of Colonial Regulations 52.

2. In view of the fact that you have previously disclosed these transactions to the head of your department, it is not proposed to take disciplinary action against you on this account, but I am directed to inform you that you must not indulge in any further activities of this kind, and that you must disengage yourself from existing activities and report when you have done so.

(sgd) A. L. Baker
For the Colonial Secretary

30

Final Thoughts

The most important thing today is to make human beings rise to a sense of inclusiveness beyond gender, race, religion, and nationhood.[1]

Procedures were set in the General Orders and Colonial Rules for the proper conduct of administrative affairs of the colony.

Almost from the moment he set foot in the department, Ram was a target of some invisible hand or hands seeking to remove him. They devised various methods, but none were successful. He loved his work and displayed an uncanny facility with figures, and his technical abilities were beyond doubt.

Legal or illegal, to them, the end justified the means; to Ram, getting justice using legal and set procedures was as frustrating as getting blood out of stone - all appeals to the governor were either ignored or dismissed without enquiry or investigation.

The General Orders did not mention that the governor had the choice to accept complaints from some officers of the civil service and to disregard complaints from others if he so pleased.

Some of Ram's "petitions" to the governor, with all the particulars of complaints that an aggrieved officer could reasonably organise, were prevented from reaching him. For this act, there was no remedy.

From 1948, over a period of thirteen years, aggression and opposition continued - almost non-stop. Two adversaries, Mr Drysdale and Mr Philbrick, *and no other officer*, it is important to note, conspired to harass him.

---

[1] *Sadhguru* Jagadish (Jaggi) Vasudev.

Final Thoughts

These two were also prime suspects in upsetting the original Secretariat terms and conditions of Ram's entry into the civil service. This act cleared their way to pursue their socio-political aims, which they ultimately failed to achieve. The reason for this may lie elsewhere.

The governor may not be as dumb as he may have appeared from his lack of response to Ram's petitions. He may have sympathised with the unwritten colonial ideology of no blacks in certain positions and aided the pair in keeping Ram's progress in check, but he would not go so far as to remove him from the service on spurious allegations.

He had won all the disciplinary cases against him and endured threats of dismissal. He won his appeal against the Commissioner's tax assessment; he was promoted despite persistent threats of insubordination and disciplinary. The Attorney-General had approved and concurred with *his* interpretations of the ordinances, which surprised the clique surrounding the Accountant-General, who had accused him of substandard work. These were momentous high points for Ram, never certain whether he would return to work the next day.

The Assistant Commissioner opened a new front in 1956. Before Ram joined the civil service, he had declared his total income from a variety of sources – his accounting clients and his property and investments portfolio – to the then Commissioner and to Mr Watson, the deputy who had negotiated his entry into the service.

An agreement was reached about how the portfolio would be managed during his government appointment. He was open and transparent during his interviews and later confirmed this in his written submission. The parties further agreed that Ram would not directly administer his estate. There were no issues or concerns raised regarding the undertakings and disclosures made by the Secretariat.

The portfolio was placed wholly in the care of his solicitors, Messrs Ellis, Munro, Warren & Leys, with Mr A. D. Leys holding power of attorney for its day-to-day management.

No break in that arrangement was reported by any officer during the period in question, and Mr Drysdale had no cause to complain on any count. No officer who had access to the files had reason to raise the issue – until Mr Drysdale decided, on a whim, to reopen his old files.

Ram was not an exception in the civil service. To his knowledge, many expatriate officers maintained farms and businesses. The Commissioner himself was known to carry out financial transactions in the private sector, including lending money. And we have already seen his displeasure at Ram's refusal to accept him as a partner in the Carnarvon Building project.

The Secretariat acknowledged that all disclosures were made as required at the time of application, and it would take no further action. Another disappointment for Messrs Drysdale and Philbrick.

Ram had a bitter experience of working among people whose word (he had assumed) was their bond, people he believed to be trustworthy and honourable heads of department, objective and perspicacious, only to discover the unsavoury aspects of racist ideology unfettered and free to dispense a version of justice unrecognised as balanced and rational. Their methods and services as British civil servants reflected the times, but the colonial policy dichotomy lay in the avowed assertions and the practicalities of executing their administrative duties.

Mr Watson acknowledged that Ram was observed for nine years, his technical skills scrutinised and approved, before the Secretariat agreed to approach him and invite him to join the department.

Ram had no desire, nor expected, to join the Inland Revenue. He was a businessman, a professional and an investor motivated to accumulate assets and achieve financial security. He never forgot his origins, the difficulties of his father, his enfeebled frame barely strong enough to sustain his energies, sapped by the toil and the kicks. The anguish his mother endured as she balanced her life between her business and her children.

So, the visit of the Assistant Commissioner to his place of employment in June 1947 was an astonishing event. He was in a place he had never imagined could or would materialise in his lifetime, but he lived in the real world where work and

Final Thoughts

perseverance are rewarded. His colleagues were equally surprised, pleased, and happy for him.

His discussions with his senior colleagues convinced him that he should accept the invitation and join the department, as it was a significant achievement to be in demand by a government department.

The government accepted his terms, and he resigned from his firm as promised. However, the colonial administration had other plans: they went back on their word, just six weeks into his appointment. He had resigned from his firm and settled into his new situation. Could he take the government to court? What would he gain if he won his case?

Ram was surprised, as were his close friends and associates, but decided to remain determined to make the best of it and deal with matters as they arose. If he decided to take legal action, his witnesses would include Mr Watson, Mr Ackland, Sir Howard Ellis and his fellow officer Mr Richardson. He was confident the original terms would be upheld.

He, however, maintained his poise. His stoicism got him through the most challenging times.

The Governor, who represented and derived his authority from the British monarch, behaved as an autocrat. Colonial Regulations, 69, stated:

> "Every officer who has any representations of a public or private nature to make to the government should address them to the Governor. The duty of the Governor is to consider and act upon each representation as public expediency or justice to the individual may appear to require, with the assistance in certain cases of the Executive Council."

Close-up, Ram had observed double standards: one set of rules for expatriate officers and another for the rest. The usual aspects of xenophobia were so embedded at the top that they defied logic and common sense in a multi-ethnic society.

The empire portrayed its dominions and colonies as being bastions of fairness, where all were treated as equals.

Perspectives of British Colonial Rule in the Fiji Islands

Freedom of movement, freedom of the press, and freedom of expression were the pillars that stood firm and secured the unity of the Commonwealth. These ideals were expressed with tongues firmly lodged in cheeks.

The government did not tolerate criticism of itself or the European settlers. In 1962/3, it forced the closure of a weekly newspaper, *The Fiji Guardian*, when it published an article describing Fiji as *"Black man's land, White man's Paradise."* The publishers, Oceania Printery, owned by Mr Mohammed Dean, were threatened with the withdrawal of government contracts if they continued to publish the weekly. Mr Dean closed the weekly.

Individuals, however well-meaning their intentions, did not escape the administration's wrath. Manilal Doctor and Sadhu Vashist Muni were banished from Fiji's shores for expressing their dismay at the government's inability to prevent the immigrants' suffering. The Republic of Fiji is today the most developed island nation in the South Pacific region.

Fijians depended wholly on the colonial dispensation, which provided them with most of their food, employment, and entertainment. Basic low-grade education was available to them; higher levels arrived later and initially catered only for the children of the chiefs and the elite. The products of these institutions never entered commerce or the professions in any meaningful way that would help make a difference in the lives of ordinary people, the *tauvanua*. Consequently, the colony's people were not adequately prepared to understand modern concepts of democracy or why some ethnic groups had higher standards of living.

Thus, Britain's unilateral decision, by the mid-1960s, to release the colony unnerved the chiefs: *they* were not prepared for freedom and above all, feared the loss of their pre-eminence, the ceremonials, the attention and adulation of the administration, and the sway they held over their people by virtue of their titular positions. They feared democracy: if it were introduced by a free nation, their sovereignty would devolve to the electorate, who would hold them, as lawmakers, accountable. The loss of their

Final Thoughts

prestige would sound the death knell for the adulation to which they had become accustomed during ninety years of colonialism.

On becoming Prime Minister in 1970, Sir Kamisese Mara was underprepared for the uncharted waters ahead. Loyally and faithfully, he adopted and followed colonial policies in the manner of an overconfident but shortsighted amateur politician.

He displayed little aptitude for bold, imaginative changes. So, it did not take long for the newly independent nation to shed tears. Those painful years ultimately culminated in policies for which some had been calling out for more than half a century. Peace and stability followed the broad-based and inclusive political settlement of 2014.

Ram, as a civil servant, never lost faith in British justice. "I struck a few bad eggs!" was all he said. During Ram's final years, Mr D. J. Barnes succeeded as the Commissioner of Inland Revenue and following Ram's early retirement in 1961, he was a frequent guest at Ram's residence, and the two discussed the Bible. Both men found common ground in the peaceful tenets of Christ and Krishna.

He settled down and successfully established his accounting practice, *Charitra Accounting & Taxation Service*, on the first floor of his property at the Carnarvon Building, Carnarvon Street, Suva. He attracted a clientele of businesses and high-net-worth individuals and worked until he passed away peacefully in November 1994.

***

The last word I leave to Harold Macmillan, a British Prime Minister who made this speech about the empire just ten years before Fiji's independence.

It revealed the dichotomy – indeed, the hypocrisy – of British colonial policies. The "Wind of Change" speech was for public consumption. It was not a plan for changing the attitudes and mindsets of colonial administrators to liberalise those policies based on race to exploit differences purely for dogmatic reasons.

Perspectives of British Colonial Rule in the Fiji Islands

The speech boldly begins with justice and Christianity and the rule of law!

> We have tried to learn and apply the lesson of our judgement of right and wrong. Our justice is rooted in the same soil as yours – in Christianity and the rule of law as the basis of a free society. This experience of our own explains why it has been our aim in the countries for which we have borne responsibility, not only to raise the material standards of living, but also to create a society which respects the rights of individuals, a society in which men are given the opportunity to grow to their full stature – and that must in our view include the opportunity to have an increasing share in political power and responsibility, a society in which individual merit and individual merit alone is the criterion for a man's advancement, whether political or economic.
>
> Finally, in countries inhabited by several different races, it has been our aim to find means by which the community can become more of a community, and fellowship can be fostered between its various parts.
>
> I have thought you would wish me to state plainly and with full candour the policy for which we in Britain stand. It may well be that in trying to do our duty as we see it, we shall sometimes make difficulties for you. If this proves to be so, we shall regret it. But I know that even so, you would not ask us to flinch from doing our duty.
>
> As a fellow member of the Commonwealth, it is our earnest desire to give South Africa our support and encouragement, but I hope you won't mind my saying frankly that there are some aspects of your policies which make it impossible for us to do this without being false to our own deep convictions about the political destinies of free men to which, in our own territories, we are trying to give effect. I think we ought, as friends, to face together, without seeking to apportion credit

Final Thoughts

or blame, the fact that in the world of today, this difference of outlook lies between us.[2]

I end with these words, with which our father would wholeheartedly agree -

"I still believe, in spite of everything, that people are really good at heart"

Anne Frank: The Diary of a Young Girl. 1947.

<u>End</u>

---

[2] Harold Macmillan's address to members of both Houses of Parliament of the Union of South Africa, Cape Town, 3 February 1960. PDF available at https://web-archives.univ-pau.fr/english/TD2doc1.pdf, accessed 27 February 2025.

Figure 1. 73 KNOLLYS STREET, SUVA, 1957: THE AUTHOR WITH PARENTS.
[Photo: Prasad's Studios]

FIGURE 2. 73 KNOLLYS STREET, 1961:
A BUSINESS LUNCH WITH LOCAL CLIENTS. ON THE FAR RIGHT: THE BANK OF BARODA MANAGER, SUVA BRANCH.
[PHOTO: PRASAD STUDIOS]

FIGURE 3. 73 KNOLLYS STREET, 1959:
FROM THE LEFT: BACK ROW: MR RICHARDSON, MRS BING, MR A.D. LEYS, RAM AND MRS CHARITRA, MRS A.D. LEYS, DR SINGH. SEATED: MR SHIRIDHAR MAHARAJ. UNKNOWN LADY, UNKNOWN LADY, MRS RICHARDSON (WITH CHILD) MR D.J. BARNES, MRS M. PRASAD. MR J.F. GRIFFITHS.   [PHOTO PRASAD STUDIOS]

Figure 4. 73, Knollys Street, 1957:
The family: standing: from the left: Pramod "Peter" (=Shakuntala Ram Bali), Ram, the author (=Rukmini Singh) Tapeshwari, Roy (=Renuka Sharma).
Seated, from the left: Manorama (=Dr Parshu Ram), Pratima (=Sushil Chandra, Chemist), Praveena (= Dr M.J.T. Dalton). [photo:Prasad's Studios]

Figure 5.
The front garden of 73 Knollys Street, Suva, 1956. [photo: author]

FIGURE 6. 73 KNOLLYS STREET, SUVA.
THE FAMILY HOME 1954 TO 1995. THE HIGH SECURITY GATES INSTALLED FOLLOWING
DISTURBANCES ASSOCIATED WITH THE 1987 COUPS. [PHOTO: AUTHOR]

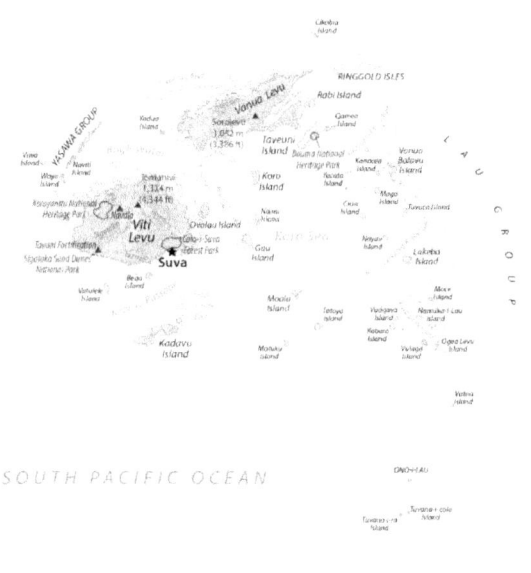

Map of Fiji Islands & Rotuma

[Courtesy of GIS Geography]

www.ingramcontent.com/pod-product-compliance
Lightning Source LLC
Chambersburg PA
CBHW052015070526
44584CB00016B/1768